Greece & Rome

NEW SURVEYS IN THE CLASSICS No. 37

COMEDY

BY

N. J. LOWE

Published for the Classical Association

CAMBRIDGE UNIVERSITY PRESS

2007

CAMBRIDGE UNIVERSITY PRESS
Cambridge, New York, Melbourne, Madrid, Cape Town, Singapore, São Paulo, Delhi

Cambridge University Press
The Edinburgh Building, Cambridge CB2 8RU, UK

Published in the United States of America by Cambridge University Press, New York

www.cambridge.org
Information on this title: www.cambridge.org/9780521706094

First published 2007 (*Greece & Rome* 54)
This edition 2008

A catalogue record for this publication is available from the British Library

ISBN 978-0-521-70609-4 paperback

Transferred to digital printing 2009

Cover illustration: Sicilian terracotta model, c 350 BC, of a comic mask
thought to represent an African slave. British Museum, Terracotta 1195.
Photograph by Marie-Lan Nguyen/Wikimedia Commons.

CONTENTS

PREFACE

This is a successor to the New Surveys on *Menander, Plautus, Terence* (W. G. Arnott, 1975) and *Aristophanes* (R. G. Ussher, 1979), but I hesitate to call it a replacement. Geoffrey Arnott's volume, in particular, remains a jewel of the series and a masterly overview of a golden era of scholarship on New Comedy, and has been a disheartening reminder throughout of how far his expertise exceeds my own. It has been an appallingly difficult project to let go; there is nothing like trying to take a snapshot of a moving subject to make one appreciate how fast the target is travelling. The new identification of Menander's *Titthe* in the Vatican palimpsest – itself testimony to the fundamental falseness of a truth peddled to students over a century, that there was no medieval tradition of Menander – has overthrown our assumptions about the scope of the Menandrean canon in later antiquity, just as those assumptions were beginning to settle comfortably into complacency. More surprises will undoubtedly be forthcoming.

I am particularly grateful to Emmanuela Bakola and Felix Budelmann for alerts on new and forthcoming publications, and to Mario Telò for an early copy of his major edition of Eupolis' *Demes*. John Taylor and Richard Hunter have been impossibly good-humoured about having the elastic limit of their patience tested. The Menander section has benefited from the insights of two remarkable doctoral students, Maria Troupi and Stavroula Kiritsi, with whom I have been privileged to work. Colin Fine suggested the translation of *Epidikazomenos* on page 120. More general debts are diffuse but deep: a global apology is probably due to Chris Carey, Edith Hall, Toph Marshall, Michael Silk, Alan Sommerstein, and David Wiles, who are all especially likely to have had their unguarded thoughts opportunistically pilfered and rendered unrecognizable to their own authors. Malcolm Willcock and Norma Miller were key figures in my own education in New Comedy; both cast a long shadow in London, and are greatly missed.

Aristophanic titles are mostly given in their more familiar English versions, but those of New Comedy in the original language, since English renderings of Menander's and Plautus's titles vary unrecognizably. Dates are BC unless otherwise stated.

Dr N.J. Lowe
Reader in Classical Literature
Royal Holloway, University of London

I COMEDY: DEFINITIONS, THEORIES, HISTORY

Q. When is a jar not a jar?
A. When it's a door.
(Q falls about. A looks puzzled.)[1]

'Comedy', from Greek *komoidia*, is a word with a complex cultural history. Its modern, as opposed to its ancient, use covers all formally marked varieties of *performed humour*, whether scripted or improvised, group or solo, in any medium: theatre, film, television, radio, stand-up, and various hybrids and mutations of these. It is also, by extension, applied more loosely to novels and other non-performance texts that share recognizable features of plot, theme, or tone with the classical tradition of comic drama; and used more loosely still as a casual synonym for 'humour'. As a countable noun, however, the word is restricted to works with a *narrative line*; thus sketch shows, stand-up, and variety acts can be 'comedy' but not 'comedies'.

Since almost everything that was called comedy in antiquity falls comfortably within the core sense of our word, it is all too easy to lose sight of the sheer weight of additional baggage that the Greek word has picked up in its long and sometimes meandering journey through the western cultural lexicon. Here, by way of illustration, is an exuberantly inclusive overview from a twentieth-century text, which self-consciously revisits ancient comedy through the lens of its modern inheritor forms – in this case, specifically the Broadway musical – annotated to gloss some of the principal generic claims made for 'comedy' as a generically distinct category of performance in line of descent from antiquity.

PROLOGUS: Something familiar, something peculiar,[1] something for everyone,[2] a comedy tonight. Something appealing, something appalling[3] . . . nothing with kings, nothing with crowns;[4] bring on the lovers,[5] liars[6] and clowns.[7] Old situations, new complications,[8] nothing portentous[9] or polite.[10] Something convulsive, something repulsive[11] . . . something aesthetic, something frenetic[12] . . . nothing with gods, nothing with fate; weighty affairs will just have to wait.[13] Nothing that's formal,[14] nothing that's normal,[15] no recitations to recite.[16] Open the curtain,[17] comedy tonight. Something erratic,[18] something dramatic[19] . . . frenzy and frolic, strictly symbolic[20] . . . anything you ask for[21] – comedy tonight. Something that's gaudy,[22]

---

[1] From the BBC spoof celebrity quiz *Shooting Stars*.

something that's bawdy,[23] something for everybawdy,[24] comedy tonight. (MILES:) Nothing that's grim.[25] (DOMINA:) Nothing that's Greek.[26] (PROLOGUS:) She plays *Medea* later this week.[27] Stunning surprises,[28] cunning disguises,[29] hundreds of actors out of sight.[30] Pantaloons and tunics,[31] courtesans and eunuchs,[32] funerals[33] and chases,[34] baritones and basses,[35] panderers, philanderers,[36] cupidity,[37] timidity,[38] mistakes,[39] fakes,[40] rhymes,[41] mimes,[42] tumblers,[43] grumblers,[44] fumblers, bumblers,[45] no royal curse, no Trojan horse[46] – and a happy ending, of course.[47] Goodness and badness, man in his madness:[48] this time it all turns out all right.[49] Tragedy tomorrow, comedy tonight.[50] [2]

[1]Sense of genre is itself part of comedy's poetics: there is a strong sense of the particular work defining its individuality within a strict genre tradition. [2]Comedy (particularly in contrast to rival genres) claims mass, populist appeal. [3]Comedy repels as well and attracts, magnifying both fears and desires. [4]Whether or not in overt opposition to tragedy, comedy's social centre of gravity lies outside the aristocratic world. [5]Heterosexual love is a strong genre trademark, as are [6]plots of deception. [7]A striking feature, lacking counterpart in tragedy, is a range of specialist buffoon characters. [8]Stereotypy of situation, and the virtuosity of improvising new figures on familiar grounds, are highly valued. [9]Comedy's generic self-image is simultaneously that of the *eiron* or wit [10]and the *bomolochos* or buffoon. [11]Comedy is 'a mimesis of inferior people' (so Aristotle, *Poetics* 5.1449a32). [12]Pacy physical action is a trademark. [13]Comedy is keen to distance itself from tragedy, even at the expense of serious self-misrepresentation. [14]Comedy encourages a Bakhtinian view of itself as anarchic, entropic, centrifugal, and [15]a carnivalesque inversion of everyday life. [16]Static, declamatory modes of performance are deprecated in favour of mobility and improvisation. [17]Metatheatre is a characteristic ingredient. [18]See 14. [19]Comedy is finely attuned to the dynamics of live performance. [20]The carnival model (see 15) is licensed by the fact that its anarchism is fantasized rather than realized. [21]Comic performance claims an element of real-time interactivity and audience empowerment. [22]Comedy welcomes the extravagant, the exaggerated, the larger-than-life. [23]It is able to engage in a non-threatening way with dangerous areas of sexual discourse. [24]Verbal play, especially puns, is prominent in its linguistic register. [25]Violence is made non-threatening. [26]Comedy subverts the classical. [27]Nevertheless, there is free commerce (sharing of personnel, audience, space, etc.) between comedy and its rival genre. [28]Plot twists are highly valued. [29]Intrigue, especially that involving impersonation, is a recurrent motif. [30]Visual spectacle is promoted. [31]Generic markers are found in costume. [32]There are stock character types, who include sexual outlaws. [33]Death is a social rather than a personal event. [34]See 12. Desire is often given manic physical expression. [35]Music is often integral to the dramatic texture. [36]Providers and customers of sexual services are key figures in the situational repertoire. [37]Plots centre on desire: physical, sexual, commercial, social. [38]Human weakness is exposed and ridiculed. [39]Errors, cognitive and practical, are major plot elements. [40]See 6, 29. [41]The discursive register is free to oscillate between the bound and the unbound, the formal and the naturalistic. [42]Non-verbal signification plays a part, and [43]exotic physical displays are especially welcomed. [44]Characters with a misanthropic or surly disposition

---

[2] Stephen Sondheim, 'Comedy Tonight', from *A Funny Thing Happened on the Way to the Forum* (1962).

are useful to the social and satiric chemistry. [45]See 38–9. [46]See 13. [47]The fulfilment of the narrative lies in order emerging triumphantly out of disorder and sympathetic characters decisively attaining their desires. [48]Comedy at its most professionally ambitious aspires to a distinctive vision of the human condition that claims to be global, humanistic, and life-affirming. [49]Comedy's vision of the world is closural, teleological, and feelgood; but [50]this may be interpreted as a mere deferral of the (possibly, but not necessarily, truer) tragic world-model.

Three general features of this account deserve slightly fuller comment. First, although Sondheim's show tune is a knowingly modern text, the cultural tradition it describes is emphatically classical. His musical is set in ancient Rome and based on five Latin comedies by Plautus;[3] and this famous opening song not only continues a classical tradition of generic self-reflexiveness, but boldly asserts that every element of its expansive definition is already, and archetypally, to be found within the world of Roman comedy itself. Indeed, the theory of comedy is one of the few areas of modern literary theory in which classical scholars can claim to have played a central part. Cornford's 1914 *Origins of Attic Comedy*, one of the landmark works of the group nowadays known as the 'Cambridge ritualists', argued for a ritual basis to the plot patterns of Aristophanic comedy; it was swiftly discredited in classical circles by the criticisms of Pickard-Cambridge (1927) and others,[4] but its basic model, abstracted from the historical claims of actual ritual origins, became the basis of Frye's formal plot pattern, still the most influential grand unified theory of comedy yet proposed. More recently, the studies of Segal and Silk have attempted to use an understanding of the complexities of ancient comedy's own history and generic positioning to address larger definitional questions about comedy's place in the western tradition.

Second, Sondheim is responding to what we can now see to have been the last major phase of the theorization of comedy as a genre, summing up two millennia's accumulated sense of comedy's nature at the very point when its intellectual history may have been coming to an end. The last widely influential attempt at an overall poetics of the mode was Frye's in 1957, though its key elements date from 1948;

[3] Three are normally credited (*Pseudolus*, *Miles Gloriosus*, and *Mostellaria*) but *Casina* has clearly been used for the wedding scene and *Poenulus* for the Erronius storyline. The project originated with librettist Burt Shevelove, who had studied Plautus at Yale and would go on to write the book for Sondheim's 1974 musical version of Aristophanes' *Frogs*. Shevelove introduced co-writer Larry Gelbart, the future screenwriter of *M*A*S*H* and *Tootsie*, to the material; both Gelbart and Sondheim read widely in the corpus. See Gelbart 1998 and Malamud 2001.

[4] More recent appraisal has been more sympathetic, against a background of deeper appreciation of the ritual elements in fifth-century drama generally; see especially Reckford 1987: 441–98; Jeffrey Henderson 1993b: xi–xxxiii; E. Segal 2001: 1–26.

Bakhtin's concept of the carnivalesque, formulated in 1941, reached the attention of English-speaking scholarship only in 1968; and in the poststructuralist and postmodern eras the focus of theory has moved from comedy as an ideal form to humour as a psychological and cultural process.[5] The reasons for this shift are complex, but one environmental factor has been the rise in cultural prominence of television comedy, which tends to open-ended serial form of a kind difficult to accommodate within traditional notions of the contained comic storyline with its strongly closural festive ending, or else to short sketches and vignettes, which come closer in form to the single joke than to the full-length comic work imagined by classical theories of comedy ancient and modern. The resurgence of non-narrative forms of performed comedy, particularly stand-up, has also been a challenge to the boundaries of traditional formalist models; and in his provocatively titled *The Death of Comedy* (2001) Erich Segal, himself a classical scholar with professional experience in the writing of musicals, articulates the widespread recent view that the Cornford–Frye model of comedy as rite of spring is specifically undermined by the twentieth-century turn to darker, even apocalyptic, comic effects.[6]

Finally, Sondheim brilliantly captures the sheer centrifugality of the definitional project, which is principally due to two things: (i) a struggle to unify the radically different Aristophanic and Menandrean models in a single generic definition; and (ii) a difficulty in clearly disengaging a theory of *comedy* from a theory of *the comic*, or humour.

(i) Essentialist models of comedy tend to underplay the complexity of ancient comedy's own history, both as an evolving cultural form and as an object of reception in later tradition. In 486 BC, a kind of play called *komoidia* was granted its own competition in the Athenian festival of the City Dionysia. It was not the only kind of comic drama at the festivals; at around the same time a kind of mythological romp called satyr-play became an official feature of the competition in tragedy. But, whereas satyr-play remained subordinate to tragedy, *komoidia* remained distinct. By 425 it had developed into a complex popular art form, which used the resources of the Greek theatre in startlingly different ways to its more conservative sibling *tragoidia*, which was performed at the same festivals in the same theatres but never composed by the same poets. Over the course of the fourth century it developed into what would be, for the rest of antiquity, its

---

[5] Hokenson 2006: 173–265. The major works since Frye have been E. Olson 1968; Gurewitch 1975; Torrance 1978; Simon 1985; Patrick O'Neill 1993; Purdie 1993.

[6] On the emergence of this view, see Hokenson 2006: 126–7.

classical form: the so-called New Comedy of Menander and his contemporaries, which was translated into Latin in the second half of the third century and the first half of the second. Complete Latin plays by Plautus and Terence survived into the Latin west and seeded the classical tradition in comic drama from the Renaissance on.

But the story of that tradition is one of fracture rather than continuity. The Greek plays on which the Latin comedies had been based only began to be rediscovered in the late 1890s, when archaeologists began to dig in Egypt for ancient papyrus rolls preserved by the dry desert climate. Menander was one of the great beneficiaries of the new philological science of papyrology, because the heyday of his popularity from roughly 200 BC to 200 AD meant that copies were still being made in the period from which actual texts can be recovered. Aristophanes, meanwhile, had disappeared early on from the performance repertoire, and though his plays were extensively studied and edited in the Hellenistic era, it was only under the Roman empire that he began at last to displace Menander in the literary canon. The main reason for this was linguistic: in one of the fits of cultural cleansing to which the Greek language has been occasionally subject in its long history, prose writers from the late first century AD adopted a purist stance that deprecated Hellenistic and later linguistic innovations and modelled itself on the Athenian writers of the fifth and fourth century. Menander, with his exquisitely nuanced early Hellenistic *koine*, was too late and decadent to qualify; the models were the historians, orators, and dramatists of earlier generations, and Aristophanes was of special value as the principal surviving repository of conversational Attic speech, as well as of sub-literary and fantastic vocabulary that would never otherwise have survived.

The upshot of all this is that Menander, arguably the most influential single dramatist in history, was unknown to the later western dramatic tradition he seeded until that tradition's classical phase was already entering its twilight; while Aristophanes, whose direct influence on ancient drama was already long over by the time of Menander's birth, was the one Greek comedian who survived to be read, copied, and preserved throughout the Byzantine middle ages, thus to be rediscovered by humanists and become part of the western classical tradition – yet without ever being part of the living performance tradition, until his belated reabsorption into the theatrical repertoire in the nineteenth and twentieth centuries. Menander remains the direct ancestor of the classical western comedy of romantic intrigue, mistaken identity, and farcical convolutions of plotting: a tradition so successful that its ancient prototypes have become increasingly marginal to the performance repertoire and are now almost never staged. But Aristophanes' legacy is more complex and diffuse, and lies more outside theatre history than within it, particularly in verse and prose satire and the latter's legacy; his master plot of the visionary hero's fantasy quest to rewrite the laws of the universe in his favour is the seed of the fantastic-voyage tradition in prose fiction that runs through Lucian to to Swift, Baron Münchhausen, and the lineage of science fiction.[7]

What comedy meant for its *ancient* audiences is thus a question bound up with its history. The Greek word *komoidia* means, not altogether illuminatingly, '*komos* song'; the untranslatable *komos* is a loose term for a processional revel or mobile party such as we find in a variety of contexts formal and informal, religious and secular, civic and private (though always *in* public).[8] When the word *komoidia* first appears to our view in the fifth century, it refers to a particular kind of play that had its own distinct competition at the Athenian city dramatic festivals, differentiated from its sister genre tragedy in a number of theatrical respects. Its chorus was large (twenty-four as opposed to the twelve or fifteen of tragedy); its masks were cartoonish and ugly rather than naturalistic and dignified, and its costume grotesquely padded, with some or all male characters equipped with a distinctive costume phallus. Competing poets produced a single play each rather than the tragedians' two (at the Lenaea) or four (Dionysia), and there was no overlap of authorship between comedy and tragedy. In the time of Aristophanes at least, plays were shaped around elaborate musical set-pieces, often involving structures of metrical and choreographic symmetry, which had no counterpart in tragedy at all. The subject matter could be, and more usually was, contemporary in setting and fictional in plot, in contrast to tragedy's fixation with retelling myths of the heroic age; and time, space, causality, dramatic illusion were all susceptible to kinds of rupture avoided by tragedy's much more literalistic representational system.

It is far from easy to see how or why these particular differences between comedy and tragedy emerged, and indeed many of them would be eroded or obliterated over the course of the century leading up to Menander's first production in the late 320s. But the effect was

---

[7] For the continuity of the tradition of the *voyage extraordinaire* from Lucian to Verne, see especially now Roberts 2006.

[8] On the *komos* and comedy, see most recently Rothwell 2007: esp. 7 f. and bibliography at 214 n. 3.

to create a distinctive look, form, and grammar of performance for a kind of festival entertainment whose central feature was the invitation to laughter; and comedy's history in antiquity can be viewed as a series of far-reaching experiments in how to assemble a series of comic moments into a larger performance whose armature is essentially *narrative*. These large-scale, storylined performances we call 'comedies' are in essence a series of explorations of how to scale up the things that humour does at the level of the individual joke – what we might call 'simple' humour – to more complex and extended forms of articulation. And the ancient world's invention of comedy, whose cumulative subsequent history in the western tradition is so amply described in the Sondheim lyric from which we began, comes ultimately from the attempt to discover how humour works as a specifically theatrical activity with a mass audience and an extended narrative line.

(ii) Indifference to the distinction between comedy in particular and humour in general has been the second major impediment to a coherent theory of either. Even today, critics of comedy, classical and otherwise, still tend to take surprisingly little account of the vibrant interdisciplinary field of contemporary humour research,[9] which has largely assimilated or displaced the various reinventions of the wheel in the nineteenth and twentieth centuries.[10] Since the foundation of the journal *Humor* in 1988, there has been significant convergence between what had previously been rival approaches, and a recognition that what in the past have been different kinds of theories of humour are in fact complementary lines of inquiry into a single complex phenomenon. Thus, Attardo's metacritical overview classifies the major categories of humour theory as shown in Table 1.

Like the blind men's elephant, these four categories of theory represent different parts of a single humour process. We may not for literary purposes be much concerned with the physiological aspects of laughter, but a full account of the operations of humour will certainly need to consider its *initial conditions* in the social frame within which humour acts are set, and the relationships thereby constructed between the performer, audience, and target; the cognitive mechanisms, including linguistic processing, then involved in the actual

---

[9] Robson 2006 is the major classical exception. See especially McGhee and Goldstein 1983; Morreall 1983, 1987; Raskin 1985; Mulkay 1988; P. Lewis 1989; Orin 1992; Nilsen 1993; Norrick 1993; R. I. Williams 1993; and, above all, Attardo 1994 and Ruch 1998.

[10] The canon of classics comprises Meredith 1877; Bergson 1900; Freud 1905; Langer 1953: 326–50; Frye 1957; Koestler 1964; Bakhtin 1984.

Table 1 Four families of theories (after Attardo [1994: 47], after Raskin [1985: 31–40])

Social	Cognitive	Psychoanalytical	Physiological
Hostility	Incongruity	Release	Neurological
Aggression	Contrast	Sublimation	Muscular
Superiority		Liberation	
Triumph		Economy	
Derision			
Disparagement			

structure and processing of comic texts; and the psychology of comic *response*, and in particular the involuntary or sub-cognitive operation of comic arousal. The four kinds of theories, in other words, address different stages in an essentially sequential process, as shown in Figure 1:

Figure 1

The integration of these different theories has been the aim of the most influential recent model, Raskin and Attardo's General Theory of Verbal Humour (GTVH), which explains the process of recognizing and resolving incongruity through a mechanism of 'script opposition': significantly contrasted frames of reference, which a joke brings into collision. The process looks something like Figure 2.

Such a convergence of approaches has made it possible to integrate the pioneer studies of Bergson, Freud, and Koestler into what is by now, whether or not we endorse the GTVH model itself, at least a broadly agreed general picture of how humour can be analysed using the tools of social and cognitive linguistics. Such an approach has the power to clarify some central issues in the criticism of comedy, for example by helping us to distinguish at least three different kinds of literary question we may want to ask in thinking about the job it does and how it achieves its effect. If we accept that comedy's defining feature is the targeting of the humour response, then this staged model immediately poses three questions:

- What *social tensions* are being identified and negotiated? (A question of contextual, usually historicist, positioning.)

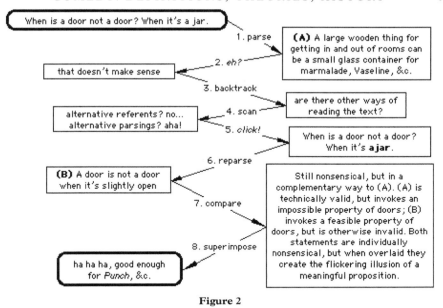

When is a door not a door? When it's a jar.

1. parse

(A) A large wooden thing for getting in and out of rooms can be a small glass container for marmalade, Vaseline, &c.

2. *eh?*

that doesn't make sense

3. backtrack

are there other ways of reading the text?

4. scan

alternative referents? no...
alternative parsings? aha!

5. *click!*

When is a door not a door?
When it's **a jar**.

6. reparse

(B) A door is not a door when it's slightly open

7. compare

8. superimpose

Still nonsensical, but in a complementary way to (A). (A) is technically valid, but invokes an impossible property of doors; (B) invokes a feasible property of doors, but is otherwise invalid. Both statements are individually nonsensical, but when overlaid they create the flickering illusion of a meaningful proposition.

ha ha ha, good enough for *Punch*, &c.

Figure 2

- How is the humorous effect *constructed in the text*? (A question centred in close reading of the actual text against that background.)

- What kind of therapeutic or other *psychological response* is provoked from the audience or reader? (A question that puts text and context back together to confront the effect of humour at the point of reception.)

These are questions that literary models of comedy have not always been very successful at connecting up. Yet the shift in focus from theories of comedy to theories of humour has also left the study of comedy underequipped for a number of its traditional tasks. For one thing, it is a truism that not all comedy is particularly funny. The medieval reconfiguration of the concept of 'comedy', centred on the happy ending as the form's defining feature rather than on the necessary presence of an attempt at humour, is only vestigially present in modern usage. But it remains the case that comic effect is highly vulnerable to nuances of cultural translation, and that a large part of the criticism of comedy, perhaps especially of ancient comedy, lies in unpacking kinds of meaning from the text that transcend any actual impulse to laughter. Menander's *Dyskolos* has a reputation, though largely among those who have not seen it performed, as a play without jokes; but, even if true, it would not diminish the importance of the text as a complex expression of citizen ideology in early Hellenistic Athens, to say nothing of its technical accomplishments as a piece of finely constructed theatrical clockwork. This is not to say that comedy is primarily interesting for its serious content; there would at least be something of a paradox in claiming that comedy is significant precisely when it is not being funny. But a humour-centred model risks loading the emphasis too heavily in the other direction.

More seriously still, a recognized limitation in humour research to date has been the fixation on the individual joke rather than the construction of complex extended comic performances or routines of the kind likely to interest students of comedy. There has also been a related tendency to underestimate the complexity of individual jokes, which very often operate on several levels simultaneously, some of them recursive or metacomic. Thus a GTVH-type model is good at explaining simple jokes such as the one presented in the diagram above, but rather poorer with more Aristophanic kinds of surrealism, such as the variation at the head of this chapter (asked of an unwary celebrity contestant on a spoof quiz show of the 1990s that set up its guests for genial ridicule).

To appreciate just how much is going on in a single moderately complex comic moment, it may help to sit down with a relatively straightforward case. (I use a purely textual example here to sidestep contingent issues of performance and other outside variables.) *Monty Python's Big Red Book* ends with a 'Bibliography', whose first two items are:

> *Mowing the Lawn* by H.R.H. The Duke of Edinburgh
> *How to Spell* by The Quoon[11]

Consider the second line. This is not in any simple sense a joke: rather, it is an item in an ongoing comic sequence, shown in the diagram below as the stepped arrows coming down from the upper left, with dotted lines marking the individual units in the sequence. Each of the three preceding steps is a humorous item in itself, but in the total sequence they are all preparation, part of the frame, for the central item, which is funny in an extremely wide diversity of different but simultaneous respects. It is a profoundly non-linear diagram, traversable in many different ways – something that underpins much of what we would think of as 'complex', 'rich', 'interesting', or

[11] Idle 1971.

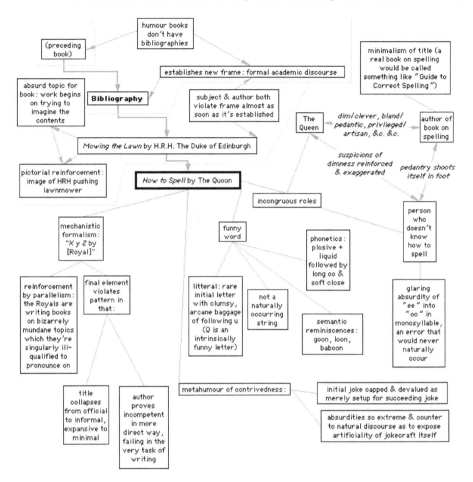

Figure 3

'literary' humour. At the same time, the diagram is far from closed: once we start turning the comic moment over in our minds, we become (as Koestler, in particular, saw) part of the creative process ourselves, extending the mental map with our own further additions (Figure 3). Crucially, although the Quoon gag itself looks like a piece of innocent nonsense, it in fact engages with some highly charged contextual issues:

(i) The British royal family are perceived as over-rewarded, resented as being out of touch with the everyday realities of their subjects, embodiments of undeserving power, and widely perceived as idle; but ambivalence is compounded by the continuing social and ideological investment of commitment in the institution of monarchy, as well as by widespread public regard for the Queen herself, and the perception of a disjunction between the Queen and other royals.

(ii) Spelling errors are a source of potential anxiety about how others might perceive and judge one's intelligence, class, professional competence, authority, etc., etc.

Even brief consideration of such a comparatively straightforward example – and jokes in Aristophanes are routinely a great deal more complex than this – shows the limitations of models of humour that treat jokes reductively, as semantically, psychologically, and textually closed or finite entities. In general, jokes perceived to be 'rich' or 'complex' will tend to depend on one or more of five factors:

sequencing:	the sustained manipulation of the audience's arousal state as part of a *series* of jokes linked in a process of cumulative escalation and pacing
concept:	danger (charged subject matter) and/or complexity (significant intellectual or propositional content – though this on its own has no guaranteed *humorous* effect)
multiplicity:	abundance of simultaneous and overlapping incongruities or other invitations to laughter
aperture:	the absence of clearly defined limits to the audience's or reader's imaginative work
metahumour:	self-reflexive exploitation and subversion of comic form, pragmatics, etc.

There is still an oddly persistent belief that comedy is intrinsically impervious to analysis, on the grounds either that humour is irreducibly subjective or that comic effect is irreparably destroyed by the act of dissection. Practical experience suggests that the reverse is true: that close analysis of complex humour if anything deepens appreciation of the comic effect, both as an experience of funniness and as a work of artifice. Such analysis, it is probably fair to say, is still in its intellectual infancy. But, for that very reason, the prospect for comic criticism is an exciting one, with important work waiting to be done.

Scholarship on comedy in antiquity

In antiquity at least, comedy had a central place in intellectual history. Comedy was second only to Homer in the ancient scholarly effort expended on its interpretation, from the fourth-century Peripatetics to the abundance of interesting if unreliable treatises preserved among the Byzantine paraphernalia that have accreted round the texts. Chief among the latter are the collections of material known as the *Prolegomena on Comedy*, particularly the comparatively well-informed *Prolegomena III* and the two treatises of unknown date by Platonius *On the Different Kinds of Comedy* and *On the Different Styles of Comic Dramatists*. Like the Aristophanic scholia, these draw ultimately on the work of Alexandrian scholars in the third to first centuries, who in turn drew on the published works of Aristotle – particularly his seminal *Didascaliae* or 'Production Records', a chronology of Athenian drama researched from the official archives, which became the basis for all subsequent dating of tragedy and comedy.[12] Aristotle also reports on his researches into the early history of comedy in his extant *Poetics*, and draws a number of suggestive contrasts in the course of his discussion of tragedy. A passage in the *Rhetoric* (1.11.1371b35) promises a discussion of laughter in the *Poetics* that does not appear in our text, but the case for a lost second book on comedy remains unclosed, notwithstanding Janko's bravura revival (1984) of the suggestion that the remarkable Peripatetic outline known as the *Tractatus Coislinianus* may be a summary of the putative missing book, rather than an extension of Aristotle's argument by another hand.

There was no official text of comic poets corresponding to the Lycurgan text of the tragedians, but Old Comedy fascinated the great Hellenistic scholars of Alexandria and Pergamum. Alexandrian scholarship on Old Comedy began as early as the 270s, when the second generation of poets of New Comedy was still productive; the Ptolemaic tragedian Lycophron, ostensible author of the extant poem *Alexandra*, was the first to write a specialist treatise, though his nine books *On Comedy* seem to have been principally concerned with linguistic and textual minutiae. Meanwhile, Aristotle's work on dramatic chronology was continued by Callimachus in his *Pinakes* ('Tables'), the 120-book encyclopaedia of Greek literature that effectively served as the catalogue of the Alexandrian library. Commentaries on individual plays begin with Lycophron's fellow tragedian-scholar Euphronius, who wrote a companion to *Wealth* – an early sign of this play's special popularity; and Euphronius' pupil, the great Aristophanes of Byzantium, made an edition of the texts of Old Comedy around 200 that would be the basis for all subsequent editions, and

---

[12] The Aristotle known to the Hellenistic world was a completely different corpus from the body of privately read treatises that survive; for an engaging account, see Canfora 1989: 26–9, 51–8, 173–82.

his prefaces to each play ('hypotheses') have been preserved in the manuscript tradition. Although all this work was on Old Comedy, it was Aristophanes of Byzantium who was also largely responsible for the canonization of Menander as a classic – and who coined the famous *mot* on Menandrean realism, 'Menander, life: which imitated which?' In the first century, the prolific literary scholar Didymus compiled a commentary from the many works of his Alexandrian predecessors, which in due course became the ultimate ancestor of the marginal commentaries in Byzantine editions.[13]

As the earliest substantial generic tradition in Latin poetry, comedy was also a preoccupation of Latin literary scholars from the late second century on.[14] An early arena of debate was the authenticity of the plays attributed to Plautus, on which the first-century antiquarian Varro was able to cite half a dozen predecessors, including the trage- dian and literary historian Accius, who was also responsible for an attempt – disastrously wrongheaded, as Cicero's friend Atticus was able to show – to establish a revisionist chronology for the career of Livius Andronicus. But the first great literary historian of Latin comedy was Varro, who wrote prolifically on early comedy's history and interpretation, and became the single most influential authority on points of controversy. Major surviving monuments of Latin schol- arship on comedy include Suetonius' *Life of Terence*, whose attempt to reconcile the conflicting biographical traditions is especially useful for its explicit citation of earlier authorities and their views; the commen- tary on Terence's plays by Aelius Donatus, which has come down to us in a curious reassembled form following the original's dismember- ment into marginal notes; and the treatise *De Fabula* ascribed to Evanthius, which seeks to apply Greek theories of comedy to its Roman form and history.

Chronology and evolution

Comedy had a long run in antiquity. It was already old at the time of its first official festival performances in Athens at the City Dionysia of 486 BC, and new plays were still being written in Latin over five centuries later. In contrast, every surviving classical tragedy we know to have been performed was produced in the space of a single lifetime;

[13] For overviews of ancient scholarship on Aristophanes, see Dunbar 1995: 31–42; Dickey 2007: 28–31.
[14] See Rawson 1985: 268, 271–9.

and in the half-century spanned by the career of Euripides and the surviving plays of Sophocles, the genre's formal development had already stabilized to the extent that some of Sophocles' plays could come from almost anywhere within that span. But comedy's story is many times longer, and spans a succession of radical transformations that reinvent the genre almost beyond recognition, sometimes within the space of a single generation. Aristotle claimed that tragedy stopped developing because it had by this time reached its mature stage, like a living thing growing to adulthood. But comedy was a much less conservative genre, capable of transforming itself several times over into something unrecognizably different from its ancestral form, and it was not until the early Hellenistic period that the subject matter and conventions of comedy reached the kind of stability that had been reached in tragedy some 130 years earlier.

Further, while we may miss the survival of such seminal tragedies as Aeschylus' *Myrmidons*, Sophocles' *Tereus*, or Euripides' *Telephus*, our picture of fifth-century tragedy as a genre does not seem significantly gappy; whereas our picture of comedy is composed almost entirely of gaps. While for tragedy we can study the work of three dramatists from the same century whose careers overlapped, our two surviving Greek comic dramatists were working a century apart, in phases of the genre so different that, if we did not know that Menander's plays were a direct descendant of the kind of play written by Aristophanes, it would be hard to recognize them as part of the same history at all. What is more, each of these surviving authors is himself the end product of a long evolution whose early stages are known only from fragments and hints. By the time of Aristophanes' earliest surviving plays, comedy already had a rich history behind it stretching back at least sixty years, and probably much, much longer. Of the other great comic dramatists of his day, we have only titles and the odd text fragment. Even over the four decades spanned by the surviving plays of Aristophanes, the kind of play he and his lost contemporaries were writing changed almost beyond recognition. The two crucial generations of experiment and innovation that divide Aristophanes from Menander are known only from titles, ancient quotations, and a small scattering of papyrus fragments; and the other great comedians of Menander's age, some of whom were more successful than Menander himself, survive only in very free Latin adaptations composed a century or more after the Greek originals for a very different world and audience. Thus our two surviving Roman dramatists, who also belonged to different generations, adapted their plays from Greek texts a century or more old – all of them now lost – and did so in a theatrical culture that teemed with other, more home-grown forms of popular comedy that do not survive at all.

The history of ancient comedy is thus a fundamentally different *kind* of history from that of tragedy: longer, more complex, and above all more fragmentary. As far as the Greek phase was concerned, Hellenistic scholars tried to impose some shape on the story so far by periodizing it into three ages, which they called Old, Middle, and New. The formal and chronological boundaries between these phases were ill-defined,[15] and each in any case spanned two or three distinct generations of poets and further shorter-lived trends within each, whose detailed history is only very imperfectly recoverable, while some careers, including that of Aristophanes, cut across the divisions anyway. Nevertheless, the terminology is retained by modern scholarship, and the dates conventionally distinguished as follows – with the fifth-century plays of Aristophanes belonging to the tail end of 'Old Comedy' and his last two surviving plays *Assemblywomen* and *Wealth* falling within the early decades of 'Middle Comedy'. At the time of his death, what later generations would view as the golden age of Greek comedy still lay some seventy years in the future, with the 'New Comedy' of Menander and his contemporaries in the early Hellenistic period.

Bibliographic note

Hokenson 2006 is a metacritical history of theories of comedy from Plato to Genette, though sometimes unreliable on classical material and entirely unaware of the new discipline of humour studies (for which, see Attardo 1994 and Ruch 1998). Nelson 1990 is an accessible traditionalist overview, and Erich Segal 2001 an ambitious long history of comedy's life cycle in the western tradition from the classicist's perspective. Two Aristophanists to engage frontally with the larger theoretical debate are Silk (1988, 2000) and Robson (2006).

For ancient comedy in general, the chapters on comedy in the *Cambridge History of Classical Literature*, by Handley (1985) and Gratwick (1982) in the Greek and Latin volumes respectively, remain the outstanding short accounts. Sandbach's concise introductory volume (1977) is the only broad survey in English of Greek and

---

[15] For some of the problems, see Csapo 2000; Sidwell 2000.

Roman comedy as a whole; Maurach 2005 is on a similar scale. Erich Segal's two *Oxford Readings* collections (1996, 2002) assemble strong selections of reprinted articles, including some first English translations of important continental items. Konstan's two collections of essays on individual plays (1983, 1995) offer probing readings of ancient comedy's negotiation of complex unresolved tensions in civic and ethical values, and apply an impressively consistent and compelling critical approach across the whole corpus from Aristophanes to Terence. Important cross-generic histories of ancient theatre with significant material on comedy include Easterling and Hall 2002, and MacDonald and Walton 2007. The sourcebook by Csapo and Slater (1995) collects and translates a wealth of primary documents on the organization and performance of ancient drama, tragic as well as comic. Walton 2006 surveys the translation history of ancient comedy in English, with a full listing of known translations of Aristophanes and Menander.

The best survey history of Greek comedy is Zimmermann 2006; in English, Norwood 1931 is a sparkling performance that still has much to recommend it, though it is outdated on Menander and overenthusiastic in the reconstruction of lost works. On Greek and Roman New Comedy, Hunter 1985 is especially valuable for its unified view of the genre across languages, centuries, cultures, and authors, while Wiles 1991 unpacks the theatrical codes in what is perhaps the single most significant critical work of modern times on post-Aristophanic comedy.

Greek and Latin comedy and tragedy: outline chronology

Historical events	BC	Comedy	Tragedy
	540		first tragic contest c. 535–533
	530		birth of Aeschylus 525
	520		
Pisistratids expelled 510	510		
	500		Aeschylus' first production early 490s; birth of Sophocles 495
1st Persian War; battle of Marathon 490	490	first comic contest 486	birth of Euripides c. 485–480; Aeschylus' first victory 484
2nd Persian War; battle of Salamis 480	480		Aeschylus, *Persians* 472
ascendancy of Pericles 461–429	470		Sophocles' first production 468
	460		Aeschylus, *Oresteia* 458; death of Aeschylus 456; Euripides' 1st production 455
Parthenon built 447–432	450	birth of Aristophanes c. 450–445?	earliest extant Sophocles (*Ajax, Antigone*) 440s
Peloponnesian War 431–404	440		earliest extant Euripides (*Alcestis* 438, *Medea* 431)
death of Pericles 429	430	Aristophanes' early plays 427–421	Euripides, *Hippolytus* 428; Sophocles, *Oedipus Tyrannus* c. 425
	420	Aristophanes, *Birds* 414; *Lysistrata, Thesmophoriazusae* 411	Euripides, *Trojan Women* 415
Athens surrenders to Sparta 404	410	Aristophanes, *Frogs* 405	Sophocles, *Philoctetes* 409; deaths of Euripides (spring) and Sophocles (autumn) 406
Socrates executed 399	400		
Gauls sack Rome 390; birth of Aristotle 384	390	Aristophanes, *Wealth* 388; death of Aristophanes c. 385	
	380		

Historical events	BC	Comedy	Tragedy
	370		
Philip of Macedon crowned 359; birth of Alexander 356	360		
death of Plato 347	350	birth of Menander 342/341	
Philip assassinated, Alexander crowned 336	340		Aristotle's *Poetics* 335–323(?)
deaths of Alexander 323, Aristotle and Demosthenes 322	330	Menander's first play (*Orge*) 321?	
Demetrius of Phalerum 317–307	320	Menander, *Dyskolos* 316; *Samia* c. 320–310	
	310		
	300	death of Menander c. 292	
	290		birth of Livius Andronicus 290?
Rome at war with Pyrrhus 280–275	280		
1st Punic War 264–241	270		
	260		
	250		
	240		Livius' first Latin versions of Greek tragedy and comedy 240
	230		
2nd Punic War 218–202	220	Plautus' early plays c. 215–205	birth of Pacuvius 220
Hannibal defeated 202	210		death of Livius Andronicus 205?; Ennius' first tragedies c. 204
2nd Macedonian War 200–197	200	Plautus, *Stichus* 200; Plautus, *Pseudolus* 191	
	190	death of Plautus and birth of Terence c. 184	
3rd Macedonian War 172–168	180		

Historical events	BC	Comedy	Tragedy
	170	Terence's six plays 166–160	birth of Accius 170; death of Ennius 169
	160	death of Terence 159?	

II OLD COMEDY AND ARISTOPHANES

Origins and cognates

The development of tragedy and those responsible for it have not been forgotten, but comedy was neglected from the start because it was not taken seriously; only at a late date did comic choruses, which had been volunteers, become assigned by the archon. Comedy's recorded poets date from a time when some of its characteristics were already established. Who introduced masks, prologues, additional actors and the like is unknown; but Epicharmus and Phormis introduced plots, which came originally from Sicily, and in Athens were introduced by Crates, who abandoned the lampoon form in favour of coherent storylines and plots.[16]

Although the competition for comedies at the Athenian City Dionysia was made official in 486, the genre itself is certainly older, probably by generations. In this much-discussed passage from the *Poetics*, Aristotle complains that his research into the early history of Attic drama was hampered in the case of comedy by a shortage of documentation, making it impossible to construct the kind of developmental history that he was able to piece together for tragedy. Only with the generation of Crates, whose career began around 450, did a clear sequence of innovation start to become traceable, and for the earlier period Aristotle himself seems to have been driven back on what would have appeared to him a plausible inference: that comedy had evolved in the same way as tragedy, from a pre-dramatic mode of performance through the separation of chorus and soloist. He saw a credible ancestor in the 'phallic songs' performed at Dionysiac festivals around Attica, such as the one staged in *Acharnians* (237 ff.), and suggested that the lead voice in such processional songs (taken by Dicaeopolis in the *Acharnians* scene) was the origin of the comic solo actor.

Yet Aristotle was also aware that comedy's origins were more complex, diverse, and contested. Tragedy was an Athenian invention, but it is far from clear to what extent the same was true of comedy and, in arguing for autochthonous origins, Aristotle had to fend off rival claims from other parts of the Greek world. From the mid-sixth century, Attic vases were already starting to show costumed choruses that strikingly anticipate those of fifth-century comedy, and a Thespis-like

---

[16] Aristotle, *Poetics* 5.1449a37–b9.

figure by the name of Susarion, claimed variously by Megara and by the Attic deme of Icaria, was credited with inventing comedy in the 560s or thereabouts. But there is still earlier evidence, from the late seventh century onwards, for popular comic mummery in the Dorian dialect zone of the Peloponnese and Greek west. Early vases, showing padded dancers with or without costume phalli, tend to be associated especially with Corinth, but two fifth-century instances are of particular interest: the local comedy of Megara, Athens' closest Dorian neighbour city to the south, and a byword in Aristophanes for weak and lowbrow humour; and the Sicilian comic plays of Epicharmus and his successors early in the fifth century.

Epicharmus is something of a puzzle.[17] Aristotle dates him 'much earlier' than Chionides and Magnes, the pioneers of the comic competition in Athens from 486 onwards, but he was certainly active into the 470s, and may simply have had a very long career. Ancient writers regularly confused or identified him with a Pythagorean philosopher of the same name who may or may not have existed, and many of the putative fragments clearly belong to this apocryphal tradition. Even the plausibly authentic play-fragments give little clue about the storylines or form of the plays; but their style is strikingly reminiscent of Athenian Old Comedy, and the titles are tantalizingly suggestive. Mythological comedy dominated, perhaps exclusively; among the forty or so titles attested for Epicharmus are such familiar names as *Amycus, Atalanta, Cyclops, Philoctetes, Sciron, The Trojans*, and the intriguing *Pyrrha and Prometheus* (also known as *Deucalion*); while from Phormis we hear of *Admetus, The Sack of Troy, Cepheus or Perseus*; and the later Dinolochus offers *Althaea, Medea*, and *Telephus*. Two staple figures of Athenian Old Comedy, Heracles and Odysseus, already appear repeatedly: *Heracles and the Girdle, Heracles and Pholus, Busiris, Hebe's Wedding*, and perhaps also Dinolochus' *The Amazons*; *The Sirens, The Cyclops, Odysseus Shipwrecked, Odysseus Doing a Bunk*, and Phormis' *Alcinous*. Other of Epicharmus' titles are more enigmatic: *Earth and Sea, Hope or Wealth*, and the cryptic *Logos kai Logina* ('The Word and his Wife'?). There is no sign of a chorus in the fragments, though many of the plays have plural titles that suggest one, and indeed in some cases were actually used of Athenian tragedies or comedies named after their choruses: *Persians, Bacchants, Islands, Muses*. Epicharmus' *Dionusoi* ('Dionysuses') has a curious form of pluralized celebrity name that in the mid-century Athenian comedy of

---

[17] Useful recent discussions in Cassio 2002; Kerkhof 2003.

Cratinus refers to a chorus of followers of the named hero: *Archilochoi* ('The Archilochus Boys'), *Odysseis* ('The Odysseus Boys'). One title attested for the second-generation playwright Dinolochus, *Komoido-tragoidia* ('Comitragedy'), refers tantalizingly to the proprietary Athenian genre of tragedy, and seems to anticipate the metadramatic comedies of Aristophanes and his younger contemporaries.

How all this bore on Athenian comedy is far from clear. Dramatic links between Athens and Syracuse were well established in the time of Aeschylus, who toured productions there in the 470s and 450s, and the similarities between Epicharmean and Cratinean comedy suggest that some cross-fertilization has taken place, though when, how, and in which direction is hard to determine.[18] Aristotle notes Sicilian claims that Athenian comedy was a straight derivative of their own, but he was aware that the chronology seemed to rule out anything so tidy; his solution, quoted above, was to credit Epicharmus and Phormis with the innovation of giving comic performances a narrative spine in the form of an actual storyline, something that, in his judgment, Athenian comedy did not adopt until the time of Crates in mid-century. What its earlier 'lampoon form' (*iambike idea*) looked like is unclear; the term looks back to the tradition of scurrilous personal poetry in iambic metres from Archilochus to Hipponax, which seems to have been at least an influence on the tone and style of comedy's spoken dialogue.[19] But Aristotle may not have had much to go on for this early period; it is unlikely that scripts from before the age of Crates actually survived.

All that can really be concluded from this is that comedy's origins were more diffuse than those of tragedy; that they lay at least partly outside Athens; that comedy was probably the older genre; and that such similarities as we do find between tragedy and comedy in the period of the surviving scripts were probably the result less of common origins than of a long process of mutual influence and convergence.

Old Comedy and tragedy

Whatever their prehistory, comedy and tragedy remained in a paradoxical state of mutual segregation. They were produced at the same

---

[18] See in particular Dearden 1999.

[19] The case for a more fundamental and pervasive debt of comedy to archaic iambic poetry is put by Rosen 1988.

festivals, in the same theatres, in front of the same audiences, and apparently on the same days, and yet there was no formal interaction between them. They had completely separate competitions – a tragedy and a comedy could never compete for the same prize – and, most remarkably, were composed by entirely different people. There were no ancient Shakespeares: nobody who wrote tragedy ever wrote comedy, and once a young writer like Aristophanes had had a comedy accepted for a festival, he never wrote anything else so long as he lived. The reasons for this are complex and somewhat elusive; there was no actual prohibition against writing in both genres, and the tragedians' exclusive custody of satyr-play shows that the skills of comic writing were not so specialized as to be beyond the tragedians' reach. Yet the professional separation of genres in the archaic and classical period seems to have been so ingrained that the very notion of writing both was taken as a self-evident absurdity. The famous end of Plato's *Symposium* has Socrates trying to persuade Aristophanes and Agathon that, in theory at least, it was possible for the same person to write both tragedy and comedy, but the point of the episode is that the idea is presented as a joke: the only person who would seriously pretend to argue such a notion is the fifth century's most notorious intellectual *provocateur*, and on grounds which even Plato does not take seriously enough to feel them worth setting out at length.

This fundamental separateness of the two genres must be part of the reason why their performance conventions are so radically different. Considering that the plays were being put on in the same theatres in front of the same audiences, it is astonishing how different they manage to be in the basic grammar of performance that each develops. In general, tragedy was a much more restrictive performance system than comedy. Where tragedy put limits on what it could do with the form and medium of theatre, comedy made a virtue of its freedom to transgress those limits. It is not that comedy could not choose, when it suited, to abide by tragedy's conventions; but it never felt that it had to. Some of the more striking examples:

(i) **Myth and reality**. After Aeschylus' *Persians*, tragedy confined its subject matter to myth. There were no more historical tragedies, let alone a tragedy about fictional characters set in the contemporary world. But this is what comedy was able to do in play after play. All eleven surviving plays of Aristophanes tell original stories set in the time of the here and now. Even when mythological characters and settings are involved, the time setting is the present and the story is a fresh one. *Peace* is set in heaven, *Frogs* in the underworld, yet they are specifically and crucially the heaven of March 421 BC and the under-world of January 405. This is not to say that Aristophanes did not write mythological comedies set in the age of heroes and retelling stories familiar from epic and tragedy; it just happens that none of his famous mythological comedies, which made up perhaps a quarter of his output, is among the eleven that survive. The point, rather, is that Aristophanes could do *both*: he could recycle a story from myth, or he could make up a story set in the streets of contemporary Athens, or he could combine the two in any number of imaginative ways. Where tragedy was locked into telling the same stories over and over again, comedy was free to break loose – one reason why its creative lifetime was so much longer than that of tragedy.[20]

(ii) **Topicality**. One consequence of this was that tragedy had no way of referring directly to the world of the audience, since the plays were set hundreds of years before they were even born. Comedy had no such difficulty, and made the most of its freedom to deal directly with issues of satirical interest in contemporary Athenian life, culture, and politics. It could caricature real people on the stage; it could comment on current affairs; it could base its plots around matters of topical concern. The best that tragedy could do was to present a mythological story in ways that made it possible to see pointed parallels with contemporary events; but even that is so obliquely done in the surviving plays that it is seriously possible to question whether any of them is doing it at all. Old Comedy's fondness for subjects of immediate topical concern was one of the factors that militated against its long-term survival, as it made plays very difficult for actors to revive for later production, or even for later readers to understand, once the original topical references had lost their resonance.

(iii) **Fantasy**. Where tragedy tried to keep magic and the super-natural at arm's length, comedy positively revelled in suspending the laws of physics, logic, and naturalism on every available level. Aristophanes' plots are founded on deliberately bizarre and impossible premises, such as making a one-man peace treaty with Sparta while the rest of Athens is at war, or founding a city of birds between heaven and earth and imposing a trade blockade on the commerce in prayers and sacrifice between humans and gods. Characterization, too, is uninterested in the kinds of intense psychological realism that tragedy found so important; Aristophanes' characters are larger-than-life cartoon figures, their motivation determined less by nuances of

---

[20] A fuller discussion of these issues is in N. J. Lowe 2000b.

personality than by the dictates of theme, plot, and comic possibility.[21] This is mirrored in the costume: tragic actors' masks and costume were dignified and naturalistic, whereas comic costume was distorted and deliberately grotesque, with leering masks and exaggerated belly, buttocks, and phallus.

(iv) **Language**. One area where comedy's greater freedom and range, and its disdain for naturalism, has spectacular consequences is in its verbal style. Tragedy has a fairly uniform, restrained, highly artificial poetic diction of its own; there are differences between the Greek of the spoken dialogue and the Greek of the choral odes, but all the characters speak within a homogeneous linguistic register. Comedy is quite different: its poetry spans a wider range of styles of Greek than any other literature the ancient world produced, ranging all the way from gutter obscenities at one extreme to high-flown tragic parody at the other, with a licence to soar beyond existing lexical horizons to invent exuberant new words, usages, and expressions of its own. Aristophanic verse is dizzily inventive, mixing styles and metaphors in relentlessly unpredictable ways; he can capture the idioms and speech patterns of everyday spoken Attic with a precision that only Menander ever surpassed, but he can also mix it up with bizarre poetic coinages of his own creation – and do both within the space of a single phrase.

(v) **Production values**. Comedy was a more extravagant theatrical form than tragedy. It was more expensive to put on: the figures quoted in the orators suggest that a tragic production cost about twice as much as a comic production, but the tragic production comprised four plays as against the comic production's one, so that, play for play, a single comedy required double the budget of a single tragedy.[22] From the texts of Aristophanes' plays, it is not hard to see where the money is going. A major part of the expense was the chorus, which was double the size in comedy – twenty-four members as against tragedy's twelve or fifteen – and far more spectacularly characterized, costumed, and choreographed. Fantasy choruses such as clouds or frogs abound; Aristophanes' most lavish surviving play, *Birds*, seems to have had a chorus representing twenty-four different species of bird.[23] There is also much more use made of props, stage machinery and

---

[21] On 'imagist' characterization, see especially Silk 1990, 2000: 207–55.

[22] The speaker of Lysias 21 laid out 3000 drachmae as tragic *choregos* (for a production of four plays) but 1600 for a (single) comedy; analysis of the figures in P. Wilson 2000: 89–95 (who perhaps overemphasizes the expense of costume relative to other per-capita expenditure).

[23] This has sometimes been disputed, but Dunbar 1995: at lines 267–326 notes the precedent of the twenty-four individualized members of Eupolis' chorus of *Cities*.

special effects, additional speaking and non-speaking actors, and extra costumes and masks for further characters (*Birds* manages an astonishing twenty-one from the three main actors alone).

(vi) **Dramatic illusion**. Tragedy never openly breaches the 'fourth wall' dividing the world of the play from the world of its spectators. The closest it comes is to use language or to set up situations that might implicitly invite the audience to think about their own role as spectators of a performance; but no character in a tragedy ever acknowledges the audience directly or refers directly to the fact that they are watching a play. Comedy has no such restraints. Characters in Aristophanes are constantly acknowledging the audience, making jokes about individuals in the audience, and referring to their own status as characters in a play by Aristophanes at an Athenian dramatic festival. The one thing that they cannot do, interestingly, is to take off their masks or name the actor beneath.[24]

(vii) **Space and time**. Tragedy insists on literalism in the treatment of space and time. Scene changes are largely avoided, and the action presents at least the pretence of real-time continuity. In fifth-century comedy, there is no such insistence; scene changes are freely permitted, and the action can skip ahead days in time if it happens to suit the story. Interestingly, Aristophanes takes much less advantage of this freedom than we might expect, and a couple of plays retain unity of time, place, and action throughout. But it is still possible to have a character fly from earth to heaven, or travel through the underworld, in real time, live on stage, and the identity of the stage building can be dissolved and reassigned repeatedly throughout the play if desired.[25]

(viii) **Formal structure**. Comedy has a much more elaborate formal structure than tragedy, with even the shared elements used in different ways. Both normally begin with a *prologue* (simply the opening scene before the chorus arrives) and *parodos* (a big entry song where the chorus first arrive), and end with an *exodos* (mass exit of all characters, including the chorus, by one or more routes off stage). But the main body of the play, as the diagram below shows, is structurally very simple in tragedy (merely alternating dialogue scenes or *episodes*, with choral odes or *stasima*) but extremely complex in comedy. An important option that does not exist in tragedy at all is the *epirrhematic syzygy*, a strictly symmetrical, two-part musical routine, which can itself take a number of further forms in the course of the

---

[24] Occasional claims that something like this happens in *Acharnians* should be viewed with grave scepticism.

[25] See more on this in N. J. Lowe 2006; Revermann 2006: 107–29.

play as alternatives to the dialogue episode. One variation is the *agon* or comic 'contest', a symmetrical debate scene in which the two sides of the central conflict square up and argue their case in formal presentations; another is the *parabasis*, a long set piece in the middle of the play where the chorus get the stage to themselves and are able to drop out of character to speak in wider terms about the play and its author. Much of this gets lost in the layout of translations, but it is a vitally important feature of comedy's performance structure, and to a large extent can determine the actual shaping of the plot (see below, pp. 54–6).

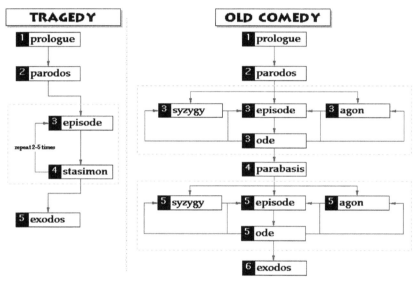

Figure 4

Yet, despite these fundamental differences of performance convention, and despite the professional and institutional segregation of the two genres, comedy could not help but be influenced by what was going on in its sister genre. (It is a great deal harder to argue for any influence of comedy on tragedy.[26]) The genre in which Aristophanes began writing in the 420s was already the product of sixty years (and probably many more) of convergent evolution, and one of the things that seems to have distinguished Aristophanes and his generation from their predecessors is a more direct interest in tragedy as a source

[26] For interesting recent attempts, see Sommerstein 2002b; Kirkpatrick and Dunn 2002.

of plot ideas, parodic opportunities, and general theatrical inspiration. Over the course of Aristophanes' forty-year career, we can already see comedy beginning to adopt more of tragedy's techniques and conventions; by the time of Menander, another sixty years' influence and convergence have changed the whole shape and character of comedy almost beyond recognition.

Attic comedy before Aristophanes

The first generation of Athenian comic poets is irrecoverable beyond a handful of names and titles and a handful of suspect fragments. The titles of plays will have been preserved in the festival records, but it seems unlikely that scripts survived. **Chionides** seems to have competed, and presumably taken first prize, in the first official competition in 486; the plays that survived under his name in antiquity (*Heroes*, *Beggars*) may have been fabrications, but their choral-sounding titles (there was also a *Persians* or *Assyrians*) may be authentic, since they would have been documented in the festival records that were later edited by Aristotle and published. **Magnes** is a more substantial figure: he won first prize in 472, and a long career is implied by Aristophanes' typically back-handed tribute to him in the *parabasis* of *Knights* (520–5) as one of three once-celebrated poets who in old age outlived their audience's enthusiasm for their plays. He is widely suspected to be the enigmatic early comic playwright ending in -s who is credited with a record-breaking eleven victories in an inscription (*IG* ii^2.2318.7). Aristophanes seems to allude to plays called *Lyre-Players*, *Birds*, *Fruit-Flies*, and *Frogs*, as well as the independently attested *Lydians*; we hear also of two versions of a *Dionysus* and the more mysterious *Grass-Cutter* and *Pytacides* (a character name, perhaps garbled). Particularly notable is the anticipation of Aristophanic titles and subjects: Dionysus is already a recurrent comic lead, and fantasy choruses of birds and frogs are an established tradition on which Aristophanes is building his own variations.

Magnes' later plays would have overlapped with the comedians of the period 450–430, the first generation from whom we have sufficiently extensive and illuminating fragments to be able to characterise their output. **Crates**, as we saw above, was credited by Aristotle as a major innovator, the pioneer of comedies with logical plots instead of loose satirical sketches (if this is what is meant by the problem term *iambike idea*, 'lampoon form'). The fragments give us little opportunity to assess the basis for this verdict, but the preserved titles suggest contemporary rather than mythological settings: *Heroes, Neighbours, Samians, Games*, as well as *Lamia* and the utopian fantasy *Beasts*, from which we have a handful of fragments describing a new dispensation under which humans will no longer need to work. Aristotle implies that Crates refrained from political engagement with current events and individuals, which seems, from the 300 or so fragments, to have been true also of Crates' supposed disciple **Pherecrates**. His long career began around 440 and lasted perhaps to the end of the century; the titles and fragments include several golden-age and underworld fantasies, as well as a number of female names and choral titles that suggest an Aristophanic interest in comedies of gender; whether Pherecrates or Aristophanes was the pioneer here remains unclear, but Pherecrates' underworld comedy *Krapataloi* ('Small Change'), in which the dead Aeschylus was a character, seems to have preceded, and presumably influenced, *Frogs*. Several other plays had a literary or musical theme: an extraordinary and brilliant long fragment from *Chiron* has Music complaining in sexual terms of her abuse at the hands of the avant-garde composers of the so-called 'New Music'. Another figure from the same era was **Callias**, who may or may not be the same as the author of the fascinating *Alphabet Tragedy*.[27] This is also the generation in which political comedy first emerges to clear view: two key figures here were **Teleclides** and **Hermippus**, both of whom seem to have pursued particular comic vendettas against Pericles and Aspasia.

But the titan of this era was **Cratinus**, who was still producing annually in the years of Aristophanes' earliest surviving plays (425–422), and defeated him in 423 with the extraordinary *Putine* ('Hipflask'), which responded to Aristophanes' dismissal of him in the *Knights* as a washed-up drunk by presenting Cratinus himself as torn between the rival mistresses of Poetry and Booze. Among other plays whose storyline is not completely obscure, *Odysseis* ('The Odysseus Boys') was a mythological comedy reworking the episode of Odysseus and the Cyclops, previously staged by Epicharmus and also an enduring staple of satyr-play; the fragments all fit neatly into identifiable moments in the Homeric storyline, though there was doubtless more to it. *Archilochoi* ('The Archilochus Boys') featured the founder of iambic satirical poetry, perhaps in some kind of competition with

----

[27] Rosen 1999.

Homer and other founding fathers of Greek poetry. *Dionysalexandros* ('Dionysus/Paris') is relatively sparsely represented by fragments, but a papyrus synopsis of the second half of the play tells us that the god assumed the role of Paris of Troy, judged the goddesses' beauty pageant in his place, and carried off Helen of Sparta as Aphrodite's reward – only for the real Paris (referred to here, as often in drama, under his Homeric name Alexandros) to track the impostor down, confiscate Helen, and fall in love with her himself. Two further details are especially tantalizing. First, the papyrus concludes by interpreting the play as an ingenious political satire accusing Pericles of 'bringing the war on Athens', which seems to imply that Paris, Helen, and the Trojan War were open, or at least fairly transparent, mythological allegories of Pericles, Aspasia, and the Peloponnesian War (or possibly the Samian War of ten years earlier; the play is only dated by this reference). Second, the papyrus opens at a point where the chorus of satyrs are addressing the audience, presumably in a *parabasis*, 'about the poets' – which, if the text is correctly supplemented, would appear to be an early example of the kind of literary polemic familiar from Aristophanes' *parabases*. But the papyrus is damaged at this point, and the correct reading may be 'about the making of sons' – perhaps in connection with Pericles' citizenship law of 451.

Aristophanes himself belonged to a fertile new generation of young comic poets who emerged in close succession in the early years of the Archidamian war. One such was **Phrynichus**, who would go on to compete against *Birds* with his *Monotropos* or 'Hermit' – apparently an ancestor of the misanthrope leads in Menander's *Dyskolos* and Plautus' *Aulularia* – and against *Frogs* with the intriguing but mysterious literary comedy *Muses*.[28] Phrynichus probably made his bow in the same year (429) as the seventeen-year-old **Eupolis**, whose seven victories in his short career left his sparring-partner Aristophanes standing in his shade until Eupolis' early death (probably in the sea-battle of Cynossema) in 411. His *Demes* is the best-preserved comedy on papyrus and had its hero resurrect four great Athenians from different past eras to put a degenerate Athens to rights; *Baptai* (apparently 'Dyers') was a satire on the vogue for foreign ecstatic cults and somehow attacked Alcibiades; *Marikas* (421) was a *Knights*-style attack on Cleon's demagogic successor, Hyperbolus, portrayed as the titular Persian slave, with a split chorus in the manner of *Lysistrata*; *Kolakes* ('Flatterers', also 421) satirized the intellectual and social life

---

[28] Harvey 2000.

of the phenomenally wealthy Callias. Unusually, perhaps uniquely, Eupolis specialized in political comedy, and seems not to have shared Aristophanes' taste for mythological or literary comedy – unlike their versatile contemporary **Plato** (no known relation to the philosopher), whose particular fondness for mythological sex comedies may be one reason why ancient critics sometimes classed him as a, sometimes *the*, representative of Middle Comedy. The somewhat younger **Archippus** similarly dramatized the amours of Heracles and Zeus, but of greatest interest is his *Birds*-like utopian comedy *Fishes* from the post-war years. Also making their débuts in the teens were **Theopompus**, a third or more of whose plays took their subjects from non-tragic myth, and the fascinating paratragic specialist **Strattis**.

But it was the 420s that were Old Comedy's golden decade, when the three canonical masters of the genre – Cratinus, Eupolis, and Aristophanes – were all in regular and increasingly hard-fought competition. The intense professional rivalry between these three escalated over the decade in a number of ways: in the Aristophanic *parabases*, which engage in open self-advertisement, disparagement of rivals, and competition for audience support; in the emergence of a new class of metatheatrical comedy, such as Cratinus' *Putine* and Aristophanes' mysterious *Proagon*; in rival attempts at the same subject matter, and back-and-forth accusations of plagiarism; and in a fascinating succession of more-or-less veiled self-representations by the playwrights in the plays themselves. All this came to a head at the Dionysia of 423, when Aristophanes' most ambitious play to date, *Clouds*, found itself up against a rival Socrates play in the form of Ameipsias' *Connus*, which beat *Clouds* into third place (of three) but was itself beaten by Cratinus' late masterpiece *Putine*. Cratinus disappears from the scene around this time, and 421's *Peace* jokes about him as already dead (which perhaps he was).[29]

Aristophanes: life

The ancient biographical tradition on Aristophanes, represented in the *Life* preserved in the manuscripts and assorted notes in the

---

[29] A series of important recent studies (Sidwell 1993, 1994; Biles 2002; Ruffell 2002; and see also Heath 1990; Luppe 2000; Storey 2003; Kyriakidi 2007) has challenged what we once thought we knew about the dynamics of comic intertextual rivalry in the 420s and by implication beyond, with the competition of 423 the climactic battleground. Further contributions to this debate are forthcoming.

scholia, is, as usual, built largely out of naively biographical readings of incidents and passages in the plays, but does at least embed some raw prosopographical information. Aristophanes was the son of Philippus of Cydathenaeum, one of the four Attic demes nucleated in the city itself; fellow-demesmen included Aristophanes' political *bête noire* Cleon and a number of figures from Aristophanes' early career who appear as members of a *thiasos* or religious association in honour of Heracles in the remarkable inscription IG ii².2343, including Aristophanes' frequent producer Philonides and the singularly named Amphitheus, who appears as a character in *Acharnians*.[30] The chorus of Aristophanes' first play, *Banqueters*, seems to have been modelled on or inspired by this club; the implications, and the extent of such in-jokes and characterizations *à clef* in the plays of the twenties, remain something of an enigma, but *Clouds* 528–31 thanks an unspecified group of early enthusiasts who were apparently responsible for getting *Banqueters* produced, and it is plausibly inferred that Aristophanes' career was launched with the help of these contacts. There was some connection with Aegina (*Ach.* 653–4); possibly Philippus held property on the island as a windfall from the Athenian clearances in 431.

Aristophanes' birth and death are undated. The low birth-date of 444 that is still occasionally found in derivative modern sources is the product of an emendation and a chain of inference too shaky to stand,[31] and Aristophanes (who was already bald by the time of *Peace*, 767–74) could have been born any time from 460, though a first production at seventeen is not entirely unthinkable for a comic poet; Aristophanes' rival Eupolis is said to have produced his first play at that age in 429, and Menander's career began at a similar age. Aristophanes may be playing up his youth and inexperience in the *Clouds* passage, but that he was at least more comfortable writing than rehearsing is suggested by his frequent use, especially early in his career, of such figures as Philonides and Callistratus in a role approximating to that of theatre director – something that caused understandable confusion in the competition records, though it is also attested for Eupolis and perhaps Plato. The *parabasis* of *Clouds* paints a possibly disingenuous self-portrait of a tyro playwright only gradually and coyly emerging into the spotlight in his own right, but Mastromarco and Halliwell have suggested that references to

---

[30] Dow 1969, Welsh 1983a, N. G. Wilson 2007a: 17, cf. 83.
[31] Dover 1968: xix n. 1.

collaborative writing preserve traces of a typical pattern of comic apprenticeship, which would begin with the contribution of material to others' plays and only gradually work up to the composition and production of a full-scale work under one's own name.[32] At any rate, Aristophanes' first plays were produced by the Callistratus who continued to direct some of Aristophanes' later plays as late as *Lysistrata*, and perhaps also by the still longer-serving Philonides, who directed *Wasps* and *Frogs* as well as at least three comedies of his own. Aristophanes' own first production as director was *Knights* in 424; this was the play for which he remained most celebrated until *Frogs*.

About a quarter of Aristophanes' total output survives.[33] As also for Aeschylus and Menander, a Hellenistic catalogue of titles is preserved; it lists forty-four plays, of which four were of debated authorship. Some titles existed in more than one version; in some cases (such as the two plays *Thesmophoriazusae*) these seem to have been titles reused for different plays, while in others they were revisions (*diaskeuaí*) of plays previously produced. The most interesting case is *Clouds*, which appears to be an unproduced partial revision, for book circulation only, of the unsuccessful production version; but *Peace* and *Wealth*, as well as the lost *Aeolosicon* and perhaps *Plays*, seem to have been staged competitively in revised versions, although the details are difficult to untangle and ancient scholars were easily confused by this practice. One particularly regrettable loss is the substantial subcorpus of mythological comedies amounting to nearly a quarter of Aristophanes' attested production.

The eleven extant plays fall into three chronological clusters: five plays from 425–421, four from 414–405, and two from the end of his career in 393–388. The majority of Aristophanes' undated plays are at least assignable to a general period on the basis of topical references to named individuals whose careers in the spotlight have more or less firm limits, and, with the significant exception of the revised text of *Clouds*, no known play is plausibly datable to the years 420–415, when the comic stage seems to have been heavily dominated by Eupolis. There is no such discontinuity apparent in the post-war period, though Aristophanes' final years seem to have seen a renewal of activity after a slowdown. He seems to have died in the mid–380s; the last firm dates are a stint on the city's Council around 390 (IG ii².1720.24) and the production of *Wealth* in 388. Two subsequent

---

[32] *Wasps* 1018–50 as interpreted by Mastromarco 1979; Halliwell 1980. Storey 2003: 280–1 surveys views since.

[33] For the full list, see Silk 2000: 16–17; Harvey and Wilkins 2000: 510–11.

plays, *Aeolosicon II* and *Cocalus*, were directed by his son Araros and may have been posthumously produced. Like Aeschylus, Sophocles, and Euripides, Aristophanes founded a theatrical dynasty – Araros and two other sons had careers as comic dramatists in their own right – which was probably influential in keeping his plays in circulation during the critical period between their first (and, in the case of comedy, generally their only) productions and the collected editions assembled at Alexandria as much as two centuries later. Despite their intense topicality, some of the plays were still sufficiently appreciated a generation after his death for a scene from *Thesmophoriazusae* to be represented in close theatrical detail on an Italian vase around 370, and other illustrations from the same period are plausibly tied to *Frogs* and to Eupolis' *Demes*.[34]

Historical events		Aristophanes: plays (+ producer, festival, prize)
revolt of Mytilene	427	*Banqueters* (Philonides or Callistratus,[35] ?Lenaea, ?2nd)
Cleon prosecutes Aristophanes	426	*Babylonians* (Callistratus, Dionysia, ?1st)
Pylos campaign	425	***Acharnians*** (Callistratus, Lenaea, 1st)
battle of Delium; Brasidas in Thrace	424	***Knights*** (Aristophanes, Lenaea, 1st)
1-year truce	423	***Clouds*** (?Aristophanes, Dionysia, 3rd)
battle of Amphipolis; deaths of Cleon, Brasidas	422	*Proagon* (Philonides, Lenaea, 1st); ***Wasps*** (?Aristophanes, Lenaea, 2nd)
Peace of Nicias	421	***Peace I*** (Dionysia, 2nd)
negotiations with Argos	420	
Alcibiades in Peloponnese	419	
Mantinea campaign	418	
Hyperbolus ostracized	417	
revolt of Melos	416	
Sicilian expedition sails	415	
siege of Syracuse	414	*Amphiaraus* (Philonides, Lenaea); ***Birds*** (Callistratus, Dionysia, 2nd)

[34] *Frogs*: the 'Berlin Heracles' (Taplin 1993: 45–7), lost and presumed destroyed in the Second World War. *Demes*: Assteas (Salerno, Museo Provinciale Pc 1812; Taplin 1993: 42; Storey 2003: 117).

[35] Callistratus according to *Prolegomena* III (9.38 Koster), Philonides in Schol. *Clouds* 531. Sommerstein 1980–2002: vol. 11 (2001) 219 favours Callistratus, but Welsh 1983b: 52–3, MacDowell 1995: 35, and Storey 2003: 280 favour Philonides.

Historical events		Aristophanes: plays (+ producer, festival, prize)
Spartans occupy Decelea; Sicilian expedition wiped out	413	
allies revolt; Spartans woo Persia	412	
oligarchic coup in Athens	411	*Lysistrata* (Callistratus, ?Lenaea); *Thesmophoriazusae* (?Dionysia)
Athenian democracy restored	410	
Athens loses Pylos	409	
Thracian campaign	408	*Wealth I*
Alcibiades returns to Athens	407	
Alcibiades exiled; battle of Arginusae	406	
fleet destroyed at Aegospotami	405	*Frogs* (Philonides, Lenaea, 1st)
Athens surrenders; 'Thirty Tyrants' puppet regime	404	
democracy restored	403	
	402	
march of the Ten Thousand	401	
Spartan war with Persia	400	
trial and execution of Socrates	399	
Sparta negotiates with Persia	398	
Conon commands Persian fleet against Spartans	397	
Agesilaus invades Phrygia	396	
Agesilaus in Lydia	395	
Athenian–Boeotian alliance against Sparta; battle of Coronea	394	
Athenian Long Walls rebuilt	393	
	392	*Assemblywomen* (?)
	391	
	390	
Thrasybulus killed on campaign	389	
	388	*Wealth II* (Aristophanes, ?1st)
'King's Peace'	387	*Cocalus* (Araros)?
	386	*Aeolosicon II* (Araros)?

The early group (427–421)

Aristophanes' early career was both prolific and successful. As well as the five extant plays from successive years, at least half a dozen others can be assigned with confidence to the same eight-year period. On one curious occasion (Lenaea, 422), he seems to have exploited a loophole in the festival regulations to enter two plays, one under his own name and one under its producer's; one of these was *Wasps*, which took second prize to the lost paratheatrical comedy *Proagon*. With *Acharnians* and *Knights*, this puts three of his four securely attested victories in this period, and he may also have taken first prize with *Babylonians*.

The plays of this period are, for all their layeredness and complexity, essentially single-issue plays, heavily topical comedies on a well-defined matter of current concern: the war with Sparta (*Acharnians*), domestic demagogic politics (*Knights*), the impact of the new intellectuals (*Clouds*), the democratic legal system and its abuse (*Wasps*), the imminent peace treaty of spring 421 (*Peace*). The plots are happy to shape themselves more around the traditional elements of formal structure than any sustained logic of cause and effect; *Acharnians* and *Peace* resolve their conflicts by the time of the *parabasis* and devote the second half to a loose series of sketches illustrating the consequence of that resolution through a succession of new characters trooping to the hero's door. Nevertheless, the great plays of this period – especially *Clouds* and *Wasps* – are already starting to move beyond this, using transgenerational conflicts to dramatize major contemporary social and cultural changes as seen through the eyes of Aristophanes' own generation and that of his elders. Several of these plays (*Banqueters, Clouds, Wasps*) fasten on father–son conflicts as a means to dramatize cultural change, by aligning the generations with old and new sets of ideas or values that are then shown at work within an existing structure of family bonds and problems.

Banqueters and Babylonians.[36] Aristophanes' two earliest plays are the best documented of his lost works. *Banqueters* was an early generational comedy in the mould of *Clouds* and *Wasps*, though here with two sons embodying the effects of traditional versus sophistic education. The surviving fragments give more sense of situation than of plot, but there seems to have been a strong agonistic element between the contrasting brothers, whom Aristophanes calls 'the

[36] Cassio 1977; Welsh 1983a, 1983b; MacDowell 1995: 27–45.

decent and the indecent' (*ho sophron kai ho katapugon*, *Clouds* 529). The scandalous *Babylonians* is more of an enigma. Something in the play about Athens and its subject allies seems to have provoked Cleon to the legal procedure known as *eisangelia*, though the details of pretext, charge, and outcome are all extremely unclear, as indeed is the situation of the play, which somehow involved the god Dionysus and a chorus of tattooed Babylonian slaves working in a mill. At any rate the legal and political fallout, which seems to have done Aristophanes' fledgling career no harm at all, was sufficiently fresh to be repeatedly invoked in the extant play from the next available festival.

Acharnians (Lenaea, 425, 1st prize).[37] This hugely complex political and literary comedy is framed, as is *Thesmophoriazusae*, around a burlesque of Euripides' lost tragedy *Telephus* (438), in which the hero, responding to an oracle instructing him to seek a cure for the crippling wound inflicted by Achilles' spear, infiltrated the Greek camp at Aulis in a beggar disguise, Odysseus-style, and made a speech arguing that the Trojans were not wholly to blame for the war; cornered, he forced a standoff by holding a sword to the infant Orestes. In Aristophanes' version, the Telephus figure is the war-weary farmer Dicaeopolis who, frustrated by official resistance and public apathy towards peace negotiations with Sparta, arranges a private peace treaty for himself and his family while the rest of Attica remains at war; the Trojan War becomes the current war with Sparta, and the role of the hostile Greeks is taken by the chorus of charcoal-makers from the village of Acharnae, whose hostility to Sparta has been stoked by five years of invasion and crop-burning. After costuming himself from Euripides' own character wardrobe, Dicaeopolis makes his scandalous speech defending Sparta, performs the hostage scene with a basket of charcoal, and spends the second half of the play enjoying the fruits of trade monopoly with Athens' enemies while the real-life general Lamachus suffers the consequences of pursuing the war.

---

[37] As well as the editions by Sommerstein (1980–2002, vol. 1 [1980]), S. D. Olson (2002), the reading commentary by Platter (2003), and the chapters in Dover 1972, Russo 1994, and MacDowell 1995, see Forrest 1963; Edmunds 1980; Sommerstein 1980; A. M. Bowie 1982; Harriott 1982; MacDowell 1983; E. L. Bowie 1988; Foley 1988; Sutton 1988; S. D. Olson 1990a, 1991b; Goldhill 1991: 185–8; L. P. E. Parker 1991; Carey 1993; N. R. E. Fisher 1993; Slater 1993; Sidwell 1994; Van Steen 1994; Habash 1995; Compton-Engle 1999; Moorton 1999; Hesk 2000: 237–43; Lanza 2000; Pelling 2000: 141–63; Dobrov 2001: 47–97; McGlew 2002: 57–85; Brockmann 2003; Whitehorne 2005.

Acharnians paints a compelling picture of the mood of Athens six years into a war that had seen no significant successes and two desperate hardships: the annual spring invasions of Attica, with their attendant evacuations of the rural population within the city walls while their crops and livestock were ravaged by the Peloponnesian army, and the plague outbreaks of 430 and 429. Against this background, rural demes like Acharnae might seem like a tough constituency to try to win to the cause of peace; but, from the outset, the play is built around issues of democratic accountability and the individual's right to power. A dazzling prologue stages a meeting of the Athenian assembly, in which it becomes clear to the heckling Dicaeopolis that peace is being deliberately kept off the agenda by the city's officials, who are lining their own pockets by continuing the war; and it is this failure of the machinery of democracy to enact the actual will of the people that drives Dicaeopolis to his individualistic solution.

Like his play, the character of Dicaeopolis operates on several levels at once. The imaginary speaking name Dicaeopolis, 'just-[in-respect-of-his]-city', is calqued on the suggestive name of Aristophanes' rival (but also, apparently, intermittent collaborator) Eupolis, yet Dicaeopolis is not Eupolis in any simple sense: he is a middle-aged farmer from the deme of Cholleidae, albeit one who perplexingly identifies himself at one point as a comic poet. What we seem to have here is an early example of Aristophanes' onomastic play with the names of real public figures whose identity is lightly and partially invoked by a name which plays on, but substitutes one element of, its real-world counterpart; so with 'Lysistrata' and the priestess of Athena Polias, Lysimache, and with the figure of Amphitheus (whose rare name means 'god on both sides') in this very play. Dicaeopolis has a notional name, life, and family of his own, but he is also, as a specimen of the middle-aged, self-assertive, everyman hero, a representative of the comic genre, who at times can seem to speak with the voice of its makers; and on to this are further overlaid the intertextual role of a comic Telephus, the onomastic role of a civic benefactor, and the metadramatic role of a spokesman for comedy itself.

Knights (Lenaea, 424, 1st prize).[38] This was the defining play of Aristophanes' early career: a relentless personal onslaught on

---

[38] See Sommerstein's edition (1980–2002, vol. 2 [1981]), and Brock 1986; Littlefield 1968a; also Edmunds 1987a, 1987b; Worthington 1987; C. A. Anderson 1989; Bennett and Tyrrell 1990; Welsh 1990; S. D. Olson 1990c; Sidwell 1993; Cannata 1995; McGlew 1996, 2002: 86–111; Hesk 2000: 248–60; Biles 2001; Reinders 2001; Scholtz 2004.

Aristophanes' arch-nemesis Cleon, building a full-blown allegorical satire on the conceit that populist politicians were slaves and/or lovers (the metaphors slip and mix as the play unfolds) of the *demos* – perhaps a contemporary political catchphrase. Here Demos ('the people') has been himself effectively enslaved by the shameless toadying and manipulation of his own favoured slave, Paphlagon, until the other slaves come up with an even more grotesque rival in the form of a street hawker flogging low-grade meat products. The duel for Demos' favours takes up the rest of the unusually tight and minimalist play, with a series of twists towards the end as Demos is revealed to be only play-acting dementia (but is rejuvenated nevertheless) and the sausage-seller emerges as a natural statesman.

In later years, Aristophanes would claim, apparently with some justice, that in devoting a play to an all-out onslaught on a single political figure he had pioneered a kind of comedy that would keep his rivals in business long after he himself had moved on.[39] Certainly it is Cleon's historical misfortune to have managed personally to alienate both of our two major sources for the period. Whatever exactly happened in the aftermath of *Babylonians*, no individual receives as sustained or savage treatment in Aristophanes' plays; his name and reputation are still being traduced in *Frogs*, eighteen years after his actual death. Yet Cleon at this time was a popular hero following his personal role in the Pylos campaign the previous autumn, when 120 Spartan citizens had unprecedentedly been captured alive in a brilliant operation in the south-west Peloponnese. Like Thucydides, whose bravura narrative of the episode (iv.1–41) is one of the sustained dramatic highlights of his history, Aristophanes presents Cleon as stealing the credit that rightfully belonged to the main architect of the victory, the general Demosthenes. But at the very least Cleon gambled and won on Demosthenes' talent against the more cautious stance of his domestic rival Nicias, whose generalship he dramatically took over in the process; and the Spartan hostages gave Athens an upper hand in negotiations, among other things putting an end to the annual spring invasions of Attica.

---

[39] The *parabasis* of *Clouds* claims that Eupolis' *Maricas* and Hermippus' *Breadsellers* were straight knock-offs of *Knights*, attacking Cleon's successor, Hyperbolus. A fragment of Eupolis seems to respond to this, claiming that *Knights* was his work in the first place and that he had made a gift of it to Aristophanes – implying, no doubt disingenuously, that he was the author and Aristophanes merely the director.

Clouds (Dionysia, 423, 3rd prize).[40] Aristophanes' dark, Faustian comedy about the dangers of too much cleverness has the dim-witted farmer Strepsiades, in hock for his son's debts, turn to Socrates' Brain Shop to help him outwit his creditors, only to find that the reduction of persuasiveness to a set of teachable and entirely truth-free techniques has unleashed a genie that refuses to go back in the bottle.

This first appearance of Socrates in literature is notoriously unlike the portrait we find in Xenophon and Plato. Plato, in particular, is keen to demonstrate that, far from being representative of the sophists as a whole, Socrates is not actually a sophist at all, lacking as he does three essential qualifications: he does not teach rhetoric, and indeed does not claim to be a teacher of anything at all; he does not have a school or charge fees; and he is entirely uninterested in the scientific researches and speculation with which Aristophanes has so much fun in *Clouds*. There is no particular reason to doubt Plato's account on the matters of fact – though a famous article by Nussbaum makes a strong case for Aristophanes' portrait as showing a surprisingly close and deep understanding of Socratic ideas, and we may in any case doubt whether Plato's highly tendentious attempt to deny Socrates the label 'sophist' would have convinced even his contemporaries who remembered him, let alone the Athenians of the 420s. Probably, Socrates is made the comic figurehead of the sophistic movement for no better reason than that he was the most publicly visible, was a native Athenian, and had a face that was already halfway to being a comic mask.[41]

The play's notorious failure (on its production in 423) and revision (around 418) have both been picked over without conclusion. Aristophanes himself, in the revised part of the *parabasis*, blames the flop on his play's sophistication; but it was perhaps not the best moment to attack Socrates, who seems to have been something of a war hero after his conduct at the battle of Delium the previous summer, which included saving the life of the young Alcibiades. It is also notable that Strepsiades is the first and last of Aristophanes' heroes to be a loser rather than a winner, a brilliantly realized but

---

[40] Editions by Dover (1968) and Sommerstein (1980–2002, vol. 3 [1982]), and see C. Segal 1969; Adkins 1970; Green 1979; Nussbaum 1980; R. K. Fisher 1984, 1988; R. Olson 1984; Hubbard 1986; Davies 1990; Kopff 1990; Nevola 1990–3; Tarrant 1991; Marianetti 1992, 1993; O'Regan 1992; Jeffrey Henderson 1993a; Storey 1993; S. D. Olson 1994; Vander Waerdt 1994; Reckford 1987; Rosen 1997; Gaertner 1999; Meineck 2000; Erbse 2002; Papageorgiou 2004; Major 2006; Revermann 2006: 179–235, 326–32.

[41] How widely, and even whether, 'portrait masks' were used remains debated; but it would be astonishing if a generic mask were used in this case.

unsettling prototype of Homer Simpson; and the sheer darkness of the ending, which at least in the revised version has the hero burn down the stage building, is so unlike anything else in Aristophanes that it is hard not to wonder whether the play was simply asking its audience to forge too unfamiliar a relationship with its hero and his scheme. Aristophanes, at least, refused to let the play die, and partly reworked it: the first of his attested *diaskeuai* or revisions, though if he ever intended for it to be staged he must have been refused a chorus before the revision was complete, as part of the *parabasis* remains that of the 423 production while part has been completely overhauled to look back on the play's original reception and the development of comedy over the intervening half-decade or so. The scholia also seem to iden- tify the *agon* (between the personifications of Straight and Crooked, in reasoning and morals alike) and the ending as among the parts of the play that differed significantly in their original version.

Wasps (Lenaea, 422, 2nd prize).[42] Young Bdelycleon ('Loathe- Cleon') tries to reform his father Philocleon ('Love-Cleon') from his addiction to the exercise of his democratic power through jury service by redirecting his activity from the civic to the domestic sphere; but the old dog learns his new tricks imperfectly, and by the end of the play the anarchic comic energies that had previously been contained by being channelled into civic participation have been unleashed in their full force on household and city alike.

Often felt to be the most accomplished of the early plays, *Wasps* packages a blistering satire on the failures of popular democracy as a generation-gap comedy of manners in the mould of *Banqueters*. The key scene is the *agon*, in which Philocleon's argument that his democratic power is *arche*, imperial dominion, is overthrown by Bdelycleon's paradoxical demonstration that it is in fact *douleia*, slavery: that the demos is being fobbed off with the illusion of power while the real power, and wealth, resides with Cleon and other radical-democratic politicians who use that illusion to control them. This is strong stuff, and the final third of the play, like the closing scenes of *Knights*, knows well enough to retreat gracefully from its implication that the very institutions of democracy are fundamentally flawed. In notable contrast to the treatment of Strepsiades in *Clouds*, *Wasps* allows the incorrigible Philocleon to traverse the full path from

---

[42] Editions by MacDowell (1971) and Sommerstein (1980–2002, vol. 4 [1983], revised 2007), and see Borthwick 1968, 1992; Vaio 1971; MacCary 1979; Banks 1980; Horsley 1982; Konstan 1985; Storey 1985; A. M. Bowie 1987; Sidwell 1990, 1995; Crichton 1991–3; S. D. Olson 1996; McGlew 2004; Jedrkiewicz 2006.

sneakily lovable villain of the piece to comic hero triumphant. The play modulates with astonishing deftness from an initially domestic comedy of psychopathology to a rabble-rousing demonstration that the failings of the legal system are merely symptoms of a wider corruption endemic in the operations of democracy itself, only to settle back into a domestic comedy of personalities, slapstick, and a barnstorming close that reaffirms the old man as the embodiment of the irrepressible energy of comedy itself.

Peace (Dionysia, 421, 2nd prize).[43] The most fantastic of the early plays reworks themes from *Acharnians* for a world now on the brink of peace, as the Dicaeopolis-like farmer hero Trygaeus flies to heaven on a giant dung-beetle (spoofing Euripides' *Bellerophon*) to find out why the gods have allowed the war to drag on; there he rescues the goddess Peace from her dungeon with the help of a Panhellenic chorus of farmers, and, on his return to earth, marries the goddess of Harvest as a reward.

The military and diplomatic obstacles to a peace settlement had fallen dramatically away with the deaths at Amphipolis the previous summer of Cleon and the Spartan general Brasidas, each a popular and successful advocate of continued hostilities. In both Sparta and Athens the doves seized the opportunity to establish a climate for negotiation and, by the time of *Peace*, the treaty known as the 'Peace of Nicias' (after Cleon's old rival, eclipsed in the Pylos affair) was a done deal, ratified within days of the festival. The play addresses this transitional situation by allegorizing the peace process as the result of a comic hero's adventure behind the scenes, and following up with an *Acharnians*-style second half back in the real world, where the hero enjoys what is now a merely temporary monopoly on the benefits of peace before her release into the wider community.

Other plays. Several lost plays from this period are of interest in addition to *Banqueters* and *Babylonians*. The plot of **Proagon** (Lenaea, 422) remains mysterious, but Euripides featured as a character and the title refers to the pre-festival preview day at which the competing tragedians introduced their choruses out of costume as a kind of live trailer; the play may have been the first full-length comedy about tragic theatre and its making. **Farmers** and **Merchant-Ships** were both peace plays in the mould of *Acharnians* and *Peace*; the interesting chorus of *Merchant-Ships* comprised the vessels of Athens'

[43] Editions: Platnauer 1964; S. D. Olson 1998; Sommerstein 1980–2002, vol. 5 (1985), revised 2005; and see Cassio 1985; Slater 1988b; McGlew 2001; Whitehorne 2001; Hall 2006: 321–52.

trading fleet, presumably as victims of the war and beneficiaries of a truce, and the fragments seem to show an Athenian sympathizing with a Spartan over their mutual sufferings.

The middle group (414–405)

The four plays that survive from this decade, the zenith of Aristophanes' powers, are more complex and ambitious in their choice of theme – no longer single-issue plays but multi-layered satires, which find poetic connections between a range of targets and ideas in a way that can make it significantly more difficult now to say what each play is really 'about'. Plotting is tighter, and the tyranny of elements such as the *agon* and *parabasis* over the shape of the play is beginning to give way to a much more sustained dramatic control, with stories that resolve in the closing minutes rather than halfway through. There is less intertextual reference to, and criticism of, the plays of his rivals, who were by now mostly younger and less established – though the decline of the anapaestic section of the *parabasis* may also be a factor here.

Birds (Dionysia, 414, 2nd prize).[44] The ethereal plot has much in common with *Peace*: the speakingly named Peisthetaerus ('Persuasion-Friend') seeks a utopian refuge from the madness of Athenian life but instead ends up founding a city of birds, and imposes an embargo on traffic between earth and heaven until the gods hand over Zeus's sceptre to the birds and award our hero the goddess of Sovereignty in marriage.

Birds is Aristophanes' most expansive play, its length and production values presumably reflecting a larger choregic budgetary pot after seven years of formal peace. It has also been, even by the standards of middle Aristophanes, the most impervious to interpretation, viewed variously as topical satire or escapist fantasy, comic utopia or dark Thucydidean parable. Political readings have tended to founder on the combination of a notable lack of specific topical references and the difficulty of chronological fit with Thucydidean time-mates (the Melian massacre, the Sicilian expedition, and Alcibiades' recall and defection). Arrowsmith's reading remains broadly attractive at one of the play's levels, seeing it as a panoramic satire on the Athenian

---

[44] Editions: Sommerstein 1980–2002, vol. 6 (1987), revised 2007; Dunbar 1995. See also Arrowsmith 1961, 1973; Epstein 1981; Pozzi 1986; Craik 1987; Zannini-Quirini 1987; Dobrov 1990, 1993, 1997; Konstan 1990; Perkell 1993; Vickers 1995; Dunbar 1996.

national character and its virtue/vice of *polypragmosyne* or inability to mind one's own business. But it is also hard to deny the play's Thucydidean resonances, particularly in its central situation of third-party states exploited by Athenian (as by Spartan) military advisers to fight others' wars for them on dubious claims of ultimate local self-interest. Already a familiar feature of the Archidamian war and the more recent Mantinean campaign, this pattern would be used against Athens with devastating success within weeks of the play's premiere, as Sparta dispatched the dauntingly effective Gylippus to mobilize Syracusan resistance to the rudderless Athenian attack – a decision prompted in turn by the still more Peisthetaerean figure of Alcibiades. Aristophanes and his audience could hardly have imagined these developments, and would hardly have borne so airy a treatment if they had; but the play is embedded in a deep and brutal realist understanding of how the world of late fifth-century warfare worked.

Lysistrata (411, probably Lenaea; prize unknown).[45] Under the leadership of the visionary heroine Lysistrata, the women of Athens force their menfolk to make peace with Sparta by occupying the Acropolis and imposing an international sex strike.

This (probable) first of Aristophanes' plays on contemporary women's lives mingles earnest Panhellenism with wall-to-wall sex jokes and *double entendres*, characteristically developing poetic mappings between the politics of gender and of war, and offering a surprisingly complex and thoughtful analysis of Athens' situation in the immediate aftermath of the Sicilian debacle of 413 and the subsequent revolt of allies, Persian involvement in the war, and anti-democratic stirrings at home.

Generalization from silence is dangerous, but Aristophanes' plays of 411 seem to have been the first fully female-centred comedies; plays with mythical or allegorical females go back to Epicharmus, and hetaera comedies such as Pherecrates' *Corianno* were probably an established subgenre, but there is no trace of a comedy centred on respectable citizen females before *Lysistrata*, and it seems quite probable that the opening-up of comedy to the female was Aristophanes'

---

[45] Editions: Jeffrey Henderson 1987; Sommerstein 1980–2002, vol. 7 (1990), revised 2007. See also D. M. Lewis 1955; Hulton 1972; Vaio 1973; Sommerstein 1977, 1980; Rosellini 1979; Jeffrey Henderson 1980b; Loraux 1981; N. G. Wilson 1982; Harriott 1985; Dillon 1987a; Levine 1987; R. P. Martin 1987; Konstan 1993a; Taaffe 1993: 48–73; F. D. Harvey 1994; Fowler 1996; Faraone 1997, 2006; Fletcher 1999; Ruden 2003; Stroup 2004; Revermann 2006: 236–60.

own invention in the plays we have from 411.[46] *Lysistrata* pioneers the distinctive Aristophanic vision of Athenian women's segregated world as a society-within-society from which men are paradoxically the ones excluded – particularly at the women's festivals at which their great conspiracy plots are hatched – and which is collectively bonded by its housewifely networks of gossip, mutual assistance, and *de facto* collusion against their menfolk. Like its successors, *Thesmophoriazusae* and *Ecclesiazusae*, *Lysistrata* spins from this comic observation a fantasy of conspiracy, revolution, and the radical inversion of gendered worlds, playing on male citizens' latent paranoia both domestic and political, at a time when the air was thick with real and imagined plots to overthrow the democracy.

The speaking name Lysistrata, 'Army-Dissolver', alludes to the celebrated priestess of Athena Polias, Lysimache, whose name means 'Battle-Dissolver'. But it is a misunderstanding of the nuances of Aristophanic play with names to claim that she is in any meaningful sense 'based on' the real-life priestess; we are in Dicaeopolis territory here, with a fictional character referencing a real one in name and some attributes, but with the substitution of one name-element for a close synonym to make it clear that this is something more complex and flexible than a mere stage version of that real-life individual. In developing a female counterpart to the traditional male 'comic hero', Aristophanes plays safer than he will in later plays, allowing Lysistrata the comic vision and civic initiative of Dicaeopolis and Trygaeus without the appetitive enthusiasms for food, sex, and power, and keeping her character high-minded and largely humourless as a foil to the other women's surrender to what will be a stereotype of alcoholism, sex addiction, and shameless duplicity.

Thesmophoriazusae ('**Women at the Thesmophoria**') (411, probably Dionysia; prize unknown).[47] Euripides tries to forestall a plot against him by the women of Athens, who are outraged at his notorious representation of female conduct in the tragedies, by sending a dubious relative along to infiltrate their festival in drag, only to have to rescue him once the ruse is exposed.

Aristophanes' second comedy of gender is a wildly surreal literary fantasy in which the reassuringly segregated worlds of male and female, comedy and tragedy, and theatre and reality are all turned

---

[46] So Jeffrey Henderson 1987: xxviii; reservations in Storey 2003: 315–17.

[47] Editions: Sommerstein 1980–2002, vol. 8 (1994); Austin and Olson 2004. See also Hansen 1976; Sommerstein 1977; Muecke 1982; Zeitlin 1982; Hall 1989; Taaffe 1993: 74–102; Habash 1997; Gamel 2001.

upside-down by a series of actual and metaphoric transvestisms. As in *Acharnians*, the first half is traced over Euripides' own *Telephus*, with the disguised hero delivering a speech in Euripides' defence in the midst of his enemies and fending off exposure by playing the hostage scene with a baby that turns out to be a wineskin. But, as infiltration becomes captivity, the second half of the play rewrites the swash-buckling rescue tragedies with which Euripides had recently been experimenting, and specifically his two extraordinary plays of the previous Dionysia, *Andromeda* and *Helen* – casting the transvestite hero as the successive damsels in distress, and Euripides himself as the would-be heroic rescuer. Particularly fascinating is the extended parody of Euripides' extant *Helen*, whose text has been taken apart (Aristophanes is evidently working from an actual script) and reas-sembled in comically reduced form as a two-hander, with a third character unwittingly written in as the scene unfolds.

Frogs (Lenaea, 405, 1st prize).[48] Dionysus, god of theatre, descends to the underworld to bring back the recently deceased Euripides and save tragedy (and Athens itself) but, after a hotly fought literary debate, decides to take Aeschylus back instead.

Frogs uses the history of tragedy as an opportunistic metaphor for the state of Athenian politics in what were to prove the fateful closing months of the Peloponnesian War, while simultaneously making fun with (and of) contemporary literary-critical ideas about the nature and function of poetry. Two key events are repeatedly invoked: the abor-tive oligarchic coup of 411, with the dispossession of the surviving participants after democracy was restored; and the naval battle of Arginusae in 406, where slaves were permitted to make up the man-power shortage by rowing in the fleet at the reward of their freedom, and where an Athenian victory was clouded by the commanders' decision not to risk further losses by picking up survivors from the choppy seas. Back in Athens, the assembly approved a motion of the Council that the generals involved should be executed for dereliction. Socrates' famous solitary dissent from his fellow councillors' decision was not enough to prevent the executions, which probably contrib-uted to the disastrous decisions at Aegospotami the following year,

---

[48] Editions: Dover 1993; Sommerstein 1980–2002, vol. 9 (1996). See also C. Segal 1961; Stanford 1963; Littlefield 1968b; Higgins 1977; Hooker 1980; Havelock 1982; Allison 1983; Epstein 1985; Vaio 1985; R. P. Martin 1988–9; Goldhill 1991; Heiden 1991; Padilla 1992; Borthwick 1994; Lada-Richards 1999; Vickers 2001; Habash 2002; R. Edmonds 2004; Rosen 2004.

which saw the fleet destroyed and Athens besieged into unconditional surrender.

Frogs was granted the rare, perhaps unique, privilege of a second production 'because of its *parabasis*' (*Hypothesis* I), which argues for the restoration of citizenship to the exiled oligarchs on the grounds that Athens needs all the talent it can muster and is already extending citizen rights even to slaves. It is no coincidence that the first half of the play centres on the first of western comedy's great master–servant double acts, with the slave Xanthias sharing the spotlight and the laughs on even terms with his master Dionysus, culminating in a superbly constructed first-act climax in which master and slave repeatedly exchange roles to the point where no reliable way can be found to distinguish them. Throughout the play, the mythical pattern of *catabasis* or descent to the underworld is used as a powerful metaphor for political death and rebirth, with the recall of Aeschylus to life symbolizing the return of Athens' most gifted political exiles. In the event, the amnesty came too late to save the city, and merely led to the still bloodier oligarchic regime of the 'Thirty Tyrants'. If the second production of *Frogs* took place at the Lenaea or City Dionysia of 404, it is hard to avoid the implication that Aristophanes, never a vocal enthusiast for radical democracy, was uncomfortably complicit in these high-stakes games.

Other plays. The lost plays of the middle period are less easy to pin down, but ***Phoenician Women*** appears to have been a full-length parody of Euripides' compendious tragedy on the Theban civil war, which was produced around 410; Aristophanes' play probably appeared soon after (compare the parody of two 412 tragedies in 411's *Thesmophoriazusae*), and seems to have been part of a general vogue for full-length mythological paratragedies. The lost second ***Thesmophoriazusae*** [49] does not seem to have been a reworking of the play we have; the prologue was spoken by the goddess Calligenia, personification of the final day of the festival, and an alternative title, *Thesmophoriasasae* ('Women after the Thesmophoria'), suggests that the rites were essentially over at the time of the play's action, which has resisted reconstruction despite the relatively abundant and indicative fragments.

---

[49] Butrica's bold suggestion (2001) that the lost play was a work of the 420s has not found acceptance; see Austin & Olson 2004: lxxvii–lxxxix, with Butrica's response to their points (2004).

The late group (393–385)

After *Frogs*, there is an even longer gap – not this time in Aristophanes' writing, although his output does seem to have fallen off somewhat in the early post-war years. Some twelve years separate *Frogs* from the next surviving play, *Assemblywomen*, but the final years of Aristophanes' life were a third phase of high productivity and innovation. His most influential plays from this period were mythological comedies that seem to have anticipated some of the features of later fourth-century comedy, though these are unfortunately lost. What we do have is two fascinating plays that show the genre already starting to reinvent itself for the changed world of a post-imperial Athens. *Assemblywomen* and *Wealth* are less theatrically extravagant plays than their predecessors, reflecting the comparative lack of cash available to spend on theatrical performances. The chorus not only has its theatrical and formal presence severely reduced but is beginning to disappear from the script, with a stage direction *CHOROU* ('[song] of the chorus') marking in the manuscript tradition some points in the later part of the play where ancient scholars understood a choral song to have been performed.

But what these plays lack in production values they make up in intellectual ambition: both are fantasies of social revolution, apparently reflecting a contemporary climate of speculative social engineering among early fourth-century intellectuals in an Athens that was consciously rebuilding itself after the loss of its empire and the restoration of democracy following Spartan occupation. Both explore issues of poverty and inequality in contemporary Athenian society, and scholars have been divided over whether or not to see this as a response to serious and widespread deprivation in the post-war condition of Athens, notwithstanding the elements of fantasy and illogic in both plays' scenarios, which imagine the social consequences of radical redistribution of wealth: in *Assemblywomen*, through the establishment of a new communist utopia in which all property (including the family) is held in common; in *Wealth*, through the mythological fantasy of applying modern medical techniques to the eyesight of the god of wealth himself, so that now he can tell the difference between the deserving and the undeserving. How seriously these unsettlingly thoughtful, yet problematically coherent, plays ask to be taken is one of the great cruces of Aristophanic criticism, with readings largely polarized between face-value and 'ironic' interpretations; the insufficiencies of these polarities to make sense of these plays are the subject of important discussions by McGlew (2002) and Ruffell (2006).[50]

Ecclesiazusae ('**Women in the Assembly**') (393?).[51] Led by the resourceful Praxagora, the women of Athens infiltrate the assembly in male disguise and persuade the city to turn power over to them, whereupon they institute a radical and increasingly bizarre communistic utopia.

This intricately worked-out fantasy of feminist conspiracy and utopian social engineering has curious parallels to Plato's (as yet unwritten) *Republic*, which have been variously explained in terms of a putative influence of Aristophanes on Plato, of Plato's embryonic project on Aristophanes, of a lost common source on both, of generalized roots in a wider intellectual context of utopian social models, and of meaningless coincidence; none is very convincing, but no new solution seems forthcoming. The surprising details of the women's utopia, which emerge only after they have been handed a constitutional blank cheque, centre on the abolition of personal property, including familial and sexual forms of ownership – not entirely inappropriately, in view of Athenian women's restricted property rights and their status as virtual chattels, but it is far from clear what response the play seeks to the scenario proposed. Ironic readings see the various incoherences and dissident sentiments of the final third of the play as indicating that the new utopia is doomed to failure; others relate the measures closely to the state of post-war Athens as a fantastic but intellectually ambitious response to serious social and economic hardship.

Wealth (388).[52] An ingenious citizen uses the modern medical technique of incubation to cure the legendary blindness of the god of wealth, overnight creating a world in which only the righteous are wealthy.

A sober, moralistic, often unfunny play ('the possibility that Aristophanes had had a stroke,' wrote Dover, 'cannot be entirely discounted'[53]), for most of the history of Aristophanes' reception this

---

[50] The key discussions of the plays as a pair are Flashar 1967; Sommerstein 1984; McGlew 2002: 171–211; and Ruffell 2006.

[51] Editions: Ussher 1973; Sommerstein 1980–2002, vol. 10 (1998), revised 2007. See also Ussher 1969; Saïd 1979; Foley 1982; S. D. Olson 1988, 1989c, 1991a; Rothwell 1990; Taaffe 1991, 1993: 103–33; Slater 1997; Dettenhofer 1999; Zeitlin 1999; Compton-Engle 2005.

[52] Editions: Sommerstein 1980–2002, vol. 11 (2001); and note the student commentary by S. D. Olson (1989a). See further Barkhuisen 1981; Konstan and Dillon 1981; David 1984; Dillon 1987b; S. D. Olson 1989b, 1990b; Groton 1990–1; Sfyroeras 1995; McGlew 1997; Revermann 2006: 261–95.

[53] Dover 1974: 195 n. 7.

has nevertheless – or rather for that very reason – been by a huge margin his most popular play. Like *Ecclesiazusae*, it is a puzzling work, which presents a fascinating thought-experiment in terms so ambivalent that modern criticism is divided on how it intends itself to be taken or indeed how coherent or successful is the attempt. Discussion has centred on two particular problems: the debate between Chremylus and the personified Poverty, whose articulate points in defence of her own essential role in society are never really answered; and the shift from a conception of the consequences of Wealth's cure in which only the righteous are wealthy to one in which the blessings extend to all alike. A fruitful approach has been to see the play as attempting to articulate, but not necessarily to resolve, tensions and contradictions in popular conceptions of wealth: in effect, the first sustained text in economic theory, as *Frogs* is the first sustained text in the history of western literary criticism.

Other plays. Two major lost mythological plays from the years after *Wealth* were seen by ancient critics as anticipating the plots of New Comedy. ***Cocalus*** is said by the ancient *Life of Aristophanes* to have introduced 'rape and recognition and all the other things imitated by Menander', though it is far from clear how these fitted into a play named after the mythological Sicilian ruler who took in the fugitive Cretan inventor Daedalus and had his daughters execute the Cretan king Minos when he came in pursuit. ***Aeolosicon*** means 'Sicon as Aeolus', and follows a pattern of title familiar from such comedies as Cratinus' *Dionysalexandros* or 'Dionysus as Paris'. Evidently it had a low-life character called Sicon (probably a comedy cook, like other characters of this name in later drama) somehow taking on the role of the hero of Euripides' notorious tragedy of forbidden love, *Aeolus*. Like *Wealth*, it was apparently a *diaskeue* or updated revision of a play from twenty years earlier, which would place its first version in the period of *Thesmophoriazusae* and *Phoenissae* when extended Euripidean comedy seems to have been something of a fad.

Some constants

Aristophanes was working in a fast-evolving genre, and seems himself to have been one of the main forces pushing it in new directions. But, despite the many changes in the genre itself over the course of his career, and with due allowance for the way our sense of Aristophanes' distinctiveness is limited by the loss of the plays of his contemporaries, there are a number of consistent qualities we can observe across his surviving work taken as a whole.

Staging ideas. Aristophanes is particularly adept at finding ways of *making ideas theatrical* – of giving complex, abstruse concepts or themes a concrete and dynamic dramatic form, working with the strengths of Old Comedy's traditional patterns and conventions. A key technique is to build the play around a confrontation between opposing forces or interests, represented by a pair of antagonists who can compete both in formal debate (the comic *agon*) and in other kinds of personal rivalry; a recurrent device in the early plays is to embody the outlooks of different generations in a father and son in conflict. Often the rewards of success for the victor are encapsulated in a specific prize that gratifies the physical appetites for food, sex, power, and pleasure: a wedding, a feast, a celebration of newfound wealth or status.

Verbal and theatrical invention. The ingenuity with which Aristophanic comedy finds ways to turn themes into theatre is part of a wider quality of inventiveness in language and staging. The style of Old Comedy covered an enormously wide range, and Aristophanes clearly relishes the opportunity for relentless wordplay, verbal coinages, and dislocations of style and register. But he is no less inventive in the non-verbal business of comedy: stage routines, sight gags, the communication of theme and meaning through the concrete language of performance.

Intellectual dexterity. Aristophanes was a clever writer. He liked to say so himself, and for his rivals it may have been one of his less attractive trademarks; a famous fragment of Cratinus (342) describes someone as 'an oversubtle *bon-mot*-making[54] Euripidaristophanizer', implying that Aristophanes could be recognizably caricatured to the traditional comic audience as appealing to the same intellectual faddists whom he presents as the admirers of Euripides, particularly in his play with words and ideas. Nor is this limited to the way he writes; Aristophanes engages in surprisingly deep ways with new-wave intellectual figures, ideas, and arguments. Sophists and poets were familiar targets of Aristophanes' rivals as well, but *Clouds* includes some remarkably adroit satire on actual sophists' teaching (which quite possibly amused its author more than his audience); and he

---

[54] A less likely reading has '-chasing'; see Kassel and Austin 1983–2001: ad loc., and Luppe 2000: 19.

seems to have been the first comedian to make extensive use of contemporary tragedy, particularly that of Euripides, as a target for satire and a source of story ideas.

Metaphoric richness. The plays are rich in both verbal and visual metaphors. Like the choral lyric poetry of Pindar and tragedy, Old Comedy is uninhibited by any worries about mixing metaphors, and likes to surprise its audience with bold, striking combinations of imagery. But Aristophanes is also intensely aware of theatre's special power to create images from the stage action as well as from the words, and to link verbal metaphor with theatrical image. Because Old Comedy is relatively unconstrained by real-world logic, the range of possible visual images is wide. Thus, in *Acharnians*, peace treaties of different durations are physically embodied as wines of different vintages, and the flavour of each is characterized in terms of the real-world associations conjured up by the different lengths of truce. This single image allows ideas to become physical props, abstract qualities to become sensory experiences, and the political to be assimilated to the vividly sensual.

Comic coherence. Yet Aristophanes is also remarkably adroit at keeping his material under purposeful control. Comedy's very licence to do as it will with the laws of logic, character, and stage convention makes it a particular challenge to maintain focus and coherence. But Aristophanes' comic routines are carefully structured, and segue together with a sense of overall direction; the play is careful to give a sense of where it is heading from moment to moment; the stage space is organized in a shapely, intelligible way; the conflict is kept in view; different targets and kinds of comic material are united by an overall coherence of theme, complex though this often is.

Finger on the pulse of change. Finally, Aristophanes is an extremely astute observer of his times and, as well as a rich source for social history,[55] is often the principal contemporary analyst of momentous historical and cultural changes of the era. The extant plays engage directly with some of what remain the most significant and intensely analysed developments of his age: the use and abuse of radical democracy (*Knights*, *Wasps*); the impact of the sophists, and the implications of a teachable art of verbal persuasion (*Clouds*); the birth of literary criticism (*Frogs*); the rise of constitutional theory and the principles of social engineering (*Assemblywomen*); the emergent

---

[55] Ehrenberg 1951 remains a classic, and see Sparkes 1975.

theory of monetary economics (*Wealth*).[56] He is also an important witness to the rise of the book as a technology with far-reaching implications for the way information is used in society, including drama itself.[57] No other ancient writer shows so wide an awareness of the significance of the changes going on in the world around him – changes that we can see in hindsight to have been fundamental to the formation of western culture and thought.

Formal and theatrical structure[58]

As we have seen, the formal organization of Aristophanic comedy is highly complex – far more so than that of tragedy – and shapes both plot and performance values in fundamental ways, though this is generally obscured in translations. We have also seen that comedy is free to breach the essentially illusionistic conventions of tragic space, time, logic, and theatricality. Aristophanes is master rather than servant of these formal and theatrical frameworks, but he is also alert to their usefulness in shaping action and theme in a genre denied the convenience of pre-existing characters and plots.[59]

The most important theatrical fact about Old Comedy is the size of its chorus: twenty-four members in contrast to the twelve or fifteen of tragedy and satyr-play. This is reflected in the higher preponderance of choral titles (nine out of the extant eleven), particularly when the identity of the chorus promises fantastic, exotic, or otherwise spectacular costume and choreography. Two particular choral moments acquire disproportionate theatrical force: the *parodos*, when the chorus is introduced to the audience in a theatrical set piece that shows off their distinctive character and performance; and the *parabasis*, when the plot stops midway through for an extended choral routine with its own distinctive form and conventions. Because the choral impact is particularly strong in the first half of the play, there is some tendency for the chorus's identity and significance in the plot to recede somewhat in later scenes. Even the comic prologue and *exodos* are pulled into non-tragic shapes by the chorus's sheer gravitational mass. The prologue, as the one part of the play in which the chorus are not yet

---

[56] Spielvogel 2001.
[57] N. J. Lowe 1993; Slater 1996.
[58] See especially Gelzer 1960, 1993; Sifakis 1971; Zimmermann 1984–7; Totaro 2000; and, on plot structure generally, Sifakis 1992; Silk 2000: 256–300.
[59] On this aspect of comedy, see the famous fragment of Antiphanes' *Poiesis* (189 K.–A.).

on stage, is much longer than its tragic counterpart and tends to build up the story and its setting more gradually rather than plunging the audience straight into a pre-existing world; there are warm-up routines, in monologue or two-hander form, in which the dramatic illusion is especially light and the audience liberally acknowledged, and the setting can be dissolved and reconstituted freely before the chorus arrives and fixes the identity of the setting.[60] The comic *exodos*, where everyone including the chorus leaves the stage, will overwhelmingly tend to be dramatized as a *komos* or processional revel – one reason why comedy becomes so keen on weddings, whose central ritual was the escort of the bride to her new home.

The chorus is also central to those formal elements that have no parallel at all in tragedy. At the heart of these lies the *epirrhematic syzygy*: a symmetrical scene alternating responding recitative sequences with the two halves (strophe and antistrophe) of a lyric ode. On its own, this is merely a powerful incentive to the organization of the action in a way that will lend itself to symmetrical or antithetic structures involving the chorus – such as the splitting of the chorus into two battling factions in *Lysistrata* (where the epirrhematic passages reveal elaborately symmetrical choreography in the fight scenes) and (more briefly) *Acharnians*. But it is also the basis for two further formal sequences whose effect on the shape of the play is more profound. The *parabasis* expands the epirrhematic nucleus by prefixing an extended sequence in anapaestic metre, in which the chorus drop their specific characterization and address the audience directly on behalf of Aristophanes himself; the epirrhematic section then marks the resumption of the chorus's stage identity with a continuation of the appeal, but now on their own behalf and in character rather than on the poet's behalf and as a generic comic chorus. The *agon* expands the epirrhematic nucleus into a formal debate between two opposing solo voices, in which the play's central thematic conflict is spelled out and brought to a head, with the second speaker triumphing over the first and winning the chorus round.

Both of these elements pull the play into a particular kind of shape around them. The *parabasis* introduces a protracted break in the action that effectively splits the play into two distinct movements, and requires a degree of closure at the end of the first and a new phase to be opened up in the second. Early plays especially favour a solution in which the hero's plan is essentially fulfilled by the end of the first

---

[60] For a fuller discussion, see N. J. Lowe 2006.

movement, and the second then illustrates its consequences with a series of sketches in which he interacts with a succession of new characters in turn: so in *Acharnians*, *Peace*, and *Birds*, and the pattern persists as late as *Wealth*, though other plays find more ingenious solutions. The *agon* pushes the play towards a clash of antagonists who embody the play's conflictual thematics – yet not as part of a final resolution, but somehow as a midpoint of the plot's progress, presenting the poet with the challenge of how to make the *agon* simultaneously decisive and yet non-final. The simplest solution is that found in the plays just mentioned: to use the *agon* to engineer the first-movement close, and to devote a more episodic second movement to the consequences that ensue. But only a minority of plays are content to settle for this, and in practice each has to crank up a new conflict to give the second phase a dramatic spine.

Both the *parabasis* and *agon* start to mutate early on. Only early plays have the full *parabasis* structure, and even *Clouds* is already experimenting with alternatives to the traditional metre of the anapaestic section. From *Peace* on, the *parabasis* is starting to be truncated of some of its full-form features, and by the time of the late plays has disappeared altogether; a *parabasis*-like epirrhematic sequence in the second half of the play, sometimes known as a 'second *parabasis*', also disappears after *Birds*. The *agon* is even more varied: some early plays (*Knights* and *Clouds*) have two, but the still-earlier *Acharnians* is already abandoning the epirrhematic nucleus for a freer structure using the metre and spoken form of less formally marked iambic dialogue.

Epirrhematic and related structures in Aristophanes

(A) BASIC EPIRRHEMATIC SYZYGY

A	*epirrhema*	recitative by chorus leader
B	*ode*	short lyric segment by whole chorus
A'	*antepirrhema*	responding recitative by chorus leader
B'	*antode*	responding lyric segment by whole chorus

(B) THE *PARABASIS*: FULL STRUCTURE

1	*kommation*	2-line farewell to main characters
2	*anapaests*	chorus drop stage persona
3	*pnigos*	climax to anapaests in short, fast lines

4	*epirrhema*	recitative by chorus leader
5	*ode*	short lyric segment by whole chorus
6	*antepirrhema*	responding recitative by chorus leader
7	*antode*	responding lyric segment by whole chorus

(C) THE *AGON*: FULL STRUCTURE

0	(The sequence usually begins with the antagonists entering in mid-dispute.)
1	*ode*
2	*katakeleusmos*: 2 introductory lines in A's metre from chorus
3	A's speech (with interruptions)
4	*pnigos* (climax to A's speech in short, fast lines)
5	*antode*
6	*antikatakeleusmos*: 2 introductory lines in B's metre from chorus
7	B's speech (with interruptions)
8	*antipnigos* (climax to B's speech in short, fast lines)

Play	*Parabasis*	**2nd** *parabasis*	*Agon*
Acharn.	full	(quasi: 971–99)	loose iambic *syzygy* (490–625)
Knights	full	1264–1315	one in each half of play: 303–460, 756–941
Clouds	Eupolideans for *anapaests* and *pnigos*	1115–30	two in 2nd half: 949–1104 (Straight and Crooked); 1345–1451 (father-beating debate)
Wasps	full	1265–91	526–724
Peace	no *epirrhemes*	1127–90	none as such
Birds	full	1058–1117	303–460
Lys.	2 pairs of 10-line *epirrhemes*	none	476–607
Thesm.	single odeless *epirrheme* for *syzygy*	none	none as such
Frogs	no *anapaests*, just the *syzygy*	none	895–1098 (part of larger contest sequence)
Eccles.	none	none	one side only
Wealth	none	none	one side only, without *ode*

Politics and the problem of 'seriousness'

No issue has bedevilled Aristophanic criticism like the question of how we should read comedy's engagement with issues of social or political concern. A seminal article by Gomme (1938) argued that the political content of Aristophanic comedy was entirely explicable in terms of its entertainment function and should not be regarded as attempting to persuade its audience on matters of politics, let alone to assert its author's private views; and in recent years a more sophisticated version of this position has been powerfully argued by Malcolm Heath (1987, 1997). On the other hand, the plays do appear to show consistent political and other value-laden biases that would not seem natural crowd-pleasers given the constitution of Aristophanes' audience; and, however much comedy's claims to civic didacticism are taken as part of its rhetoric of professional self-advertisement, the genre did perform de facto a unique civic function of public free speech (so Jeffrey Henderson 1989).

Politically, de Ste Croix's reading (1972) of Aristophanes' self-positioning has not been substantially refuted.[61] It is hard to deny that the plays of the fifth century, at least, do choose their targets selectively, with a broadly consistent bias, across a number of issues, that de Ste Croix termed 'Cimonian'. Radical democrat politicians are satirized, while conservative figures such as Nicias are comparatively spared; the 'Knights' are commended rather than resented; Sparta is viewed with sympathy even at times of war, Athens' natural partner in a joint hegemony over the lesser poleis; the era of the Persian wars is nostalgically idealized as a political golden age. None of this is particularly surprising for someone of Aristophanes' generation and background; it is, for example, essentially the outlook of Thucydides, whose list of heroes and villains would look very similar to Aristophanes'.

What is less clear is how far this position is personal rather than generic. The fragments of Aristophanes' rivals show a similar tendency to attack democrats such as Pericles and Hyperbolus preferentially, to view the Cimonian era as Athens' finest hour, and to attack avant-garde intellectual, artistic, and musical fashions. If it seems surprising that an essentially popular art form should take an essentially anti-popular stance, it is worth reflecting that the *choregoi* or 'angels', who were assigned by the archon to fund the performance, would by

---

[61] It is now essentially restated in Jeffrey Henderson 2007: 188–9; for a critique, see Chapman 1978.

definition have belonged to the propertied class, and there is no
reason to imagine that the poets themselves came from any but elite
backgrounds. But biographical interpretation is neither necessary nor
safe. Avant-garde music, tragedy, and teachers are targets in a way
that establishment intellectual and artistic figures (notably Sophocles)
are not; and audiences may simply have regarded comedy's gentle
conservative bias as an appropriate part of its civic role and voice.
Certainly there is no indication that comedy ever had the slightest
effect on actual voting, even if it did succeed in irritating some of its
victims; and the various attempts at legislative control, whose number
and scope were in any case exaggerated in ancient tradition, all proved
ineffective and short-lived.[62]

As Silk pointedly observes, much of the problem lies in the word
'serious' itself, which is a very blunt tool indeed with which to chip at
the intricacies of comic drama's construction of relationships between
play, author, audience, and subject of discourse: 'The whole discussion of "seriousness in Aristophanes" is bound to be complicated by
the fact that there are different kinds of seriousness.'[63] The term
invites particular confusion between issues and intentions – the latter
always problematic, but particularly so in a public, populist, competitive art form whose defining affective feature, humour, is evoked by a
poetics of irony. We saw in the first chapter that comedy that deals in
charged issues is likely to seem edgier than comedy that makes jokes
from safer material. But, even on a personal level, Aristophanes may
personally be deeply serious about his art without being serious about
the things his art professes to be serious about; he may be perfectly
sincere in his personal political opinions without feeling the need to
use his comedies to persuade anyone else of them; and, conversely, he
may be absolutely committed to the proposition that comedy has a
claim to a civic voice without feeling any concomitant obligation to
use that voice to express personal opinions. Nor is it clear that the
positions taken on different topics should be accounted for in the
same way, and indeed many scholars have, in practice, been happy to
see, for example, Aristophanes' attack on Cleon as personally felt but
his similarly consistent attacks on Euripides as affectionate opport-
unism. This is not simply, as might be felt, a case of scholarly self-
projection; Aristophanes shows quite a wide, deep, and close understanding of Euripidean drama on many different levels and can be

---

[62] Sommerstein 1986, 2004; Halliwell 1991; Carey 1994; MacDowell 1996.
[63] Silk 2000: 305.

seen working from personal copies of the texts,[64] whereas his treatment of Aeschylus in *Frogs* is much less penetrating, and seems largely determined by the needs of the play in conjunction with very broadbrush contemporary impressions of the poet's theatrical trademarks, so that it is not absurd to conclude that Aristophanes is interested in the detailed workings of Euripidean tragedy in a way that Aeschylus does not inspire.

One fruitful approach, particularly when we are confronted with apparent incoherence, is to view the difficulty not as a flaw but as an expression of significant tensions and essential contradictions in the desires the play attempts to address and exploit. On this reading, the striking inconsistencies of *Knights* reveal deep tensions in the ideology of democracy in the 420s; those of *Ecclesiazusae* in the unresolved gaps between the radical aspirations of post-democratic social engineering and the resistant actuality of real-world human desire; those of *Wealth* in unreconciled popular conceptions of public and personal wealth. This ideological approach, championed most visibly and influentially by Konstan, can sometimes run the risk of underplaying the plays' polemical, argumentative, and didactic rhetoric of engagement. But it does offer a way of talking about comedy's engagement with issues of social concern that avoids the difficulties both of authorial intention and of the language of 'seriousness', and has already become more or less standard in the criticism of Roman comedy, which has generally felt comfortable to do without either.

Bibliographic note

The bibliographic surveys of Storey (1987, 1992) are an invaluable resource. After a century of weary deprecation, the Oxford Classical Text by Hall and Geldart (1900–1) has been decisively replaced by a far superior edition by Nigel Wilson (2007b), with an important companion volume of notes on textual points (2007a). For the fragments, the edition of Kassel and Austin (1983–2001) supersedes all predecessors; a generous selection in translation is forthcoming from Rusten et al. J. M. Edmonds' notorious *Fragments of Attic Comedy* (1957–61) cannot be recommended for any purpose; it would be easier to learn Greek to an appropriate level than to fathom Edmonds' impenetrable English renderings of his impulsive and chaotic text.

---

[64] N. J. Lowe 1993.

The great Groningen edition of the scholia by Koster et al. (1960–) now covers all eleven plays, with the 2007 volume including *Thesmophoriazusae* and *Ecclesiazusae*.

Of the first wave of Clarendon editions of individual plays, MacDowell's *Wasps* (1971), Dover's *Clouds* (1968), and Jeffrey Henderson's *Lysistrata* (1987) remain essential, and Ussher's *Ecclesiazusae* (1973) by default; the series rebooted in a larger format with Dover's *Frogs* (1993) and Dunbar's *Birds* (1995), S. D. Olson's *Peace* (1998) and *Acharnians* (2002), and Austin and Olson's *Thesmophoriazusae* (2004), with Henderson's *Knights* forthcoming. Each is now the key edition of its play, but Sommerstein's editions of all eleven comedies for Aris & Phillips (1980–2002) offer text, translation, and commentaries of increasing expansiveness and significance; the last four (*Thesmophoriazusae, Frogs, Ecclesiazusae, Wealth*) are especially full, while the separate index volume is the single most useful reference tool on Aristophanes for non-linguistic purposes. *Wealth* includes extensive addenda to previous volumes, including bibliographies for the early volumes that lacked them; *Clouds, Wasps, Peace, Lysistrata,* and *Ecclesiazusae* have since been individually reissued with the supplementary material and further addenda. Note also the series of Italian editions from the Fondazione Lorenzo Valla by del Corno et al. (1985–), which now cover *Clouds, Birds, Thesmophoriazusae, Frogs,* and *Ecclesiazusae*.

Aristophanes does not translate easily, but Barrett 1964 is a small classic, and Halliwell 1998 strikes an unusual and impressive balance between fidelity and performability; Sommerstein's solo Penguin volume (2002a) should only be used in its second edition. For study purposes, Sommerstein's Aris & Phillips translations (1980–2002, revised 2005–) vie with Jeffrey Henderson's Loeb (1998–2002) – as well they might, given that they were originally commissioned for that same series. (The story is engagingly told in Sommerstein 2006.)

Among general works on Aristophanes, Dover 1972 remains unsurpassed as a single-volume overview, while Cartledge 1990 is an excellent single-sitting introduction, and von Möllendorff 2002 a helpful introductory guide. MacDowell 1995 is especially lucid and helpful on the complex political background, though it probably simplifies the complexities of Aristophanes' own engagement with it. The major literary study is now Silk 2000; Revermann 2006 is a wide-ranging and sophisticated theatrical treatment, though there is still much of value in Dearden 1976 and Russo 1992, translated 1994, and Wiles 1997 offers an outstanding synthetic introduction to fifth-century tragic and comic performance. Note also the specialized studies by Bierl (2001) (chorus), Stone (1981) (costume), and L. P. E. Parker (1997) (lyric). Other notable book-length treatments include McLeish 1980, Harriott 1986, Thiercy 1986; and Hubbard 1991 on the authorial persona, Taaffe 1993 on women, A. M. Bowie 1993 on intertexts with myth and ritual, Slater 2002 on theatricality, Robson 2006 on Aristophanes and modern humour theory, and the Bakhtinian studies of von Möllendorff (1995) and Platter (2006). Dover, Russo, MacDowell, and Slater all devote a chapter to each of the eleven plays. Three important collections of essays are Bonnamour and Delevault 1979, Bremer and Handley 1993, Thiercy and Menu 1997.

Aristophanes' rivals, and his own lost plays, have been a subject of renewed interest with the effective completion of Kassel and Austin's edition, and wider study of the fragments will be boosted by S. D. Olson's commentary (2007) and the translation by Rusten et al. (in press); Olson's volume also includes translations as an appendix. As well as the monographs of Storey (2003) on Eupolis and Bakola (forthcoming, based on Bakola 2006) on Cratinus, the collection by Harvey and Wilkins (2000) includes a number of important snapshots of the field, and Eupolis' *Demes* is now the subject of an important large-scale edition by Telò (2007). There is an excellent short survey by Storey in Storey and Allan 2005: 195–208.

Aristophanes' reception, briefly surveyed in Louis Lord 1925 and Pauw 1996, is the subject of important studies by Hall and Wrigley (2007), van Steen (2000) (modern Greece) and Holtermann (2004) (Germany).

III NEW COMEDY AND MENANDER

After Aristophanes' *Wealth* (388), our next complete surviving comedy
is Menander's *Dyskolos* from 316: a gap longer than the period
spanned by our entire corpus of surviving tragedy. The lost lifetime of
'Middle Comedy' is far from a desert; though papyrus texts are
scarce, quotations in later Greek texts are very numerous, with
Athenaeus' ten-book dialogue *Deipnosophistae* or 'Dinner-Party Scholars' (c. 200 AD) a particularly rich source of snippets concerned with
all aspects of food, drink, and the symposium – themes which, even
allowing for Athenaeus' specialized interests, seem to have been
unusually prominent in the comedy of the era.[65] The relatively abundant fragments and titles fall tantalizingly short of allowing us to trace
the evolution of the genre in detail, but it is clear that, by the time
Menander began producing in 320 BC, the form and character of
comedy had changed, and the long development of Athenian comedy
had more or less stabilized. We do not see much further change over
the course of Menander's career or in the surviving remains of plays
from the following generation, and the plays of New Comedy, even
the extant Menander, largely resist attempts at specific dating.

The sheer complexity of fourth-century comedy's development
can only be fleetingly glimpsed in the surviving remains of the many
fragmentary poets known from this era. The *Suda* lexicon credits
Anaxandrides, one of a new breed of immigrant poets of non-
Athenian birth, as the first to introduce love affairs and rapes of
virgins into comedy, a claim we have seen also made for Aristophanes'
Cocalus; the rival claims can be reconciled by supposing that Anaxandrides was the first to transfer these originally tragic plot motifs from
mythological to contemporary settings.[66] But, in any case, some such
route of transmission of plot motifs seems to underlie comedy's
espousal of plots of deception and mistaken identity, since the era of
'Middle Comedy' was a golden age for mythological comedy, as
fourth-century vases confirm; of nearly sixty titles attested for
Eubulus, half are mythological, and Plautus' *Amphitruo* shows us how
one of the favourite storylines of the era would play out in practice.
The massively prolific **Antiphanes** was credited in antiquity with

---

[65] Wilkins 2001.
[66] So Webster 1970: 77, cf. Arnott 1972a; Nesselrath 1990: 195 was sceptical, but he has
since (1993) come around.

between 260 and 365 plays; if these figures are anything like correct, he must have been an early exploiter of the growing market for comedy outside Athens. A giant of the age was the long-lived **Alexis**, whose *Carthaginian* may have been the original for Plautus' *Poenulus*, and who was already winning prizes a quarter-century before Menander's debut and still managed to outlive him by nearly two decades; ancient tradition claimed a close personal association between the two, with Alexis as the younger poet's teacher or even uncle. Menander's older Athenian contemporary **Timocles** is a particularly fascinating figure, not least for the surprisingly high proportion of personal abuse in the fragments, at a time when we would otherwise imagine it virtually extinct; he is an instructive embarrassment to simplistic linear and evolutionary models of fourth-century comedy's development.[67]

The ancient triad of supreme poets of New Comedy – corresponding to the Old Comic trinity of Cratinus, Eupolis, and Aristophanes, and the tragic canon of Aeschylus, Sophocles, and Euripides – bracketed the Athenian Menander with two foreign-born contemporaries. **Diphilus**, from the Black Sea city of Sinope, is of particular interest as the source of several plays adapted by Plautus and Terence, though it is difficult to form an overall impression of his distinctiveness from the fragments and titles. **Philemon**, from Syracuse or possibly Soli, was another suspiciously long-lived figure; Apuleius' comment (*Florida* 16) that he avoided plots of sexual impropriety is borne out by the known Latin adaptations *Mercator* and *Trinummus*. From the generation after Menander, the most important were the Macedonian-born **Posidippus** and the strikingly Menandrean **Apollodorus** of Carystus, who was twice adapted into Latin by Terence.

Middle and New Comedy: the main authors

Name	Known dates	Extant Roman versions
Anaxandrides	first victory 376	
Eubulus	first victory c. 370	
Antiphanes	first play 385	
Alexis	c. 375 – c. 275	Plautus, *Poenulus* (?)
Timocles	fl. 320	

[67] On these poets and 'Middle Comedy' generally see especially Nesselrath 1990, and further 1993, 1995; the editions of Eubulus by Hunter (1983) and of Alexis by Arnott (1996); and, for the vase-painting evidence, Taplin 1993, 2007.

Name	Known dates	Extant Roman versions	
Philemon	c. 365 – c. 265	Plautus,	*Mercator* *Trinummus* ?*Mostellaria*
Diphilus	c. 355 – c. 295	Plautus,	*Casina* *Rudens* *Vidularia* (?)
		Terence,	*Adelphoe* (one scene only)
Menander	342 – c. 293	Plautus,	*Bacchides* *Cistellaria* *Stichus*
		Terence,	*Adelphoe* *Andria* *Eunuchus* *Heautontimorumenos*
Posidippus	first victory 288		
Apollodorus	first play c. 285	Terence,	*Hecyra* *Phormio*

The distinctive profile of New Comedy as we see it from Menander and his Roman adapters is most easily understood as the hybrid product of three elements: (i) surviving elements from earlier comedy itself, extending back to Aristophanes and the fifth century; (ii) the increasing influence of tragedy, whose conventions have in some cases supplanted those of earlier comedy; and (iii) the design and organization of the fourth-century theatre, which has affected the fundamental shape of both genres in performance.

In two important respects the comedy of Menander's age is the direct heir of its fifth-century ancestor. The language is still that of everyday Attic speech, albeit cast into artificial verse dialogue forms; and the plays are still set in the contemporary world of the audience's own time, featuring fictional characters and storylines in real-world settings. But there are important differences in the way these defining features of the comic tradition are used. The dialogue is much more strictly naturalistic, closer than ever to the cadences of everyday speech – but without Old Comedy's freedom to range more widely across the stylistic spectrum. Both the element of obscenity and the verbal fireworks have been eliminated; there are no rude words in Menander, and none of the exuberant comic wordplay that character-izes Aristophanic poetry. Instead, we find a brilliant distillation of contemporary speech patterns into iambic verse – right down to the unfinished sentences, incoherent syntax, and favourite phrases or personal habits of expression that characterize different individuals' ways of speaking. It is a similar story with the settings: so scrupulously real-world are the settings that the element of fantasy has now been entirely banished. There are no suspensions of natural logic or causality, unless we count the laws of coincidence – no more flying to heaven on the backs of giant dung-beetles, or founding cities of cuckoos in the clouds. The most we can expect is for a god to sneak out on stage, tragedy-fashion, to speak the prologue when nobody else is around. Also lost is the element of topical satire; Athens under Macedonian rule was a politically volatile and dangerous place, and Menander does not take the risk of commenting on charged contemporary history. One early play, *Samia*, includes a couple of brief jokes about living individuals, but even this last vestige of comedy's satirical edge has vanished in the later plays.

Many of these changes are the direct result of the increased influence of tragedy. Old and Middle Comedy had both experimented sporadically with mythological settings and storylines (sometimes based on particular tragic plots), but this flirtation with myth was over by Menander's day. What *had* proved influential, however, were tragedy's approaches to character, staging, and plot. Despite some memorable leading roles, Aristophanes could not be accused of an overdeveloped interest in characterization. But, in Menander, the depiction of character in all its complexity and nuance is a major dramatic value, and Menander goes further still than tragedy in trying to make individual motivation and personality intelligible to the audience through the language characters use. Menander recognized that, free of tragedy's heightened and artificial poetic diction, comedy was able to present real people with even greater fidelity and naturalism than had ever been possible in tragedy.

Meanwhile, one of the most startling changes in New Comedy is the abandonment of Old Comedy's freer stage conventions for the austere literalism of tragedy. In New Comedy, there are now no scene changes, no time-jumps, and no breaches of dramatic illusion beyond a very occasional second-person address to the audience (as 'gentlemen', *andres*). As in tragedy, everything takes place in real time, in a single location, and in a world that pretends to exist on the other side of a one-way window to the audience. Again New Comedy actually goes beyond tragedy in the devices it uses to sustain this pretence: characters will sometimes enter in mid-conversation, or address remarks to an unseen interlocutor inside the stage building. But perhaps the greatest debt to tragedy is the new kind of comic plot. It is to Menander that we owe the western comic tradition's reliance on ridiculously convoluted, coincidence-heavy, farcical plots centred on misunderstandings (especially of identity). Yet Menander did not invent this kind of plotting; all he did was give a comic spin to a long-established pattern of recognition plotting stretching all the way back to the *Odyssey*, and long established in recognition tragedies such as Euripides' *Ion* and *Helen*. Indeed, it is probably because of Menander's success in stamping such plots with a comic copyright that the selection of surviving tragedies, made in an age when Menander was already a classic, strictly avoided all such plays (which survive only among the Euripidean 'alphabeticals'), despite their continuing prominence as late as Aristotle's *Poetics*.

It would be a mistake, however, to attribute everything that is new in New Comedy to the influence of tragedy. One of the major changes between Aristophanes and Menander was in the form of the Athenian theatre itself, and there were also important changes in the way that theatrical performances were funded and organized. These were changes that affected fourth-century tragedy and comedy alike but, since the tragedy of this period has largely disappeared, it can easily look as if the developments were peculiar to comedy. No doubt some of the changes in stage design, in particular, were a response to developments in the plays themselves, rather than an unexplained external development to which the plays had to adapt. Nevertheless, it is helpful to group all these features together, particularly as they emerge most directly to our view in the major rebuilding of the Athenian theatre itself that took place from the 360s to the 330s BC, with its last phase associated with the statesman and orator Lycurgus.

First, the theatre in which Menander produced his plays had three doors instead of one – so the stage building now represents not a single house but a section out of a terraced street. The central door was larger than the two flanking ones, and tended to encourage its use to represent a shrine of a god rather than a private house. A play did not have to use all three doors, but no play by Menander uses fewer than two. This not only changes the dramatic emphasis – from one family's story to the interactions between two or more – but vastly increases the possibilities for complication and confusion in the movements of characters on and off stage (and their options for activity offstage). In particular, Menandrean comedy likes to use the movements of characters between different stage houses to express the relationships of estrangement and reconciliation between family members.[68]

Second, in the Hellenistic theatre the solo actors performed on a high platform stage a dozen feet or more above the level of the chorus down in the *orchestra*. As well as marking the increased prominence of the solo actor in this period, it enforced a total separation of actors and chorus, by preventing the kind of free movement between *orchestra* and stage building that had been normal in fifth-century tragedy and comedy. The result was that the chorus was effectively barred from even the limited involvement in the action of the play that they enjoyed in later tragedy. By Menander's time, the two-hundred-year struggle between actors and chorus for control of the play has finally been won, and not by the chorus. The chorus now only show themselves at all when the stage is empty of actors; and the songs they sing have nothing to do with the play, and were probably not even composed specifically for the production. In the papyri, the chorus is no longer part of the script at all; in its place is the one-word stage direction *CHOROU* ('[song] of the chorus'), already familiar from Aristophanes' last plays, to mark where the chorus would have performed one of its numbers.

Third, there was a standardization of theatrical resources. The fourth century was a time of straitened finances: Athens was no longer a wealthy imperial power, and the reserves of private wealth on which fifth-century drama had depended for funding no longer existed. By Menander's time, performances of tragedy and comedy were entirely funded by the state, which led to a standardization of budget and resources in the areas that had traditionally been most expensive. Thus, the chorus of a tragedy or comedy was now allocated precisely four songs per play, no more, no less – which meant that all plays now had a consistent structure of five dialogue episodes separated by the four choral songs, the origin of the five-act structure so persistent in the western classical tradition of theatre. The number of solo actors, which in Aristophanes' time could be as many as five, was now frozen at its tragic norm of three; and it appears that even the range of character masks was restricted, with the same masks (and their associated character names) turning up in play after play. Certainly we notice a striking tendency to work in character *stereotypes*, with a highly artificial system of character names, masks, and traits that rather belies the general tendency to naturalistic individual characterization. A slave

---

[68] More on this in N. J. Lowe 2000a: 191–6.

called Daos in one play is not the same actual individual as a slave
called Daos in another; but they probably looked the same, and raised
similar broad expectations in the audience of the kind of personality
beneath, which it was then up to the writer of the particular play to
refine in what this particular slave-called-Daos said or did.

The kind of theatre that emerges from this complex fusion of different influences and traditions is so instantly recognizable and familiar
as the ancestor of the classical tradition in western comedy, with its
naturalistic but complicated plots of cross purposes and mistaken
identity, that it is easy to underestimate its historical significance and
artistry. These finely observed domestic comedies of manners were a
breakthrough in theatrical technique, and the most daring experiments that the Greek language ever conducted in trying to make
poetry from the fabric of everyday speech. The innovative distillation
of everyday Attic speech patterns, and the subtlety with which he uses
this to delineate the speech and thought patterns of individual characters, were two of the qualities most admired by Menander's ancient
enthusiasts. It is this linguistic and psychological naturalism that
Menander's most influential advocate, the second-century scholar and
critic Aristophanes of Byzantium, was commending in his famous *mot*
on Menander's realism.

But Menander's drama is also the first major literary product of the
new world of the early Hellenistic era, in which democracy is dead,
the shape of the Greek world has been changed forever by Alexander's
eastern conquests, and theatre has to address itself to a new political
order under which Athens is an occupied state and the international
situation is inherently violent and unstable. What Menander's plays
focus on, with great subtlety and insight, is therefore not the transient
world of external politics but the institutions that define Greek society
as a whole. For Menander, this is a hierarchy of three levels of citizen
identity: the individual, the *oikos* or family unit of which he or she is
an element, and the wider *polis* community of other such families in
interaction. Outside all of these is the wider Greek world of other
poleis, but that is an inherently dangerous and unstable world, and the
plays are mainly concerned with the conflicts or coincidences of duty
and interest between these three levels of all Greeks' sense of their
place in their world. Not coincidentally, it is a set of themes that a
naturalistic comedy of domestic life, set against the background of an
ordinary city street, is peculiarly well equipped to explore. However,
this concern with the institutional foundations of Greekness – in
particular, with *polis*-based models of citizenship – is also a response

to the vast expansion in the geographical and cultural compass of the Greek world after Alexander.

For Menander lived in interesting times. Born in or around 342, he was a child at the time of Athens' decisive defeat by Philip of Macedon at Chaeronea in 338, and grew up under the uneasy accommodation with Macedon that held after Philip's assassination and the accession of Alexander. When Alexander died in June 323, Athens took advantage of the political chaos to revolt against Macedonian rule, only to be forced into unconditional surrender the following year. The city was garrisoned under an oligarchic regime led by Demades and Phocion, and the anti-Macedonian orator-statesmen Demosthenes and Hyperides met grim deaths in the ensuing purge. It was against this turbulent background that the teenage Menander found himself serving his two-year term of military training as an *ephebe* – alongside the future philosopher Epicurus – and it was during this service that he found time to write his debut play *Orge* ('Anger'), which was staged in or around 321. Demades was executed on Macedonian orders in 319, and a short-lived restoration of democracy the following year ended when the city was starved into surrender a few months later and placed under the rule of the puppet philosopher-king Demetrius of Phalerum, who became a friend and supporter of the young Menander; *Dyskolos* was produced in 316, in the early months of Demetrius' regime. This regime lasted ten years, and then, in 307, the Antigonid prince Demetrius Poliorcetes 'liberated' Athens from Macedonian rule; Demetrius of Phalerum fled to Alexandria, and Menander himself is said to have narrowly escaped death. After Demetrius Poliorcetes' defeat in the battle of Ipsus (301), a notionally independent government took charge under Phaedrus of Sphettus; but intrigue and violence continued with an internal coup in the early 290s suppressed by the pro-Macedonian Lachares, who then installed himself as tyrant of Athens and was overthrown in turn by Demetrius Poliorcetes, who besieged Athens into a second surrender in 295. At the time of Menander's death, Athens was once more under a puppet oligarchy supported by the Macedonian king – none other than Demetrius Poliorcetes, to whom the Macedonian throne had now fallen.

Reflections of this turbulent world in the plays are subtle but significant.[69] Such a volatile political climate was hardly hospitable to the

---

[69] Major 1997 argues for an essentially pro-Macedonian stance, Lape 2004 against; it is not clear that one of them has to be wrong.

kind of pungent topical debate that we see in Aristophanes, which had
in any case long since fallen from fashion; early plays such as *Samia*
can be seen to make brief satirical mention of named contemporary
figures, but the satire is blandly apolitical. Nevertheless, the unnerving
instability of the wars of Alexander's successors is reflected strongly in
many aspects of Menander's plays. The world beyond the *polis* is a
violent, lawless, and unstable one, in which Greeks are routinely
raped, enslaved, and traded by other Greeks; in which the principal
opportunity available to ambitious young men is a dangerous and
often short life as a mercenary soldier in the eastern wars, and such
wealthy mercenaries are typically characterized in the plays as violent,
unpredictable, and prone to irrational rages. Ordinary citizens are
politically disempowered, their sphere of social operation confined to
the family; there is recognition now that the structures of power are
largely centred outside the home community, and that the world
beyond it has grown larger and more complex and threatening. Yet, at
the same time, there is a near-utopian pride in the orderliness of the
polis and the power of its laws and values to sustain the happiness of
its citizens. Though the democratic constitution is by now a thing of
the past, the civic ideology it fostered lingers on, and Menander's
world is still in many key respects the world of the orators: obsessively
anxious over legal issues of citizenship, paternity, and inheritance;
clinging to a utopian nostalgia for city-state autonomy and cohesion
in a world where these values are increasingly under threat from the
new geopolitical order.

Significantly, all Menander's known plays are love stories. This was
not by any means the universal practice of his rivals, but Menander
has a particular fondness for stories of citizen love, culminating in a
happy marriage legally agreed between families belonging to the same
city. Some of the reason for this is no doubt sentimental, an early sign
of the new prominence in the Hellenistic poets of love as a subject of
emotional and psychological appeal in its own right. But Menander is
as much interested in citizenship and marriage as in love, because
marriage is *the* defining transaction between citizen families. Marriage
is what allows the family, and the *polis* as a whole, to perpetuate itself.
In Athens, and no doubt elsewhere, there was enormous anxiety over
issues of citizenship and legitimacy – something we see reflected especially in the large body of surviving law-court speeches on cases of
disputed citizen status. In Menander, and in Greek family life,
marriage was about more than the romantic feelings of a boy and a
girl; this is why many of the plays involve tensions between the

inclinations of individual lovers and their responsibilities to the family or the law. That they are ultimately resolved is a way of assuring the audience that they do indeed live, as Greeks in Greek cities, in the best of all possible worlds.

At the same time, at the heart of Menander's comedy lies a subtle, coherent, and sophisticated philosophical system. Menander associated with philosophers – tradition has it that he studied with Aristotle's successor Theophrastus, did his military service with the young Epicurus, and was a personal friend of the Athenian ruler and essayist Demetrius of Phalerum – and his ethical thinking in particular was clearly influenced by Aristotle and his school. Like Aristotle and the other founders of the major Hellenistic philosophical schools, he presents a view of the world in which morality is not something mysterious or supernatural; in which there are systematic, intelligible, and practical rules that anyone can implement every day of their lives, and in so doing make not only their own lives but those of others appreciably happier and more just. A key concept is that encapsulated in the Greek word *philanthropia*, 'love of people' or 'human feeling': a sensitivity to other people's concerns alongside or ahead of one's own. Again and again in the plays, characters are rewarded for selflessness, for putting the feelings of others before their own interests, and for readiness to admit their own moral failings in preference to judging others by harsher standards. Menander's plays are full of the virtues of forgiveness, generosity, and recognition of the importance of family and community. If, at the end, love conquers all, it is not merely because the Hellenistic world shows a new inclination to sentimental escapism (though that is certainly a factor), but because it is the key to a sophisticated, philosophically informed, yet also practical, way of understanding the human world.

Menander: individual plays

The conventional wisdom that Menander did not survive in a medieval manuscript tradition was turned on its head in 2004 with the discovery of the Vatican palimpsest, recycled from a fourth-century codex whose surviving portions contain parts of *Dyskolos* and *Titthe* as part of what may have been quite a substantial and capacious luxury edition – even, it has been optimistically suggested, a *Complete Works*. But it still seems that Menander stopped being copied at an early date and, until the 1890s, his works were known only from (i) the highly creative and free Roman adaptations of Plautus and Terence, and (ii) short quotations preserved in later Greek authors (so-called 'book quotations'). The bulk of our modern text derives from two remarkable papyri: the Cairo codex, published in 1908 and delivering parts of *Heros, Perikeiromene, Samia*, and *Epitrepontes*; and the Bodmer codex, published from 1959, which gave us *Dyskolos* complete, the beginning of *Aspis*, and a crucial further chunk of *Samia*. Later finds have also given us substantial parts of *Sikyonios/oi* and *Misoumenos*. We now have *Dyskolos* all but intact; more than half of *Samia* and *Epitrepontes*; substantial amounts (sufficient to reconstruct the full plot) of *Aspis, Perikeiromene, Sikyonios/oi*, and *Misoumenos*; and scenes from a dozen or so more. Dating is not easy, but *Dyskolos* took first prize at the City Dionysia in 316; *Samia* seems on formal grounds to be a work of the same general era, while *Epitrepontes* probably belongs in the 290s.

In cases below where it seems helpful – which also includes all of Terence, but none of Plautus – I include diagrams of the structure of familial and/or romantic relationships among the principal citizen characters in their relation to the stage houses (indicated by a grey square), including relationships not known to some or all of the characters. Dotted lines indicate relationships imagined, feared, or provisionally endorsed by the characters that must turn out to be superseded by a more appropriate configuration. The orientation of left and right has been determined by the need for graphical clarity and should not be taken as indicating which house was on which side of the stage (especially in the case of *Dyskolos*, where the text in fact seems to put Cnemon's house on the left). It may be useful to bear in mind that the central event of a Greek wedding was the transfer of the bride from the house of her father or other male guardian (*kyrios*) to the house of her husband, and that a divorce would reverse the process; and that Menander's dramatic world-model is built around a three-tier view of society, in which the individual's identity is defined against the successive hierarchical levels of *oikos* (family/household), *polis*, and wider Hellenistic *oikoumene*. Theatrically, these are typically represented by the individual actor's movements between the stage doors (*oikos*), the urban side-entrance (*polis*), and the opposite harbour exit, if available (accessing the world overseas, though this features mainly as a negative force).

Dyskolos (**'Miserable'**).[70] The misanthropic title character, Cnemon, has settled his household in the remote mountain village of

<hr />

[70] Besides the edition of Handley (1965) and Sandbach's commentary in Gomme and

Phyle in an attempt to maximize his isolation from the urban community; but his quest for self-sufficiency proves his undoing when a complex chain of divinely engineered synchronicities leads to his being trapped down a well in his own backyard, only to be rescued by his daughter's feckless urban suitor and the estranged stepson whom his lifestyle has condemned to poverty (Figure 5).

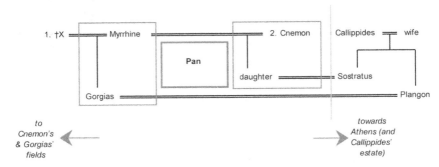

Figure 5

Dyskolos is a theatrically expansive play, with a large cast, spectacular use of props, mutes, and animals, and the only use of all three stage doors in extant Menander. Over the course of the play, the reunification of Cnemon's broken family and the continuation of his line through a double marriage with a wealthy city family is played out by the gradual funnelling of the entire cast into one great party in the central shrine of Pan, the all-controlling god unseen by any but the audience. An exceptionally complex family structure – Gorgias is Cnemon's stepson by his estranged wife's first husband – creates a legally tensioned relationship, since Gorgias must be formally adopted in order to inherit, and has no jurisdiction over his sister's welfare when he sees her apparently eyed up by what he takes to be a sexual predator. An important tragic intertext is Euripides' *Electra*, which similarly explores the uneasy relationship between rich and poor members of the same social class, and, as usual, the distance between the tragic and comic worlds is measured by the success of civic and ethical principles in averting the spectres of tragic possibility feared by the characters.

Sandbach 1973, see Arnott 1964a; Ramage 1966; Sherk 1968; Keuls 1969; Post 1969; M. Anderson 1970; Zagagi 1979, 1994: 95–113; Wiles 1984; N. J. Lowe 1987; Dedoussi 1988a; Brown 1992; Ireland 1995; Haegemans 2001; Lape 2001; Rosivach 2001; Traill 2001; Cox 2002a, 2002b.

Samia ('**The Samian Girl**').[71] Embarrassed to confess to his adoptive father, Demeas, that he has raped and impregnated the neighbour's daughter during both fathers' absence abroad, the young man Moschion conceals the truth by passing off the resulting baby as Demeas' child by his Samian mistress; but Demeas wrongly infers that Moschion has seduced the mistress himself (Figure 6).

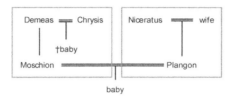

Figure 6

In contrast to *Dyskolos*, *Samia* is an extremely tight, minimalist play whose key action takes place entirely in the characters' heads, as Moschion's initial offence escalates in the imagination of the two old men into a deeper outrage, of which the original offender remains both innocent and innocently unaware. The play's fourth act is the crown jewels of Menandrean comedy so far recovered; it is instructive to compare early attempts at reconstruction, based on the parts of the play known since 1908 from the Cairo codex, with the magnificent scene of farcical cross purposes revealed by the Bodmer papyrus in 1969. But the play is also a subtle exploration of the tensions created by the Athenian institutions of adoption and concubinage within a typically Menandrean non-nuclear family unit, using intertextual intimations of tragedy (especially Euripides' *Hippolytus*) to establish a disturbing alternate reality in which the nightmare of a taboo sexual relationship, between a young stepmother and a stepson of similar age, is finally dispelled by the revelation that nothing untoward has happened beyond a rape that is itself generically healed by its transformation into married love and the propagation of the *oikos*. Moschion's reluctance to confront his father with the truth stems from a sense of an unrepayable debt: as he explains in the prologue, everything that defines him as a citizen is the result of Demeas' gift through his adoption of a non-blood heir as a socially acceptable alternative to marriage. In the final act, father and son recognize that the bond imposes a duty of trust in both directions.

---

[71] W. S. Anderson 1972; Lloyd-Jones 1972; Bain 1983; Grant 1986a; Groton 1987; Dedoussi 1988b; Zagagi 1988, 1994: 113–41; Lamagna 1998; Cusset 2000; Blanchard 2002.

Epitrepontes ('**The Arbitrants**').[72] Learning that his new bride is pregnant with a rapist's child, Charisius leaves his wife and attempts to return to a bachelor life, while his father-in-law, Smicrines, attempts to recover his daughter's dowry before it is all spent on partying; but the exposed baby survives, and a dispute over the recognition tokens found with it is arbitrated by Smicrines in a way that ultimately leads to the identification of the rapist as none other than Charisius himself (Figure 7).

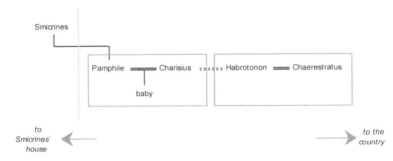

Figure 7

This major play is theatrically a counterpart of *Dyskolos*, with Charisius' young family torn apart as, one by one, its members are displaced from the family house under whose roof they must finally be united. First the baby is exposed; then Charisius himself moves out to seek consolation with the party-girl Habrotonon next door (to the consternation of his friend Chaerestratus, who has fallen for her himself); and finally Pamphile herself is put under pressure by her father, Smicrines, to abandon the marriage and return with her dowry. This has the effect of bringing her as far as the street door but no further: precisely where she needs to be in order both for Charisius to overhear her moving protestations of loyalty, and for Habrotonon to identify her visually as the victim of the festival rape. The moral ironies are strongly drawn, with the stingy Smicrines and the feckless Charisius both driven to learn the difference between preaching and practice. Smicrines unwittingly settles the fate of his grandson in advocating to the disputants at arbitration a generosity he fails to observe towards his own daughter; Charisius high-handedly blames his wife for being the victim of rape while feeling no scruple about

---

[72] W. S. Anderson 1982; Arnott 1987, 2004; Stockert 1997; Martina 1997–2000; Nünlist 1999, 2003; Porter 1999–2000; Iversen 2001.

having himself been an actual perpetrator, and it is vital to our sense of his eventual moral re-education that he repents and takes her back *before* the revelation that her child is his after all. Menander's close student Apollodorus admired these ironies, and constructed round the same bizarre situation a very different plot with an even tighter human structure: the play we know as Terence's *Hecyra*.

Aspis (**'The Shield'**).[73] When young Cleostratus is apparently killed in battle, his greedy uncle Smicrines tries to exploit the legal status of Cleostratus' orphaned sister to get his hands on the family fortune. Cleostratus' slave Daos seeks to thwart Smicrines' scheme by faking a second family tragedy, only for Cleostratus to turn up alive at the most bewildering moment possible.[74] The title refers to the spectacular procession of Cleostratus' captives and treasure across the stage, past the seething Smicrines' own door, and into his brother's house instead. Most of what survives comes from the first three acts, though we are fortunate to have key fragments of the priceless moment when the deceased turns up at another dead man's door, only for each to discover the other alive (Figure 8).

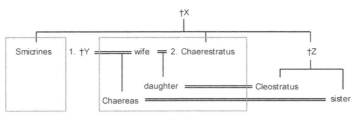

Figure 8

Menander's most elaborate legal plot is centred on the Athenian institution under which a female orphan (who could not inherit in her own right) would be attached to her late *kyrios*'s estate as an *epikleros* or 'testatory residue' and in that capacity married off to her nearest eligible male relative, who would inherit the estate as part of the package. Some details of the intricate plan, which is hatched by the one surviving Menandrean prototype of the Roman cunning slave, suggest that either Menander is alluding to legal nuances otherwise

---

[73] Lloyd-Jones 1971; MacDowell 1982; Brown 1983; Jacques 1998; Borgogno 2002; Beroutsos 2005.

[74] The diagram shows Webster's reconstruction (1974: 123), under which Chaereas and Chaerestratus' daughter are *homometrioi*, children of the same mother – which would still allow them to marry under Attic law. Others avoid this by taking Chaerestratus' present marriage to be his second, with his daughter born to his first wife; so Sandbach in his commentary (1973).

unknown or he is simply taking liberties with the strict letter of the law – though the plays generally seem to assume as high a level of legal competence as the orators, and we too easily forget the effect on mass culture of widespread experience of service on the large and numerous popular juries. MacDowell's view (1982) that the law on *epikleroi* is being criticized probably mistakes the ideological function of Menandrean comedy, which, as usual, here shows that citizen law produces the desired civic outcome even when ill-meaning characters try to use it to achieve exactly the opposite.

Perikeiromene (**'The Girl Cropped Short'**).[75] Hot-tempered soldier Polemon punishes his mistress Glycera by cutting off her hair, having misunderstood as flirtation with a stranger what is in fact her attempt to discover whether the stranger is her long-lost brother. This recognition comedy is one of three plays that explore the type-character of the professional mercenary soldier, thought of as being emotionally incontinent and prone to anger and violence, though only Polemon conforms to this type in truth. The bold opening sequence is lost, but it presented Polemon's version of events, and its con-sequence, before the goddess Ignorance (*Agnoia*) came on to explain the truth in a delayed prologue. Glycera's dilemma is that she cannot reveal her identity to Moschion without also revealing his own secret: that he, like her, is a foundling and his claim to citizenship is therefore in question unless his father can be found (which of course he quickly is).

Misoumenos (**'The Object of her Hatred'**).[76] The soldier Stratonides appears to have killed his mistress Crateia's brother; now she shuns him and her hostility drives him to despair. Menander's most paradoxical soldier character opens the play with a soliloquy lamenting the effects of his emasculation by love, which has turned him out of his own house in the middle of the night on the wish of a mere slave. A series of dramatic recognitions, triggered in turn by the brother's captured sword, eventually brings Stratophanes to confront what both he and Crateia believe to be the truth about her brother, and (probably) to surrender her to her newly discovered father – only to receive her back joyfully, not now as a slave but as a citizen wife legally bestowed by her father, when the *Aspis*-like misunderstanding is cleared up.

---

[75] Extended discussions are few, but, in addition to Goldberg 1980, see Konstan 1987.
[76] Webster 1973; Turner 1977; Giacomoni 1998.

Sikyonios/oi ('**The Sicyonian[s]**').[77] Despite the near-total loss of the play's first half, we can see that this was a remarkable recognition play of many convergent strands and elaborate doublings. The soldier Stratophanes pursues Philumene, once his property but now barred from him both by her claim of Athenian citizen birth and her sanctuary at the Eleusinian altar; his rival Moschion seems, as an Athenian, to have the stronger claim, until Stratophanes learns that he too was Athenian born, and can therefore promote Philumene from slave to wife if only he can track down the parents of both. Stratophanes' long-lost father is found to be none other than the father of his rival Moschion, and when the unscrupulous parasite Theron goes in pursuit of a bogus witness to Philumene's parentage, he unwittingly turns up her real father Cichesias – whom Theron believes his supposed stooge is merely impersonating, so that, in a glorious scene of poignant cross purposes, he interprets Cichesias' real tears and truthful recollections as uncannily convincing simulation.

Bibliographic note

The fullest bibliography of Menander is Katsouris 1995. Editions date rapidly with the arrival of new papyrus finds, but Arnott's Loeb (1979–2000) is the most complete text to date; Sandbach's Oxford text (1990) is a good second for most plays, but misses several significant recent discoveries. Translations need to be used with caution: even the benchmark prose version by Miller (1987) has been superseded in places, so that, for *Epitrepontes* and *Misoumenos*, Arnott's Loeb and Balme's World's Classics (2001) are more complete, though neither has the very latest on *Epitrepontes* (for which see Nünlist 2003 and Furley's forthcoming volume). No translation other than these three should be used for any academic purpose; the Pennsylvania volume (Slavitt and Bovie 1998) in particular needs warning against, since its free translations are themselves liberally supplemented with free invention where the papyri give out, and the shifts between loosely translated and sheerly invented Menander are entirely undocumented. There are few full commentaries in English; the monumental 'Gomme and Sandbach' 1973 is mostly Sandbach solo, Gomme having died before the Bodmer papyrus appeared. *Dyskolos* has the authoritative Handley 1965 and a good Aris & Phillips by Ireland (1995); Bain's

---

[77] See Lloyd-Jones 1966.

Samia (1983) in the same series is more austere. Ireland's Bristol *Companion* (1993) to Miller's translation is brief but useful.

The most penetrating critical monographs on Menander are Wiles 1991 (exploring how the performance codes construct and negotiate complex ideological models of the citizen and his world) and Lape 2004 (the fullest analysis of the legal heart of the plays, on which see also Scafuro 1997). The most useful general studies are Blume 1998 and Blanchard 2007; in English, Webster 1974 and Goldberg 1980 remain valuable overviews, with the latter devoting a chapter each to the major texts, and the former including characteristically fascinating, if wildly speculative, reconstructions of many lost plays. Webster's earlier books (notably 1960) are superseded by later papyrus finds, though the very boldness of the chapters on Menander's rivals in Webster 1970 has left them without any significant successor in English. Note also Vogt-Spira 1992, Zagagi 1994 (with an excellent chapter on *Samia*), and Walton and Arnott 1996. Two useful collections of essays are Turner 1969 and Handley and Hurst 1990. On Menander and tragedy, the key works are Katsouris 1975 and Cusset 2003. Frost 1988 is concerned with staging rather than stagecraft, but is still a concise and helpful companion. On women in New Comedy, see the seminal article by Wiles (1989), as well as Henry 1985, Brown 1990, 1993, and Rosivach 1998. Chapters 3 and 5 of Green 1990 offer helpful accounts of the complex Athenian political background to Menander's career – as well as the classic modern statement of the case *against* Menander's ancient estimation.

IV FROM GREECE TO ROME

The origins of Roman comedy are, in one sense, clear-cut: at the *Ludi Romani* or Roman Games of September 240, a Romanized Tarentine Greek known as Lucius Livius Andronicus, who at some point also translated the *Odyssey* into Latin, produced the first Latin translations of Greek plays on a Roman stage. This firm date, for which we have Cicero's friend Atticus to thank, marks the beginning of the establishment of a practice of translating classic Greek plays that would continue in both comedy and tragedy for at least a further century.

This is not, however, the way the Romans told the story. A first-century source used by Livy (vii.2) and Valerius Maximus (ii.4.4) spins an extraordinarily elaborate tale of home-grown dramatic evolution.[78] Here is Livy's fuller version, which Valerius closely mirrors:

[vii.2.1] There was plague in both this year and the next, the consulship of C. Sulpicius Peticus and C. Licinius Stolo (365/364). Nothing worth recording happened then except that [2] a *lectisternium* was held to try and placate the gods: the third time since the city's foundation. [3] When neither human resources nor divine help were able to mitigate the plague, the people gave way to superstition and are said, amongst their other attempts to mollify the gods, to have introduced theatrical games (*ludi scaenici*), previously unknown to a militaristic nation whose sole public entertainment had hitherto been gladiatorial. [4] As often in such cases, the games started small, and from an outside source. Players were brought in from Etruria and danced to the measures of a piper, with no singing or acting-out of songs, performing relatively dignified movements in the Etruscan style. [5] Subsequently the young men of Rome began to copy them, while at the same time exchanging jokes in improvised verse and fitting their movements to the words. [6] In this way the practice was established and developed by frequent practice. These local performers were called *histriones*, the Etruscan word for an actor being *ister*; [7] and they abandoned the exchange of impromptu badinage like the Fescennine verses, and instead began to perform musically scored medleys (*saturae*), with singing composed for pipe accompaniment and movement in time. [8] Some years later Livius, who was the first to venture away from the *satura* and compose a play with a plot, was acting in his own plays as normal for the time, [9] and is said to have lost his voice from repeated encores. With permission, he stood a boy in front of the musician to do the singing while Livius acted out the song, the more energetically now because he was not restricted by having to sing. [10] So began the practice of actors' using singers while their own voices were limited to the dialogue parts. [11] Through this kind of play, performance moved away from disconnected jokes, and theatre turned gradually into an art; and the young men abandoned the performance of plays to the professional

[78] The famous passage at Horace, *Epistles* ii.1.139–63 seems to derive from the same ultimate source (most likely Varro).

actors, and began once more to exchange extemporised jokes in verse, from which
came the so-called 'closing sketches' (*exodia*), which were connected especially to the
Atellan playlets. [12] This kind of performance, taken from the Oscans, remained the
preserve of the Roman youth and was not allowed to be tainted by professional actors
– [13] whence the practice of allowing Atellan performers to retain their tribal regis-
tration and military service on a par with non-actors.

Whatever we make of the details, two things about this account
stand out. First, it looks very much like an attempt to construct the
kind of unilinear retrospective pedigree that Aristotle's *Poetics* proposed for comedy, with an inferred prehistory based on the hypothesis
of origins from popular sub-literary improvised performance, which
could be observed still to survive in the reader's own day; an earlier
theatrical phase which prioritized comic ridicule over narrative coherence; and a later literary phase marked by the transition to 'plays with
plots'. More strikingly still, it entirely suppresses the Greek element;
even Livius Andronicus' introduction of 'plays with plots' makes no
mention of the fact that those plays were actually translated from
Greek, and the overall aim seems to be to claim Roman drama as an
autochthonous invention.

(i) Etruscan dancers are introduced in 365/364 for religious
reasons (4). This may have been recorded in the *Annales Maximi* or
other official archives, but may also have simply been attached to that
year because a persistent plague happened to be recorded for it. Livy
may be right about the Etruscan origin of the Latin word for 'actor',
and several other Latin theatre terms were thought, not implausibly,
to have come through Etruscan from Greek (such as the Latin
persona, 'mask', from Greek *prosopon*). Certainly, song and dance are
familiar elements in Etruscan art.

(ii) Young Romans imitate them, adding improvised repartee and
action (5). This looks more suspicious, and is probably a projection
back from the widely attested rural improvisations known as Fescennine verses.

(iii) *Satura* (6–7): fusion of elements in 2. The word *satura*, originally a culinary term meaning a dish with many different ingredients,
will later become the basis for the literary term 'satire' – itself a
generic label with a long and convoluted history. There is, however,
no independent evidence for Livy's lost musical *satura*, and the vague-
ness of the language and chronology only add to the impression of a
later scholarly fiction.

(iv) Livian developments: plot, mimed *cantica* (8, 9–10). This looks
like a highly tendentious description of Livius' introduction of

translated Greek tragedy and comedy from 240 onwards. Livy's source (perhaps the great Republican scholar Varro, who is, however, usually better than this) is certainly mistaken to trace the miming of sung parts back to Livius' own day; the texts of Plautus routinely give their star actors parts that are largely sung, and would look very different if all they were required to do was to mime to professional singers.

(v) Professional and amateur traditions diverge (11–13). Here Livy's source ties itself in knots trying to come up with a unified just-so story for the relationship between Greek and non-Greek genres, given that the entire narrative is hell-bent on denying any Greek input at all. The term *exodium* seems to suggest that Atellan comedy was used, at least in the late Republic, as a short closing item in a dramatic programme dominated by more substantial kinds of performance – a function, however, suspiciously analogous to that of satyr-play in the Athenian tragic competitions at the City Dionysia, so the claim may be founded on inference rather than evidence.

(vi) *Atellanae* introduced as *exodia* (also 11–13). The interesting detail here is, as so often, the one that the antiquarian narrative has been concocted to explain: that Atellan performers were exempted from the general Roman rule that prohibited citizens from performing on stage. Once again, this makes sense in terms of the separate Greek and Italian origins of the different performance traditions, but Livy's source has had to suppress the very existence of the former, and so has to explain the difference instead in terms of a long-running dialogue between amateur and professional traditions within Rome itself.

What is clear from all this is that, even in the age of Cicero, the early history of Roman drama was the subject of deep chronological confusion and cultural contestation; that the traditions of literary tragedy and comedy were understood to have grown up in a complex multicultural environment of Etruscan, Greek, Oscan, and Latin performance traditions; and that considerable cultural energy was invested in attempting to assert the Italic over the Greek elements in the archaeology of those traditions.

Greek drama in the west before Livius Andronicus

The history of Sicilian and southern Italian comic drama has something of the quality of early hominin archaeology: a vast and complex family tree that must somehow be reconstructed from a few cupfuls of random bone fragments from widely separate geological eras. (i) We have already met the sophisticated verse dramas, many or all of them mythological, composed in Syracuse in the first half of the fifth century by Epicharmus, Phormis, and Dinolochus. (ii) In 441, Athens played a central role in the foundation of the Italian city of Thurii; the historian Herodotus was involved in the foundation, and Athens now had a close cultural offshoot on the Italian mainland. (iii) By the end of the century, Sophron and Xenarchus were scripting the prose sketches from myth and life known as 'mime'. (iv) A famous anecdote in Plutarch has Athenian prisoners of war, captured by the Syracusans in 413, redeem themselves by satisfying their new masters' enthusiasm for the latest works of Euripides, whose plays were hugely popular. (v) Xenophon's *Symposium*, whose dramatic date is around this time, has a Sicilian cabaret troupe perform a succession of acrobatic and musical entertainments culminating in a two-handed erotic ballet of Dionysus and Ariadne, and (vi) from the end of the fifth century down to the time of Menander, west Greek vases show scenes from Athenian comedy on local stages, which used to be thought a precursor of (vii) the mysterious Tarentine genre of *phlyax* drama attested from Rhinthon and others in the time of Menander. Meanwhile (viii) western Greek dramatists were increasingly involved in the Athenian dramatic competitions, from the tyrant Dionysius of Syracuse in the 360s to Menander's rival Philemon (a Syracusan by birth, according to the *Suda*), who took Athenian citizenship and became one of the most successful (and longest-lived) of all Greek comic poets. His later years coincided with two third-century developments: (ix) the first appearance of the *Technitai* ('Artists') of Dionysus, the Hellenistic guilds of musical and theatrical performers who became the professional infrastructure of the theatre industry in the newly internationalized world of the expanded Greek Mediterranean, with a branch in Greek Italy and Sicily; and (x) a new poetic interest in the west Greek 'mime' tradition, which was given ambitious literary dress in the poetry of Theocritus, a Sicilian by birth, and the more shadowy Herodas.

c. 490–460 BC?	Epicharmus and Phormis active in Syracuse; Dinolochus a generation later
468 (or earlier?)	Aeschylus in Syracuse under Hieron
458–456	Aeschylus in Sicily again; dies in Gela
441	foundation of Thurii
later 5th century	Sophron active in Syracuse

422	dramatic date of Xenophon's *Symposium*
413	Athenian prisoners in Syracuse
411	Aristophanes' *Thesmophoriazusae*
c. 400	earliest Italian tragic vases and comic vases
early 4th century	Xenarchus (son of Sophron) active in Syracuse
370s	*Thesmophoriazusae* vase
368	Dionysius of Syracuse wins first prize at Athenian Lenaea
327	Philemon's first victory
c. 300	Rhinthon active in Tarentum or Syracuse
c. 300?	Theocritus born in Syracuse
c. 280	Artists of Dionysus first attested
c. 275–260?	Theocritus' *Idylls*
c. 250?	Herodas' *Mimiambi*

The pieces of this immense and perplexing jigsaw refuse to join up, but clearly there was a rich and complex tradition of comic performance in the Greek west from the fifth to the third centuries, which interacted with Athenian drama in both directions, and must in turn have influenced the early forms of Etruscan, Oscan, and Latin performance in central Italy to which the comedy of Plautus and his lost rivals is, to an unquantifiable extent, indebted. The history of Athenian tragedy and comedy, at least in the period of the surviving plays, is for all its uncertainties at least disentangled from the largely untellable story of other kinds of dramatic mimesis in other parts of the Greek world, whatever its early history might owe to outside influences. But what survives of Roman literary drama – not just the translated New Comedy of Plautus and Terence but Seneca's tragedies and the fragments of his Republican predecessors – are embedded in a much larger and more diffuse generic history of which comedy and tragedy seem not to have been even the most important parts.

Broadly speaking, the story of Roman drama is of two intertwined traditions that have quite different kinds of developmental story. On the one hand stands the tradition of literary adaptations of Athenian tragedy and comedy; on the other, the more elusive history of the various performance genres that seem to have established themselves as independent traditions in the Roman world, whatever their roots in popular west Greek and Italic performance. Thus, the Latin mime, which was certainly institutionalized at the festival of the Floralia in the second century and probably much earlier, seems to have developed at an early date into a distinct tradition from the Greek genre or genres loosely known by this name. The imperial genre of pantomime, a form of virtuoso solo mimetic dance to a sung libretto, emerges to view with the Augustan pioneers Pylades and Bathyllus, but seems to have very ancient roots in a native Roman tradition of danced drama attested under the enigmatic name *ludus talarius*. Of particular fascination is the long-lived 'Atellan' comedy rooted in the Oscan language and culture, which featured a recurrent cast of named characters such as Maccus, Pappus, and Bucco in situations reminiscent of *commedia dell'arte* or possibly of Warner Brothers cartoons, with titles such as *Maccus's Bar* or *Maccus in the Army*. Large claims are often made, especially by the 'Freiburg school' of Plautine studies, for the influence of these (at this date) improvised comedies on the distinctively Plautine elements in his adaptation of Greek comedy. In truth, we know very little indeed about what these plays were actually like, and even the attested titles come not from Plautus' time but from a literary phase a century later, when both the Atellana and the Latin mime went through a scripted form.

The tradition from which Plautus, Terence, and Roman tragedians from Ennius to Seneca emerged was quite distinct: these plays, even those of the theatrically minded Plautus, emerge out of the early history of Latin *poetry*. And, whereas the histories of the native dramatic genres go through an unscripted and largely anonymous popular phase that gives way relatively late to a more ambitious literary stage of their history with named writers and circulating scripts, the story of the poetic genres follows a quite different course: from a literature of *translation* to a series of increasingly bold experiments in the composition of original Latin works in emulation of Greek forms, and finally to the free appropriation of those forms as systems of essentially literary conventions. In the case of scripted drama, this manifests as an early phase of translated Greek plays by versatile multi-specialist poets in the Hellenistic mould; a later, but overlapping, phase of specialist translations by poets such as Plautus, Caecilius, Terence, and the tragedian Pacuvius, who work in one genre exclusively; original plays using Greek conventions, first as sporadic experiments but latterly as established genre traditions; and finally the disengagement of new tragedy and comedy from actual performance to become a vehicle for original poetic compositions on the Greek formal model but never intended to be staged.[79]

---

[79] This is not to assume any kind of stand on the question of Senecan tragedy's relationship to the stage. There is clearly stagecraft in Seneca, in the sense of significant elements, such as Hippolytus' sword, that need to be read visually rather than verbally – but recent thinking may be right to invite us to take more account of the dominance of early imperial pantomime in making sense of the performative oddities.

Roman drama: the main genres

Genre		Date	Principal authors
(a) native forms			
fabula Atellana	Atellan farce	?4th century BC to end of 1st century AD	L. Pomponius Novius (early 1st century)
mimus	mime	?later 4th century BC to Imperial times and beyond	Decimus Laberius (106–43 BC) Publilius Syrus (fl. 43 BC)
pantomimus	pantomime	Imperial (22 BC or earlier until at least 4th century AD)	Pylades, Bathyllus
(b) Greek-derived forms			
fabula palliata	comedy in Greek settings, translated from Greek originals	240 to c. 100 BC?	L. Livius Andronicus (?290–?205 BC) Gn. Naevius (died c. 200 BC) Q. Ennius (239–169 BC) T. (?) Maccius (?) Plautus (died c. 184 BC) Caecilius Statius (died 168 BC) P. Terentius Afer (?184–159 BC or after)
fabula togata or *tabernaria*	comedy in Roman settings	160 BC or earlier to early 1st century BC.	Titinius (date unknown) L. Afranius (active after 160 BC) C. Quinctius Atta (died 77 BC)
fabula crepidata	tragedy on Greek mythological plots, translated from Greek originals	240 BC to 1st century AD	Livius Andronicus Naevius Ennius M. Pacuvius (220–131 BC) L. Accius (170–after 90 BC) Varius Rufus (*Thyestes* 29 BC) P. Ovidius Naso (43 BC–17 AD) L. Annaeus Seneca (4 BC–65 AD)
fabula praetexta or *praetextata*	tragedy on Roman historical plots	sporadically from late 3rd century BC; the pseudo-Senecan *Octavia* is the last known example	Naevius Ennius Pacuvius Accius L. Cornelius Balbus (in 43 BC) anon., *Octavia* (c. 70 AD?)

Barbarous versions

Demophilus scripsit, claims the *Asinaria* prologue, *Maccus vertit barbare*: 'Demophilus authored it; Maccus turned it barbarian.' This wry formulation of the relationship between Greek play and Latin adaptation encapsulates the issue at the heart of Roman comic criticism: that the plays are highly creative adaptations of Greek plays, but the Greek plays adapted are lost. To understand the dialogue between Greek and Roman elements that is one of the principal engines of meaning in the plays, we need to appreciate something of what this process of barbarization actually involved.

As we have seen, Latin poetry was born from translation. Livius Andronicus was not just the first Latin literary dramatist but the first Latin poet, responsible for a remarkable translation of the *Odyssey* into the native Saturnian metre, through which the young Horace was still famously being dragged by his *grammaticus*, Orbilius. Cicero, generally something of a fan of the early Latin poets, gave his verdict on looking into Livius' Homer as *opus aliquod Daedali* ('a bit of a cave-painting'); but the surviving lines give a valuable glimpse of early Latin translational practice, since (unlike the few fragments of Livius' dramatic translation) nearly all can be matched to the Greek lines they translate. Livius' translation, though not verbatim, is largely versatim. One Saturnian corresponds to one line of Homer and, though there is much alteration at the verbal level, it remains a much closer level of correspondence than we find in dramatic translation. This could mean either that translators loosened up over the generation that separated Livius from Plautus, or that translation for stage performance was always freer to practice what Terence would call *neglegentia* ('casualness'), because it was never going to be compared side by side with its source. Nevertheless, there is already significant cultural translation in the *Odusia* fragments, such as the Italian *Camena* or *Moneta* substituted at different points for the Greek Muse; and Livius also shows a particular fondness for patronymic periphrases (son of Laertes, daughter of Saturn, daughter of Atlas, son of Latona) in place of a simple name in the Greek. There is heightened use of apostrophe in place of third-person naming; and there are signs of the redignification of potentially sub-heroic lines, such as Odysseus' knees being loosed with terror (5.297) and Patroclus' being compared to the gods (3.110).

But, until 1968, the most extensive direct evidence for Roman translational practice in *comedy* was Aulus Gellius' comparison of a passage of Caecilius with its Menandrean source. Gellius is probably the most interesting ancient writer on the subject of translation, certainly after Terence's prologues, and, though his views reflect the debates of a much later period, he nevertheless thinks carefully about text and register in ways that make him a useful witness to Republican practice. But Gellius' verdict was damning: Caecilius stood convicted of losing everything that was subtle, humane, and naturalistic about Menander, and replacing it with misogynistic belly-laughs and heavy-handed tragic bombast (*tragicus tumor*). Modern readers of Roman comedy might be more appreciative of things that Gellius was unlikely to value, such as the military imagery, the inversions of master/slave patterns, and the muscular way in which Roman theatrical moralizing recasts the thought in terms of the heavily keyworded Latin ideological vocabulary of *res publica* and *fortuna*.

Then, in 1968, Handley unveiled the Greek text of part of Menander's *Dis Exapaton*, already strongly suspected to be the original of Plautus' *Bacchides*.[80] The surviving Greek scene is the moment where the young man known in the Latin as Mnesilochus, whose slave Chrysalus has tricked Mnesilochus' father out of the money to pay his mistress Bacchis, has just found out that Bacchis is the mistress of his best friend Pistoclerus – not realizing that Bacchis has a twin sister of the same name, and that Pistoclerus' Bacchis is a different Bacchis from Mnesilochus' Bacchis. In the surviving passage, Mnesilochus announces his intention to confess all to his father, hand the money back, and break off with Bacchis; he then meets his father, enters the house with him, and carries out his intention, only to meet Pistoclerus on the way out and discover his ghastly mistake. Chrysalus will now have to find a way to dupe the money a second time out of a father now fully alert to his tricks. But Plautus' version of this scene was far more than just a translation. Among the mischief of which Plautus stood long suspected but now clearly convicted:

(i) The Latin is packed with wordplay, rhetorical and verbal fireworks, riddles and repartee, and punchline gags of a kind alien to the naturalistic conversational Greek of Menander's dialogue.

(ii) Characters are renamed: ordinary and colourless Greek names are replaced with longer, more grandiloquent alternatives (Pistoclerus, Mnesilochus).

---

[80] The most helpful discussions are Handley 1968; Bain 1979; Gentili 1979: 52–61; Primmer 1984; Damen 1992, 1995; W. S. Anderson 1993: 4–28; Halporn 1993; Jacques 2004.

(iii) Plautus has set most of Menander's spoken dialogue to music, in pipe-accompanied trochaic septenarii rather than the spoken iambic senarii that would correspond to the spoken iambic trimeters used through the whole passage in the Menander. But, at line 500, there is a switch from recitative into spoken senarii, only for the scene to switch back again at 526.

(iv) Plautus cuts a choral break and makes the action continuous, with the result that the whole business of finding Mnesilochus' father, explaining the trick, handing over the money, and making apologies takes up the four lines of covering dialogue spoken by Pistoclerus at 526–9.

(v) The relation between onstage and offstage action has been significantly recast: Plautus has banished the father to an entirely offstage role, and reworked the onstage dialogue between father and son as the end of a monologue by Mnesilochus announcing what he will say to his father offstage (520 ff.).

(vi) In a massive expansion, Plautus spins a whole forty-line comic routine (534 ff.) out of the dramatic misunderstanding that Menander clears up in half a dozen lines at *Dis Exapaton* 102–8.

All this spectacularly confirmed Fraenkel's careful conclusions about where to look for internal evidence of Plautus' own creativity at work. There is, in fact, a surprising amount in common between Plautine barbarization and the kinds of thing visible in the surviving fragments of his contemporary Ennius' adaptations of extant Greek tragedies, notably Euripides' *Medea*. Both show a fascination with the sound of Latin, working up the naturalistic style of the original into a highly unnaturalistic farrago of jangling verbal effects. In both we find a fondness for alliteration, assonance, rhyme, puns, etymological jingles, and rhetorical structures of expression such as anaphora, antithesis, clausal symmetry, tricolon, and climax. These are not in themselves comic effects, though in Plautus they are often *used* for comic effect; rather they are an essential part of the rhetoric of Republican dramatic verse, as is the tendency to moralize on the highly charged keywords of the Roman ideological vocabulary such as *patria, honos, virtus*.

Music and metre in Roman comedy

One of the most drastic transformations was in the musical form of the plays. First, while Roman tragedy kept the chorus, Roman comedy eliminated all trace of its presence. The reason may be no more complex than that the golden age of tragedy was the fifth century, but that of comedy the fourth, so that tragedy was frequently adapted from fifth-century texts that included choral lyric in the scripts, while comedy was adapted exclusively from fourth-century texts with only a bare *CHOROU*, if that, to mark where choral interludes would have stood. Since the chorus seems only to have been referred to in dialogue on its first appearance, it is possible that Plautus or his predecessors may have been largely unaware that there had ever been choruses at such points.

Whatever the reason, the lost musical element was made up by setting large sections of the play to music, in two quite distinct styles of delivery. We know almost nothing about how they sounded, and the terms 'recitative' and 'song' are at best approximations; but they are instantly distinguishable metrically, and they have a structural and dramatic role at least as important as the musical sequences in Aristophanic comedy. There are thus three modes of performance in Plautus and Terence:

		metre
speech	Plain spoken verse delivered without musical accompaniment.	Iambic 'senarii' or six-beat lines.
recitative	Verse intoned with accompaniment on the *tibiae* or reed-pipes.	Uniform runs of longer lines, such as iambic or trochaic septenarii or octonarii – lines of seven or eight beats.
song	Fully melodic lyric songs in the manner of operatic arias and duets; the Latin term *canticum*, which ancient writers applied to both recitative and song, is nowadays reserved for this mode (strictly *canticum mixtis modis*, 'song in mixed metres'). These, too, are accompanied by the *tibiae*.	Mixed, with no repeating structures, but may include stichic runs of identical lines (and may embed snatches of spoken and recitative metres).

The first two of these are familiar from Menander, although recitative is used much more widely than it is in Menander, where it occurs only sparingly and climactically for scenes of heightened emotion, such as the end of *Dyskolos* or the fourth act of *Samia*. Plautine lyric song has no parallel in Menandrean comedy, and seems to descend not from Greek choral lyric – with which it has little in common – but from another source entirely: perhaps from native Italian tradition, from Hellenistic Greek solo performance, or (as Fraenkel influentially argued) from the actors' monodies that were becoming a controversial fashion in later Euripidean tragedy, and were evidently adapted into Roman tragic drama. *Cantica* are astrophic: they do not fall into repeated structural units and, though the metres used can as usual be seen distantly to descend from Greek lyric metres, their combination and sequencing is quite different from anything in Greek dramatic lyric.

The three modes of delivery can be thought of as different emotional gears through which the play shifts in its modulations between higher and lower dramatic temperatures. Thus speech will tend to be used where the content of the dialogue is informative rather than emotional – it is always used for prologues, for example – whereas song will be favoured when the emotional impact of a static situation is being explored aria-style. It is common to jump a gear while shifting up (from speech directly to song, without passing through recitative), but a change down will nearly always pass through recitative. Plays normally open with a spoken prologue and then modulate directly or indirectly up to song, though a few (*Cistellaria*, *Epidicus*, *Persa*, *Stichus*) jump straight into song at the start; and they normally end in recitative, occasionally in song, never in speech. These musical divisions shape the overall dramatic contours of the play, both in the movements between more and less dramatic intensity and in the phrasing of the action, created by the divisions between them. Modulations in and out of speech tend to mark stronger dramatic shifts in tone and structure than modulations between recitative and song.[81]

Festivals, theatres, and the palliata tradition

The Roman theatrical experience of comedy was a very different one from its classical Athenian counterpart. In Athens, the performance of

---

[81] Marshall 2006: 203–44, with a full tabulation of the modulations within each play at 280–4.

drama was restricted to two festivals of Dionysus, probably both accommodated in the same permanent theatre, and with a programme centred on the competitive production of tragedy and comedy before an audience that may have been the single largest gathering of citizens in civilian life.[82] But, in Rome, performances of literary tragedy and comedy had to find a place in the numerous existing festivals, which were celebrated at different sites around the city with no permanent theatre in the city until 55 – by which time all the famous poets of Republican comedy and tragedy were long dead. Beginning with the *Ludi Romani* of 240, several of these festivals became *ludi scaenici* ('festivals with plays'); Plautus' *Stichus* was produced at the Plebeian Games of 200, and the new festival of the Great Mother, the Megalensia, introduced plays six years later and would become Terence's regular festival for the first five years of his career. We also know that Terence produced two plays at the funeral games for L. Aemilius Paullus in 160; it is unclear how far such productions at *ludi funebres* were common practice, although Livy mentions four days of dramatic performances at the funeral games for Flamininus in 174. The temporary stages erected for these performances had to fit the particular constraints of the festival space, which at the Megalensia would have meant an audience of a few thousand at most;[83] and the plays had to compete for their audience's interest against a variety of long-established popular entertainments, such as combat sports and acrobatic displays, that in the case of Terence's *Hecyra* seem to have held rather more appeal. We know very little about the stages themselves beyond what can be inferred from the texts; Pompeian wall-painting and Vitruvius' architectural handbook offer rich evidence for first-century designs, but it is optimistic to imagine that they tell us anything about Plautus' stages. Masks, costumes, personnel, seating were all organized on quite different principles to their Greek counterparts; there was none of the standardization of production resources that in Menander's theatre restricted the range and names of masks or the number of speaking actors.

Even the history of the genre is very imperfectly represented. Plautus and Terence were just two of the many poets working in their tradition of the *fabula palliata* or 'Roman theatre in Greek dress'.

---

[82] Estimates of the capacity of the Theatre of Dionysus are in the process of being revised significantly downwards (see Csapo 2007), but even the most pessimistic figure of five thousand or so would be a match for meetings of the *ekklesia*.

[83] Goldberg 1998.

Gellius quotes thirteen lines of jangling iambics from a work *On Poets* by the shadowy Volcacius Sedigitus ('Six-Fingered'), apparently a poet of the early first century, giving a personal ranking of the top ten authors of *palliatae*.[84]

> We have seen many doubtful debaters of this point:
> To which poet of comedy comes the palm?
> This uncertainty I shall undo for you with my own view,
> And if anyone dissents, he has no sense.
> I give the prize to the comic **Caecilius Statius**;
> In second place **Plautus** easily beats the rest;
> Next **Naevius** in third place, for his energy.
> If there is to be a fourth place, it is for **Licinius**;
> I rate **Atilius** next after Licinius;
> In sixth place **Terence** follows after these,
> **Turpilius** seventh, and **Trabea** takes eighth.
> I happily hand the ninth place to **Luscius**,
> Adding **Ennius** tenth for antiquarian value.

This is a large list for its kind – otherwise, only the Attic orators managed a canon of as many as ten – and still pointedly omits some famous names altogether. Notably absent are Livius Andronicus, whose plays Cicero would later dismiss as only worth reading once, and the Aquilius canvassed (perhaps by Accius) as a possible author of the *Girl from Boeotia* cited by Gellius, which Varro thought good enough to attribute to Plautus. Licinius Imbrex, Atilius, and Trabea are shadowy figures of uncertain date and output, though we have brief fragments from all three and the first two may be identical with poets known elsewhere for their work in other genres. Luscius and Turpilius are more substantial figures: the first Terence's older rival and sparring-partner in the prologues,[85] the second the last major poet of *palliatae*, active in the decades following Terence's death. Q. Ennius, a major figure across other genres of Latin poetry, was far more active and successful in tragedy than in comedy, and scrapes on to the list for historical interest. But in fact the earliest poet in the list is Gn. Naevius, who fought in the first Punic war (on which he composed the first original epic poem in Latin) and died around 200. Although he also wrote tragedy and pioneered the *fabula praetexta* or serious historical drama on Roman themes, his greatest success was as

---

[84] Gellius xv.24; see Courtney 1993: 87–96 and H. N. Parker 1996: 589–90.
[85] Donatus on *Eunuchus* 9–10 tells us a bit about Luscius' translations of Menander's *Phasma* and *Thesaurus*; for an attempt to flesh these out into a portrait of the poet, see Garton 1972.

a comedian, and the fragments seem to confirm him as the principal pioneer of the full-blooded *palliata* style of Plautus and Caecilius. Volcacius' preference for Caecilius over Plautus seems to have been the general view in antiquity; the major playwright of the generation between Plautus and Terence, he is stylistically closer to Plautus but appears to have shared Terence's, and seemingly also Turpilius', special enthusiasm for Menander.[86]

Bibliographic note

Beare 1964, while outdated on Greek New Comedy and indifferent to archaeological evidence, remains unrivalled in English as a synthesis of the literary source material, particularly on lost genres, while, for the extant comedies, Duckworth 1952 still covers more ground than any other single volume in English. Boyle 2005, though centred on tragedy, offers an extremely helpful cultural history of literary drama at Rome, with invaluable discussions of the careers of Livius, Naevius, and Ennius.

Marshall 2006 is now the fundamental text on matters of Roman comic staging and stagecraft; its focus is principally on Plautus rather than Terence. There has also been illuminating work from theatre-studies professionals: the Roman parts of Wiles 1991 present bold and important suggestions about the fundamental differences between Greek and Roman New Comedy on stage, while Beacham 1991 builds on some landmark practical experiments at reconstructionist productions, though with a more positivistic treatment of Pompeian theatrical wall-painting than that argued in his more recent and nuanced follow-up studies. Bieber 1961 assembles a rich dossier of evidence with abundant illustration, but its text needs using critically. The standard work on Roman theatre architecture is now Sear 2006, though its subject is the surviving remains and so begins with the imperial phase of the story.

On music, a series of articles by Moore (1998a, with followups in several of the ScriptOralia collections on individual Plautine plays) paves the way for his forthcoming full-length treatment. Understanding of the metres of Roman comedy (on which Questa 2007 is now the master synthesis) has been revitalized in recent years by the

---

[86] On all these figures, Wright 1974 offers detailed profiles and close reading of the fragments. New imaging techniques are slowly recovering the second half of Caecilius' *Money-Lender* from a Herculaneum papyrus: see Kleve 1996, 2001.

firm discrediting of podic, isochronous, and ictus-based models and a closer appreciation of the dynamics of the Roman versions of the Greek metra; the master exponents in English are Willcock (in his editions of Plautus' *Casina* [with MacCary, 1976] and *Pseudolus* [1987]) and Gratwick (in his editions of Plautus' *Menaechmi* [1993] and Terence's *Brothers* [1999]; see also [1982: 84–93]), and there are good accounts also in Christenson's *Amphitruo* (2000) and an excellent concise summary in Henderson's *Asinaria* (2006). Handley's alphabetic notation (originally used to describe the metres of Menandrean comedy in his *Dyskolos* edition [1965: 56–62]) has proved especially useful here and is becoming the standard shorthand, while Gratwick's system of marking the start of the *longum* with underdots is gradually gaining ground in editions; it is adopted in Henderson, as well as in Barsby's edition (1999) of Terence's *Eunuchus*.

V PLAUTUS

Life and times

If Plautus had a real name, it seems never to have been known or inquired after. 'Titus Maccius Plautus' means something like 'Willy McBozo Greasepaint', and the disquieting proliferation of variants in the manuscripts is the equivalent of indecision over whether 'McBozo' should be spelled with a 'Mac-' and a small B. *Plautus* is a variant form of *planipes* ('flatfoot'), attested as a nickname for performers in the barefoot Latin mime; *Maccius* means 'son of Maccus', the buffoonish hero of the Oscan *fabula Atellana*; while even the innocuous-looking praenomen Titus was used as a pet name for the male organ of business.[87] The strong theatrical connections are nevertheless suggestive in the light of the ancient biographical tradition on Plautus, which is a shaky-looking edifice, but on one striking central point, there seems never to have been any doubt in antiquity: unlike other early Roman dramatists, Plautus came to the writing of plays not as a poet but as a professional man of the theatre. In contrast to his contemporaries Naevius and Ennius, he specialized in a single dramatic genre, and it may be his indifference to epic and tragedy in particular that kept him out of the aristocratic patronage and politics in which the careers of others were enmeshed.

Cicero gives the date of Plautus' death as 184, though this is likely to be simply the last year for which a new production could be documented. (The birth-date of 254 still occasionally glimpsed in modern biographies has no authority, ancient or otherwise.) Only two plays are transmitted with dates: *Stichus* from the Plebeian Games of 200, and *Pseudolus* from the historic Megalensia of 191, when the temple of the Magna Mater was dedicated. Assembling the other nineteen plays into a chronological sequence is largely an exercise in self-amusement,[88] though we have Cicero's testimony (*De Senectute* 50) that *Truculentus* was a late work; *Bacchides* seems to date itself to the

---

[87] Gratwick 1973.
[88] See Gruen 1993: 125 n. 2, and Leigh 2004: 21 f. for a case study in the contradictions of apparent topicality. The most confident attempts, still useful for the arguments they collect, are Buck 1940; Sedgwick 1949; de Lorenzi 1952; and Schutter 1952 See Woytek 2001 for a recent attempt.

mid-eighties by an apparent reference to the *senatusconsultum de bacchanalibus* of 186, the decree restricting Bacchic rites at Rome, and its hero refers to *Epidicus* as an earlier work that was nevertheless recent enough for its audience to remember; *Casina* also seems to be late. These more-or-less fixed points fit with the long-held belief that the proportion of lyric song increased over the course of Plautus' career; *Casina* has the most, while *Miles Gloriosus* uniquely has none at all, and an early date for that play would synchronize with an ancient tradition that identifies the unnamed 'barbarian poet' of line 211 as Naevius. The most significant unknown is how early the earliest plays should be placed, with estimates ranging between 220 and 210 or later.

Nevertheless, and notwithstanding the uncertainties over the dating of individual plays, Plautus' career spans the most remarkable generation in the story of Rome's emergence as a Mediterranean superpower: the age of Hannibal and of Flamininus, of Carthage neutralized at Zama and Greece settled under Roman authority after the breaking of Macedonian power at Cynoscephalae. The Hannibalic war was the event that, in later cultural memory, would stand as the Republic's defining moment of triumph over its imperial nemesis at a time of darkest threat, Rome's own counterpart to what the Persian wars meant to Greeks; while the Macedonian war was a landmark in the development of Roman attitudes to Greek culture. Plautus' Rome was a highly militarized society, and the plays' complex engagement with issues of power and authority draw obsessively on military imagery and ideology. But it was also a society deeply engaged in an imperial project of cultural differentiation and self-assertion, as Roman power extended itself beyond the Italian peninsula into the wider world of old Mediterranean cultures, while a raft of domestic legislation attempted to regulate private behaviour in ways that Plautus' plays were especially well positioned to reflect.

220	starting point of Polybius' history
219	Hannibal's siege of Saguntum
218	2nd Punic War 218–202; Hannibal crosses Alps into Italy
217	Hannibal's victory at Lake Trasimene; dictatorship of Q. Fabius Maximus
216	Hannibal's victory at Cannae; revolt of Capua
215	First Macedonian War 215–205
213	Siege of Syracuse
212	Siege of Capua; fall of Syracuse

211	Hannibal's march on Rome
206	Roman conquest of Spain (from Carthage)
204	Cato brings Ennius to Rome; Megalensia founded
203	Hannibal recalled to Carthage
202	Scipio defeats Hannibal at Zama; Fabius Pictor's history
200	Plautus, *Stichus*; Second Macedonian War 200–197
196	Flamininus proclaims freedom of Greeks
195	*lex Oppia*
194	Flamininus' triumph; plays introduced at Megalensia
191	dedication of temple of Magna Mater; Plautus, *Pseudolus* (Megalensia)
186	*senatusconsultum de Bacchanalibus*
184	death of Plautus; birth of Terence; Cato censor

Works

Including the fragmentary *Vidularia*, 21 plays survive under Plautus' name, a fraction of the 130 or so that circulated in antiquity; they are surely the same as the 21 listed by Varro as of universally accepted authenticity, as opposed to his longer inventories of (i) plays whose authorship had at some point been impugned but which Varro believed to be Plautine, and (ii) plays Varro himself regarded as apocrypha.[89] Plautine authorship of all twenty-one is not in doubt, though some have suffered interpolation at an early date, and Zwierlein 1990–2 has put a case for much more extensive interpolation than has generally been suspected; his often troubling arguments have tended to be sidelined rather than answered.[90]

Latin title	English	Greek title	English	Greek author
Amphitruo	*Amphitryo*			
Asinaria	*Donkey Business*	*Onagros*	*The Donkey*	Demophilus
Aulularia	*A Crock of Gold*			
Bacchides	*Two Bacchises*	*Dis Exapaton*	*Tricking Them Twice*	Menander
Captivi	*Captives*			
Casina	*Casina*	*Kleroumenoi*	*Taking Lots*	Diphilus

[89] Gellius iii.3, quoting the example of the *Girl from Boeotia*, alternatively attributed to Aquilius and denied to Plautus by Accius.

[90] See now Deufert 2002, who bravely endorses even Zwierlein's view that most of the interpolation is the work of a single hand.

Latin title	English	Greek title	English	Greek author
Cistellaria	A Tale of a Trinket-Box	Synaristosai	The Bruncheon Club	Menander
Curculio	Curculio			
Epidicus	Epidicus			
Menaechmi	Two Menaechmuses			
Mercator	The Merchant	Emporos	The Merchant	Philemon
Miles Gloriosus	Major Bigmouth	Alazon	The Bigmouth	
Mostellaria	Ghost Story	Phasma (?)	The Ghost	Philemon?
Persa	The Persian			
Poenulus	A Little Man from Carthage[91]	Karchedonios	The Carthaginian	Alexis
Pseudolus	Pseudolus			
Rudens	Rope			Diphilus
Stichus	Stichus	Adelphoi (A)	The Brothers (I)	Menander
Trinummus	Threequidsworth	Thesauros	The Treasure	Philemon
Truculentus	Truculentus			
Vidularia	Bag Story	Schedia	The Raft	Diphilus (?)

Amphitruo.[92] The king of Thebes comes home from war to find that both he and his slave have a doppelgänger: in fact the gods Jupiter and Mercury in disguise, Jupiter having become infatuated with Amphitryo's queen, Alcmena, and fathered the infant Heracles as a twin brother to Amphitryo's unborn child.

The only fully mythological comedy extant in either Greek or Latin treats a story that we know from both literary and visual evidence to have been a (even the) staple of the subgenre, particularly in the era of Middle Comedy. The Greek source remains unidentified, but not for lack of candidates; a Middle or even Old Comic original is a possibility, though Philemon's *Long Night* has the attraction of advertising one of the unusual theatrical features of Plautus' version, the nocturnal first act caused by Jupiter's miraculous prolongation of his night of love with Alcmena. It is, as has long been recognized,[93] comedy's *Bacchae*,

---

[91] The untranslatable diminutive is part condescending, part contemptuous.

[92] See especially Galinsky 1966; Forehand 1971; Fantham 1973; Dupont 1976; Phillips 1985; Moore 1998b: 108–25; Slater 1985: 70–93; Anderson 1993: 53–9; Schoeman 1998, 1999; Baier 1999; Bond 1999; McCarthy 2000: 77–121; Christenson 2000, 2001; Peter O'Neill 2003; Schmidt 2003; Mahoney 2004.

[93] Stewart 1958.

with its disguised god, palace miracles, supernatural climax reported in a messenger speech, and *ex machina* finale, and thematically in its pervasive metatheatrical reflection on the construction of illusion, the playing of roles, and the ironic collusion with a knowing audience at the expense of an internal cast of dupes. But it is also Plautus' most unsettling essay on his recurrent theme of identity displacement, with especially close parallels to the other doppelgänger play, *Menaechmi*: a hero pointedly shut out from his house, his wife, and the citizen identity that they theatrically embody, while a double occupies his place in the world both physically and socially. (Significantly, the play is, with *Captivi*, one of only two to use a single door.) The play has a fine line to tread for a Roman audience in presenting the supreme deity of the Roman pantheon as a comic adulterer and seducer of matrons, but navigates this ideological minefield deftly by delegating the more overtly comic business to Mercury, who assimilates himself to the the role and identity of the comic slave lead, while the character of Alcmena is kept chastely clear of overt taint.

Asinaria.[94] The mercenary madam Cleareta pimps her daughter Philaenium to a pair of rival suitors, only for her preferred bidder to find himself facing a further competitor in the father who has pretended to be his ally.

As in similar bidding wars in *Bacchides*, *Curculio*, and *Pseudolus*, the impoverished hero outplays his wealthier opponent by an ingenious identity theft (though always afterwards converted into a legal transaction; Romans were sensitive on such matters). But the father's inappropriate collusion in his son's affair, using money diverted from his own wife, turns the second phase of the action into a cautionary tale of a dirty old man's comeuppance in the manner of *Casina* and *Mercator*; and, as in Terence's *Phormio*, the defrauded wife emerges as the key player in the final round, restoring the balance by deploying the cash (from an overseas sale of donkeys) in her son's interest rather than her husband's.

Aulularia.[95] The miser Euclio discovers a buried treasure in the family home, and grows so paranoid about what he believes to be others' designs on the gold that he fails to realise that his daughter is nine months' pregnant from a rape.

[94] Hough 1937; Bertini 1968; Konstan 1983: 47–56; Slater 1985: 55–69; J. C. B. Lowe 1992; W. S. Anderson 1993: 79–82; Danese 2004; Questa 2004: 1–13; John Henderson 2006.
[95] See especially Arnott 1964b, 1988; Hunter 1981; Konstan 1983: 33–46; Bain 1992; Anderson 1993: 66–8; Lefèvre 1998, 2001; Kruschwitz 2002.

The Greek play is unidentified, though the close *Dyskolos* parallels would sit plausibly with a Menandrean original.[96] The central figure is again a solitary misanthrope, violent and paranoid, with a virtuous daughter who respects the patron god her father offends. To reward her, the god explains in the prologue that he plans to marry her off to a well-to-do *adulescens* he has already caused to fall in love with her. To obtain the father's necessary permission, the hero finds himself in a position to rescue the old man from a personal calamity born of his own misanthropy – an experience that shocks him into renouncing and reforming his past ways, apparently (the ending is lost, but we have a couple of telling fragments) in a characteristically Menandrean recantation-speech such as we find in *Dyskolos*, *Samia*, *Epitrepontes*, and Terence's *Adelphoe*. The distinctively Roman figure of the *Lar Familiaris* or tutelary household god sets out the play's moral ground rules in the prologue: only the young should marry the young, and familial wealth brings only misery if hoarded rather than put to the service of the family's continuance in marriage. In attempting to keep his daughter's dowry for himself by marrying her to the unsuitable Megadorus, Euclio loses both daughter *and* gold to the young man Lyconides, leading to an artful scene of significant cross purposes where the two offences are confounded. But, in the end, the burden of the gold is lifted from Euclio as he channels it into his daughter's dowry and legitimizes his grandson through her marriage.

Bacchides.[97] Twin sisters, both named Bacchis (for reasons that have perished with the prologue), are loved by Mnesilochus and his best friend Pistoclerus but, when Mnesilochus mistakenly believes his Bacchis to be two-timing him with his best friend, he returns to his father the cash earlier tricked out of him by his slave Chrysalus to buy Bacchis' contract, only to find that Bacchis is faithful after all and Chrysalus must somehow trick the cash again from a father now fore-warned.

Plautus' adaptation of Menander's *Dis Exapaton* is our first fully extant specimen of the Menandrean double-stranded love plot so favoured by Terence, where two *adulescentes* pursue different girls without rivalry, though in this case, uniquely and significantly, neither is a citizen affair directed towards marriage. The complex multiple intrigue (there are actually three, at least in Plautus' version) is played

[96] A dissident view is in Arnott 1988 (and cf. 1989): *q.v.* 182 n. 6 for earlier discussions.
[97] Clark 1976; Slater 1985: 94–117; Barsby 1986; Goldberg 1990; Damen 1992, 1995; Owens 1994; Soubiran 2003; Salamon 2004.

out in an elaborate ballet of doubles: two youths, two sisters, two reluctant fathers who are eventually drawn into the sisters' web themselves. But the centre of all, even in Menander's title, is the versatile serial trickster Chrysalus, whose fabrications drive the plot and systematically overthrow the attempts by figures of citizen authority to assert the structures of moral and familial control.

Captivi.[98] Philocrates and his slave Tyndarus, captured together as prisoners of war, are sold to old Hegio, who aims to arrange an exchange for his own remaining son by sending the slave back to negotiate for the master's release – only to discover that master and slave have exchanged identities and he has let the valuable prisoner go and kept the slave. But Tyndarus is actually, unknown to any of them, Hegio's long-lost other son, abducted and enslaved in childhood.

This unique and unsettling play turns a probing ironic gaze on the institution of slavery itself, confounding the categories of slave and free whose utter separateness is a basic premise of New Comedy's character typology and plotting. The genre cheerfully tolerates female enslavement and emancipation through recognition, and the manumission of slaves of both sexes; but Tyndarus is a freeborn male who has been raised to adulthood in slavery, and is presented as a complex hybrid of sophisticated ethical agent and loyal slave trickster, while both dialogue and situation reflect extensively on the essentially accidental nature of enslavement. Hegio subjects his own son to brutal slave punishment for being more loyal to his lifelong master than to his present legal owner; it is Philocrates who treats Tyndarus as person rather than property, returning voluntarily to redeem him from Hegio, restore Hegio's other son, and deliver the fugitive slave Stalagmus, who abducted and enslaved his master's young son in the first place. Tyndarus resumes his rightful status, and Stalagmus is consigned to a dark and brutal end. Although the play is undated, all this resonates strikingly with the stories preserved of the fates of Roman prisoners in the Hannibalic and Macedonian wars, and it is tempting to follow Lefèvre and Leigh in connecting the production with Flamininus' triumph in 194, which featured a parade of 1200 Romans ransomed from slavery in Greece.

Casina.[99] Lysidamus and his son Euthynicus are both smitten with their slave-girl Casina, but Euthynicus is abroad and Lysidamus is

---

[98] See especially Viljoen 1963; Leach 1969b; Gosling 1983; Konstan 1983: 57–72; J. C. B. Lowe 1991; E. Segal 1991; Franko 1995; Frangoulidis 1996a, 1996b; Thalmann 1996; Benz and Lefèvre 1998; Moore 1998b: 181–96; McCarthy 2000: 167–210; Leigh 2004: 57–97.

[99] Forehand 1973a; MacCary 1973, 1974; Cody 1976; MacCary and Willcock 1976; W. S. Anderson 1983; Leadbeater 1986; O'Bryhim 1989; B. Williams 1993; Connors 1997; Gold

wary of his wife, Cleostrata (who indeed knows all about his plans, and surreptitiously supports Euthynicus), so both sides attempt to obtain Casina by using their male slaves as surrogates in an ostensible slave wedding. When Euthynicus' man loses the draw to marry Casina, Cleostrata substitutes him for the veiled bride, so that when Lysidamus attempts to consummate the wedding in his own slave's place he encounters a nasty surprise.

This major play, the rudest parts of which were suspiciously damaged in the ancestor of our modern texts, looks to be a late work: it seems to allude to the *senatusconsultum de Bacchanalibus* of 186, and its numerous mature-looking dramatic and stylistic features include the highest proportion of lyric in all of Plautus. The prologue has evidently been rewritten for a revival production a decade or two after Plautus' death, but confirms that both of the lovers have been eliminated from the stage action in Plautus' adaptation of Diphilus' Greek original. The citizen plot of recognition and marriage is relegated to a perfunctory closing announcement: Plautus' interests lie with the competition between the rival slaves and (increasingly) the middle-aged husband and wife, with Lysidamus systematically humiliated at the hands of his womenfolk and slaves as he makes the fateful choice between the house of duty and the house of pleasure, only to end up black and blue, cheated of supper and sex, stripped of his citizen costume, and barred from returning to his house and social self until his public humiliation is complete.

Cistellaria.[100] Alcesimarchus is torn between the fatherless mistress whom he has promised to marry and the neighbour's daughter arranged for him by his father; the dilemma is ultimately resolved by the recognition that the mistress too is a daughter of the same neighbour, thanks to a tangled trail of surrogate parentage that has to be pieced together from a chain of individual clues and witnesses.

An elaborate recognition comedy with affinities to *Epitrepontes*, *Epidicus*, and *Rudens*, this has been a relatively neglected play owing to the damaged state of its text; but it is of considerable interest for the domination of much of the action by female characters and the unusually systematic exploration of the ambiguities of Selenium's status as a *pseudohetaera* torn between two mothers, one a professional madam who both pimps and protects her daughter, the other a raped

1998; Moore 1998b: 158–80; Franko 1999; Fitzgerald 2000: 81–6; McCarthy 2000: 77–121; Way 2000; J. C. B. Lowe 2003; Andrews 2004; Questa 2004: 15–55, 137–54.

[100] Lange 1975; Konstan 1983: 96–114; W. S. Anderson 1993: 69–72; Goldberg 2004; Hartkamp and Hurka 2004.

citizen married late in life to the father of her lost child. In contrast, Alcesimarchus, hitherto Plautus' most melodramatically deranged lover, recedes from the stage action entirely as the recognition climax approaches.

Curculio.[101] Penniless Phaedromus needs the help of the resourceful Curculio, a professional *parasitus* or freeloader, to undo the sale of Phaedromus' girl to a soldier rival; as in the similar *Pseudolus*, this is achieved by an ingenious identity theft that diverts the transaction to Phaedromus, but here there is the further twist that the key plot device of the soldier's ring then also enables the girl to be identified as his sister, averting incest and allowing her to be given to Phaedromus in citizen marriage.

This tightly-constructed play, Plautus' shortest, is notable not just for its economy of plotting but for its radical breaches of theatrical illusion, including an astonishing speech put into the mouth of the costume manager (*choragus*), in which the surroundings of the Roman forum are superimposed on the notional Greek setting of the play in Epidaurus. It is also Plautus' only play with a parasite lead (compare Terence's *Phormio*), though in practice Curculio's capacity for legal dealing *qua* citizen is not really exploited in the Latin version, and his characterization is closely in line with Plautus' trickster heroes of slave status.

Epidicus.[102] While his young master, Stratippocles, is away at war, the wily slave Epidicus has persuaded his master, Periphanes, to buy Stratippocles' slave mistress, Acropolistis, in the belief that she is his long-lost daughter, Telestis, and has been captured and sold in the war; but now Stratippocles breezes back with the news that he is no longer interested in Acropolistis, having instead become besotted with a prisoner of war whom he has bought on credit, leaving Epidicus to unpick the results of his earlier intrigue, offload Acropolistis, and finagle the cash for the new girl out of the old man instead via a ruse of headspinning complexity under which Periphanes will believe that he is buying the real Acropolistis (actually a third girl hired to impersonate her). But what nobody, including the audience, yet knows is that Stratippocles' girl is in fact the real Telestis, who really *has* been captured and sold as a prisoner of war . . .

[101] Fantham 1965; Moore 1991, and cf. 1998b: 126–39; W. S. Anderson 1993: 72–4; Wiles 1991: 58–62; Wright 1993; Goldberg 1995.
[102] Duckworth 1940; Goldberg 1978; Slater 1985: 19–36; Willcock 1995; Auhagen 2001.

Plautus' second-shortest play bears the ancient theatre's most mind-boggling plot – perhaps a factor in its special appeal to Chrysalus (*Bacchides* 214). The confusions, coincidences, and relentless identity switches are so many and so rapid that it is hard to tell, even on determined reading, just how much sense the whole astonishing imbroglio actually makes, and it is especially bold of Plautus to dispense with a divine prologue and leave the audience to work out the probable truth for themselves. The intricate legal and political underpinnings of the plot are far from clear in Plautus' version, but it is a hugely ambitious compendium of key Plautine concerns in a virtuosically restrictive compass.

Menaechmi.[103] Syracusans Menaechmus and Sosicles were identical twins, but when their father's favourite, Menaechmus, was abducted as a child, Sosicles was renamed Menaechmus in his memory, while the real Menaechmus grew up in Epidamnus, married into the community, and inherited his abductor's estate. When the former Sosicles visits Epidamnus, he is taken for his brother and vice versa, magnifying the faultlines in Menaechmus' Epidamnian life till it threatens to fracture entirely.

Like the other doppelgänger comedy *Amphitruo*, this source for Shakespeare's *Comedy of Errors* is a play of identity usurped. Even before his twin arrives on the scene, Menaechmus' life in Epidamnus is unstable: his wife and property are a legacy of his abduction, and he is already diverting his wife's resources to fund an extra-marital liaison. Now his brother arrives to intercept Menaechmus' stolen pleasures, while Menaechmus' progressive loss of control of his social identity is played out in his exclusion from wife's and mistress's houses alike. Justice is finally restored with Menaechmus' restoration to his true Syracusan family and identity, and the decisive auctioning-off of the property inherited from his original abductor (which Plautus cheekily extends to include the wife, the marriage being apparently childless).

Mercator.[104] Demipho and his son Charinus are unknowing rival suitors for the slave Pasicompsa, each hiding behind their counterparts in the family next door; but Demipho's hard-won victory in the

---

[103] Fantham 1968a; Leach 1969c; E. Segal 1969; Haberman 1981; Jocelyn 1984; Muecke 1987; Damen 1988–9; Stärk 1989; Gratwick 1993; McCarthy 2000: 35–76; Questa 2004: 57–75.

[104] Hubka 1984; W. S. Anderson 1993: 36–41, 109–13; Lefèvre 1995: 9–59; Frangoulidis 1997: 133–43; J. C. B. Lowe 2001.

bidding quickly falls apart when his surrogate's wife returns and takes her husband's charade for the truth.

Gilbert Norwood 1932: 15–99 divided his chapters on Plautus ('the worst of all writers who have ever won permanent repute', 4) into one on *Mercator* ('shines forth magnificently . . . comes near perfection', 36) and one on 'The Other Nineteen Plays' ('mostly deplorable', 27). More recent judgment has been less polar, as the stock of the closely comparable *Casina* has risen and its more risqué and subversive treatment of the same essential situation has come to seem a strength rather than a fault. But *Mercator* is a play of great elegance and symmetry, with its mirrored houses each containing a family of father, mother, adult son, and slave, and the Oedipal rivalry pointedly contrasts the father's higher social authority with his lower moral and generic entitlement to pleasure. If Demipho is swifter than *Casina*'s Lysidamus to retire from the field once he realizes his rival is his own son, it is because this play is less interested in the systematic degradation of the adulterous offender himself and more in the tensions of paternal authority eliminated from the action of *Casina* by the deletion of the son from the onstage cast.

Miles Gloriosus.[105] The egomaniacal Pyrgopolynices has kidnapped Philocomasium from Athens, but has been tracked to Ephesus by her lover, Pleusicles, whose slave Palaestrio has fallen into the soldier's hands and is secretly working against him to reunite the lovers: first by a secret passage into Pyrgopolynices' house, and then by an elaborate adultery sting to trick him into letting Philocomasium go while placing himself in the power of his enemies.

The self-deluding boastful warrior is not unique to this play, but his systematic emasculation is, as Palaestrio's tricks draw Pyrgopolynices ever deeper into his fantasy self of epic masculinity and sexual magnetism, while his actual power is gradually taken from him as house, mistress, slave, and finally his very person are surrendered into the power of his enemies in the house next door. As in *Pseudolus*, the soldier's bamboozled disempowerment is further reflected in a leakage of military imagery from the warrior to his slave-hero antagonist. The Athenian hero Pleusicles is unable to act under Ephesian law, but finds a ready surrogate in his mature bachelor host, Periplectomenus, who willingly plays the necessary role in trapping the soldier in a staged *delictum flagrans* that will drive him to blubbering humiliation

---

[105] Fraenkel 1922, translated 2007: 174–9; G. Williams 1956a; Forehand 1973b; Leach 1980; Frangoulidis 1996d, 1998; Questa 2004: 77–97.

and a legally binding oath to seek no redress for the beating that he receives from Periplectomenus' slaves.

Mostellaria.[106] Tranio's young master, Philolaches, has been living it up in his father's absence abroad and, when the old man returns, Tranio tries to conceal the truth and service Philolaches' debt by means of an increasingly complex stack of lies in which the family house has been abandoned as haunted.

Plautus' most hopeless slave hero, Tranio finds himself constantly on the back foot to try and prop up a teetering deception that the audience can see is doomed from the start. His moments of exultation alternate with more clear-sighted moments of gibbering panic, his whole edifice in continual threat of collapse and shored up by ever more desperate and flimsy improvisations. The generic identification between house, body, and citizen identity is effectively spelled out in Philolaches' allegorical entrance-song, and developed further in the returning father's exclusion from his own door, the interior behind which has been occupied instead by a dissolute party of youths, slaves, entertainers, and whores. However, in an elegant twist, one of the guests repays Philolaches' generosity by bailing out both master and slave from his own pocket, just as Tranio is clinging to the stage altar to stave off crucifixion.

Persa.[107] In charge of his master's household while its owner is abroad, the hero Toxilus, though a slave, devises an elaborate intrigue to buy his mistress, Lemniselenis, from her pimp at the pimp's own expense, using the freeborn daughter of Toxilus' citizen parasite to impersonate a foreign chattel and entrap the pimp in an illicit traffic in persons.

Plautus' strangest play is full of generic anomalies: a masterless slave whose owner never does return from his mission abroad; who is free to conduct a pecuniary love affair of his own, notwithstanding his alienation from the legal mechanisms of property and contract; and who is attended by a citizen parasite with (uniquely) a daughter available (again uniquely) to be traded, against her inclination, in a high-stakes impersonation and legal charade. It seems fairly clear that these paradoxical inversions of convention are key to the play's meaning, but interpretation is divided between lighter and darker readings of the ethical world presented.

---

[106] Leach 1969a; J. C. B. Lowe 1985b; Frangoulidis 1997: 21–75; Milnor 2002; Questa 2004: 99–112.

[107] Woytek 1982; Hughes 1984; Slater 1985: 37–54; J. C. B. Lowe 1989; W. S. Anderson 1993: 76–8; McCarthy 2000: 122–66; Faller 2001; Hardy 2005; Richlin 2005: esp. 111–20.

Poenulus.[108] The Carthaginian Hanno arrives in the Aetolian city of Calydon in search of his two daughters, who were kidnapped in infancy and have been raised for prostitution by the pimp Lycus; a nephew, Agorastocles, was separately kidnapped and has been raised as a Calydonian in the house next door to Lycus', where he has fallen in love with one of the sisters. With his slave Milphio, Agorastocles stages a legal trap for Lycus and, on learning that the girls are free-born Carthaginians, Milphio plans a follow-up under which the newly met Hanno, now recognized as Agorastocles' uncle, will impersonate the girls' father – which of course he turns out to be in truth.

This is a fascinating if perplexing and oddly shaped play, with its pimp plot framed in the much more interesting Carthaginian plot of the prologue and finale. The comic high point is Milphio's attempt to train Hanno to play a fictitious character who turns out to be himself and marvels at his stooge's skills of simulation before the cross purposes are untangled; a similar scene in Menander's *Sikyonios/oi* may owe something to Plautus' Greek source here, perhaps a play by Menander's supposed mentor, Alexis. But the play's significance lies in its exploration of Roman views of both Aetolian and Carthaginian ethnicity in the aftermath of the Hannibalic war, which had given both the play's worlds a topicality inconceivable to the audience of Alexis' original. Like the passage of ostensible Punic in Hanno's speech, it is not easy to interpret; the most rewarding of recent readings have been those most willing to see point in puzzles rather than solutions.

Pseudolus.[109] By an elaborate imposture, the artful slave Pseudolus tricks the unscrupulous pimp Ballio, who has sold Pseudolus' young master's girl to a rival bidder, into surrendering the girl to Pseudolus instead and stumping up the cash out of his own pocket.

Plautus' most celebrated slave hero displays an exuberant meta-theatrical command of the other characters' roles in his drama and his own relationship with the audience, constructing a dizzyingly complex network of cash transactions and wagers around a characteristically Plautine act of identity theft.

---

[108] Fraenkel 1922, translated 2007: 179–90; Gratwick 1971, 1982: 101–3; Arnott 1988; Maurach 1988; Slater 1992; John Henderson 1994; Franko 1996; Starks 2000; Baier 2004; Richlin 2005: esp. 185–99.

[109] G. Williams 1956b; Wright 1975; Arnott 1982; Stehle 1984; J. C. B. Lowe 1985a; Slater 1985: 118–46; Willcock 1987; Griffith 1988; Hallett 1993; Barsby 1995; Sharrock 1996; Lefèvre 1997; Moore 1998b: 92–107; Fitzgerald 2000: 44–7; N. J. Lowe 2000a: 207–9; Questa 2004: 113–33; Tornau 2005.

Rudens.[110] In Cyrene, the slave-dealer Labrax has sold Palaestra on deposit to her lover, Plesidippus, only to swindle him by sailing off with cash and girl alike. But the storm-star Arcturus arranges a shipwreck that washes up Labrax, Palaestra, and luggage separately on the lonely stretch of African coast where Palaestra's long-lost father, Daemones, lives, and an *Epitrepontes*-style arbitration between slaves over the luggage leads to Daemones' reunion with his daughter, allowing her to marry Plesidippus while Labrax gets his legal deserts.

This expansive play takes dramatic and thematic advantage of an unusual setting where the human world meets the elemental, and where the central tug-of-war that gives the play its title turns on rival conceptions of natural ownership and justice, whose thoughtful arbitration gives the exiled Daemones back his family and his place in society.

Stichus.[111] Panegyris and Pamphila, sisters married to impoverished brothers who have been three years abroad, are under pressure from their father, Antipho, to divorce their husbands and remarry for wealth; but the brothers return in the nick of time (with the slave Stichus in tow), now wealthy men themselves.

Menander's play seems to have been taken apart and reassembled into a virtually plotless montage of festive variations on a theme of homecoming, organized less around events than in an intricate structure of mirror scenes and doubled types, with the spotlight moving progressively from the two sisters to their two husbands to their two slaves. The sisters' Penelopean predicament, noted by Panegyris in the opening lines, is fully resolved by line 409, and the resolution itself is relegated to an offstage scene recounted in a couple of lines; the remainder of the action celebrates the reunion and prosperity of both households above and below stairs, in a series of mirrored episodes attached to successive characters' arrivals from the harbour. Wiles 1988a attractively suggests that the date of 200 could link the play to the return of troops from overseas following the defeat of Hannibal at Zama; at any rate it seems to be Plautus' most radical experiment in detaching the poetics of Roman comedy from conventional Greek plot forms.

Trinummus.[112] During a business trip abroad, Charmides has charged his friend Callicles with keeping an eye on Charmides' son

---

[110] Lloyd 1963; Leach 1974; Konstan 1983: 73–95; W. S. Anderson 1993: 46–53; Louden 1999.

[111] Fraenkel 1922 translated 2007: 190–8; Arnott 1972b; Wiles 1988a; Owens 2000.

[112] J. P. Stein 1970; Fantham 1977; W. S. Anderson 1979, 1993: 41–5; Hunter 1980; Muecke 1985; Lefèvre 1995: 61–168.

Lesbonicus, and also with the secret of a family treasure buried in the house and intended for his daughter's dowry; but when the congenitally overgenerous Lesbonicus seeks to sell the house and give his sister in marriage without a dowry, Callicles buys the house from his own pocket and tries to use the treasure to supply a dowry by hiring an impostor to masquerade as a messenger from Charmides – only for the impostor to turn up on Charmides' doorstep at the same moment as the real Charmides.

Unusual both for its absence of any erotic element and for its cast dominated by elderly citizen males, this thoughtful comedy of social obligation turns on the issues of familial responsibility seen also in the more farcical *Aulularia*. Here again, the proper use for family wealth is the propagation of the *oikos* through citizen marriage, lubricated by appropriate dowries; but, where in *Aulularia* Euclio's false priorities were the obstacle, here it is the combination of Charmides' absence with Lesbonicus' excessive good nature. Callicles has no power to block Lesbonicus' transactions, so must keep house, treasure, and daughter together by clandestine means. We do not need to assume, with Erich Segal 1987a, that the play's high-mindedness was externally imposed by the circumstances of the commission; Plautine comedy was a broad church, and was as capable of celebrating the wisdom of age as it was elsewhere of exposing its folly.

Truculentus.[113] The courtesan Phronesium dangles three males on her hook: the city youth Diniarchus, bankrupted but still besotted; the soldier Stratophanes, to whom Phronesium is pretending to have borne a child; and her latest victim, Strabax, a naive but well-heeled country youth. Phronesium's supposititious baby turns out to be the product of Diniarchus' rape of a citizen's daughter, whom he reluctantly agrees to marry – though Phronesium is allowed to borrow the baby long enough to complete her extortion of Stratophanes' cash while she simultaneously fleeces Strabax, whose slave Truculentus has already fallen victim to her maid Astaphium.

A play of situation rather than of plot, this exuberantly cynical comedy of female domination over a procession of uniformly feckless males is the prostitute comedy *par excellence*, staged entirely around the independent *meretrix*'s grant or refusal of access to her door, as a whole gallery of contrasting male types are ruthlessly exploited by turns for a quick cash profit, and the norms of masculinity, male

---

[113] Enk 1964; Dessen 1977; Konstan 1983: 142–64; W. S. Anderson 1993: 82–7; Moore 1998b: 140–57; Hofmann 2001.

self-mastery, and citizen duty all crumble in the face of the women's mercenary deployment of their charms. A key word in modern criticism has been 'satiric': this most demonstratively amoral of Plautus' plays seems to celebrate a vision of society in which the traditional core values of New Comedy are systematically overthrown by the emasculating force of non-citizen desire.

Vidularia.[114] The shipwrecked Nicodemus is taken in by the fisherman Gorgines and taken on by Gorgines' neighbour Dinia as a labourer, while Nicodemus' lost luggage, probably containing recognition tokens, becomes the subject of a dispute and arbitration that leads to Nicodemus' recognition as Dinia's son. Clearly, in the little preserved of this twenty-first play, we have a situation with analogies to *Rudens*, Plautus' other play from an original by Diphilus, though there is no trace in the fragments of any romantic element or indeed of female characters.

Bibliographic note

A replacement for Lindsay's centenarian Oxford text (1903) has been slow to emerge,[115] but the *Editio Plautina Sarsinatis* so far covers *Asinaria* (Danese, 2004), *Casina* (Questa 2001), and *Vidularia* with the fragments (Monda 2004), augmented by Questa's *hors série* edition of the cantica (1995); this is the authoritative text where available. Deufert 2002 is an important history of the vicissitudes of Plautus' text in antiquity, although few will endorse his endorsement of Zwierlein's single-reviser theory (1990–2). Essential modern editions in English of single plays are MacCary and Willcock's *Casina* (1976), Willcock's solo *Pseudolus* (1987), Barsby's *Bacchides* (1986), Christenson's *Amphitruo* (2000), Gratwick's *Menaechmi* (1993), and John Henderson's *Asinaria* (2006); for other plays, Italian or German is needed.

There is no satisfactory complete translation of Plautus in English. Nixon's first-generation Loeb (1916–38) stands up better for its age than might be imagined, and is more reliable than the four-volume variorum series edited by Slavitt and Bovie (1995) for Johns Hopkins. Watling's Penguin (1973, 1975) suffers from a narrow and conservative selection of plays, skewed towards schoolroom use and so

---

[114] Dér 1987; Calderan 2004; Monda 2004.
[115] On the deficiencies of Lindsay's edition, see especially Gratwick 2000, and cf. R. J. Tarrant 1983.

excluding major plays such as *Casina* that were felt too spicy for their target users; Erich Segal's World's Classics volume (2002) offers superior, annotated translations of four of the same plays. The gap is partly filled by Tatum 1983, and a refreshingly radical approach is taken with the versions for performance of *Curculio*, *Persa*, and *Poenulus* in Richlin 2005, which includes very full notes; Henderson's *Asinaria* edition includes a similarly sparky cisatlantic translation. Note also Peter Smith 1991 and the *Miles Gloriosus*, *Menaechmi*, and *Bacchides* in Berg and Parker 1999.

Wiles 1988b is an extremely useful snapshot of trends in Plautine criticism internationally from the sixties to the mid-eighties. The cornerstone of modern Plautine criticism is Fraenkel 1922, now available in English (2007) with additional material from the 1960 Italian edition; its careful conclusions have since been largely vindicated by further papyrus discoveries, including the *Dis Exapaton* papyrus, though on structural changes Fraenkel was readier than most scholars since to believe in widespread Plautine *contaminatio* (see on Terence below) and the possibility of its detection. Plautine criticism since Fraenkel has found it hard to shake off the obsession with analyst approaches and, since the sixties, has followed different national paths, with German and British scholars generally pursuing different kinds of analyst agenda while Italian and American scholars have been more willing to read the plays as coherent compositions for a Roman audience. In Germany, Plautine studies have gone off on two near-opposite trajectories, which have both been more sceptically received abroad, with Zwierlein 1990–2 arguing that our texts are massively interpolated versions of significantly more conservative original versions of the Greek texts, while Lefèvre's Freiburg school has energetically argued (1982) for a very high level of Plautine creativity and originality under the influence of native Italian comic traditions.

Erich Segal 1968 marks something of a year zero in post-analyst Plautine studies, showing how the plays use their highly Romanized versions of Greek comedy to encode deep tensions in Roman society and culture under the comic licence of festival performance; it remains the foundational text for all subsequent Plautine criticism in North America, where the key works have been Slater 1985 (the first and most convincing Anglophone study of metatheatricality in ancient drama), W. S. Anderson 1993 (which includes pages on most of the plays, though its confidence on matters of dating should be taken with caution), Moore 1998b (a valuable introductory volume), McCarthy

2000 (on the complexities and social function of the representation of slavery, on which see now the metacritical survey in McKeown 2007: 108–19), and above all Konstan's 1983 volume of new and revised essays on individual plays, focusing on the tensions in civic ideology negotiated by their plots. Gruen's pioneering historicist analyses (1990, 1993) have had fewer successors than they deserve, but Leigh 2004 is an important casebook of in-depth readings. Of the key works in Italian criticism, special mention should be made of Petrone 1977, Chiarini 1979, and above all Bettini 1982, a brilliant tour of the corpus as a transformational system of plot relationships.

Two series of edited volumes on individual plays are the Italian *Lecturae plautinae sarsinates* by Raffaelli et al. (annually, in alphabetical order by play, begun in 1998; the series has now reached *Menaechmi*) and the volumes in the ScriptOralia series, which focus particularly on plays that members of the Freiburg school suspect to be original or at least radically Plautinized compositions: *Captivi* (Lefèvre, Stärk, and Vogt-Spira 1991), *Amphitruo* (Baier 1999), *Persa* (Faller 2001), *Epidicus* (Auhagen 2001), *Poenulus* (Baier 2004), *Cistellaria* (Hartkamp and Hurka 2004), and the earlier monograph by Stärk on *Menaechmi* (1989), as well as the wider-ranging Benz and Lefèvre 1998, which includes similar claims made for *Truculentus*.

VI TERENCE

Publius Terentius Afer is a remarkably well-documented figure about whom we nevertheless know next to nothing with any certainty. We have a reasonably secure documentary core in the *didascaliae*, the production notices attached to the plays in the manuscript tradition, whose information on original performances has survived the occasional sceptical attempts at unpicking;[116] these give not only date, festival, producer, and aediles or other commissioning magistrates, but Greek source, and even the name and owner of the slave who composed the music and which type of reed-pipes it was played on. There is also Donatus' commentary, though frustratingly shredded and reconstituted in the form in which we have it, which also preserves invaluable, if sometimes puzzling, information about the Greek source plays and their adaptation. But Terence himself remains an enigma. Suetonius' biography of Terence, one of only four survivors from his *Lives of the Poets*, is a rich and still underinvestigated document, but it tells us less about Terence's life than it does about the biographical tradition that grew up around him a century after his death.

If Suetonius' sources are to be trusted, the poet was born in Carthage and arrived in Rome as a senator's slave. The suspicion persists that the tradition of African birth is a biographical fiction from his cognomen Afer – though no alternative origin was canvassed in antiquity, and it may after all be that the man who, in later ages, became the most widely read ancient poet after Virgil was indeed a second- or third-language writer, a Conrad or Nabokov of the Roman world. It was also universally believed that Terence's career was owed to the patronage of a group of young aristocrats centred on the teenage Scipio Aemilianus, son of the conqueror of Macedon and himself the future destroyer of Carthage. The old idea of such a 'Scipionic circle' has in recent years been seen as largely a piece of Ciceronian historical fiction,[117] but this may be too sceptical. Scipio and his brother Fabius did commission Terence to produce at the funeral games for their father Aemilius Paullus; it remains possible that the entire tradition of a more extended relationship derives from

---

[116] Notably by Mattingly 1959, 1963; but see Klose 1966.
[117] Strasburger 1966; Zetzel 1972; Goldberg 1986; Parker 1996.

this single documented fact but, despite their youth, Scipio and his friend Laelius were already emerging in the years after Pydna as important literary patrons, most notably of the historian Polybius, and within at most a generation or two of Terence's death their relationship with the poet was being scurrilously interpreted as sexual.[118]

Whatever the personal background, Terence's career was a product of one of the most tumultuous decades in Roman cultural history, the years following the final Roman conquest of Greece with Aemilius Paullus' victory over the last king of Macedon at Pydna in 168. Greek spoils flooded into Rome on an unprecedented scale, including highly educated slaves and hostage aristocrats (Polybius among them) as well as the contents of the Macedonian royal library, first pick from which Paullus granted to his sons, who would be Terence's future patrons. The years that followed offer tantalizing glimpses of intensely fought culture wars over a perceived threat to Roman traditions and values from the aristocracy's influx of Greek-tinged wealth, played out in a series of triumphal shows and cultural exchanges and, by the end of the decade, provoking a backlash of reactionary legislation in the form of sumptuary laws on aristocratic displays of wealth and a remarkable decree banning Greek philosophers from the city.

It is against this background that Terence's career developed from a hesitant start to an extraordinary year and a half of unprecedented success, only for him to disappear at the height of his fame so abruptly and mysteriously that, even in antiquity, there was no agreement as to what became of him. The tradition seems to have agreed that Terence did not die or retire, but left Rome for Greece; two first-century versions claimed that he died on the homeward journey in some connection with a loss of luggage at sea, while another has him die as late as 156 in Stymphalus in Arcadia (intriguingly close to Polybius' home). It is obviously tempting to speculate that the legislative backlash of 161–160, together with Terence's newfound wealth after the success of the *Eunuch*, made a career break attractive, though the tradition also suggests that there may at this time have been a shortage of suitable untranslated Greek plays available in Rome, and that Terence's mission was in part one of professional research.

---

[118] Suetonius is able to document the story with an extended quotation from the second-century poet Porcius Licinus; see Courtney 1993: 87–90.

184	Suetonius' date for Terence's birth; Cicero's date for Plautus' death
169	death of Ennius
168	Crates of Mallos in Rome
	battle of Pydna June
	death of Caecilius Statius
167	Polybius deported to Rome
	Macedonian royal library brought to Rome
	triumph of Aemilius Paullus, November
	Anicius Gallus' triumphal show
166	*Andria* ('The Girl from Andros'), April (Megalensia)
165	*Hecyra*[1] ('The Mother in Law'), April (Megalensia, aborted)
163	*Heautontimorumenos* ('The Self-Tormentor')
161	*Eunuchus* ('The Eunuch'), April (Megalensia, twice)
	sumptuary law on *ludi*
	Pomponius' expulsion of the philosophers
	Phormio, September (Ludi Romani)
160	*Adelphoe* ('The Brothers'); *Hecyra*[2] (*ludi funebres* for Aemilius Paullus)
	Hecyra[3], probably September (Ludi Romani)
	Terence leaves Rome
156	death of Terence (according to Cosconius)
	Pergamene–Bithynian war

Terence and the palliata

Terence seems to have been as different from Plautus as it was possible to get within their common generic tradition. Where Plautus had been a professional man of the theatre, Terence came to the stage as a product of the new aristocratic patronage that had taken hold in tragedy a generation earlier but that was evidently still viewed with hostility and suspicion by comic professionals such as Luscius. Terence's distance from his peers can only have been magnified by the fact that he worked exclusively with a single production company, the troupe (*grex*) of the veteran actor-manager L. Ambivius Turpio. Indeed, this close relationship with Ambivius' team may be one reason why the plays survived as a corpus generally free from the kind of interpolation by later hands that we find in the texts of Plautus, no doubt arising out of revival productions.

What is clear is that what Terence was doing with the *palliata* differed radically not just from Plautus but from the whole Roman

comic tradition, including that of his contemporaries.[119] Terence's
theatre was a product of the world of the 160s, and responded to the
Hellenizing vogue in aristocratic culture by drastically reconstructing
the relationship between Latin comedy and its Greek models as one of
assimilation rather than appropriation. Where Plautus had gleefully
asserted his creative dominance over the dramatic and ethical values
of his Greek material, Terence was obsessed with trying to make the
qualities of Menandrean comedy speak meaningfully to a Roman
popular audience, while still exercising his own creative freedom to
improve liberally on the texts in the process of adaptation. Though no
more faithful to the letter of the text than Plautus had been, Terence
nevertheless worked hard at making the text feel like a Greek play – in
plot, in characterization, in ethics, and above all in language, where he
forged an extraordinarily beautiful, well-spoken conversational Latin
that would ensure his classic status in schoolrooms right through the
middle ages. No wonder Luscius felt threatened by the forces of
patronage lined up behind this enigmatic young revolutionary *arri-
viste*.

As an adapter of Greek New Comedy into Latin *palliatae*, Terence
inherited certain theatrical givens from the existing *palliata* tradition.
He did not reinstate a chorus, and he accepted the anti-naturalistic
convention of making up for the lost musical element by setting large
quantities of the dialogue to musical accompaniment – although the
element of lyric *canticum* is now close to non-existent, largely replaced
by a much higher proportion of recitative passages. We cannot tell
whether this was Terence's innovation or merely a change in fashion
in the twenty years since Plautus' day; the former is perhaps suggested
by the record-breaking proportion of *canticum* in the surviving text of
Casina, even though our version is that of a revival production from
around this time and has been updated to suit changing taste in other
respects. But it meant that Terence, like Plautus before him, was faced
with the challenge of successfully eliminating and camouflaging the
four choral breaks in the action of his Greek model; and in practice he
seems to have been every bit as free as Plautus with the structure and
plotting of his adaptations, though in different directions.

Although it is hard to catch either completely red-handed, the overwhelming impression of Plautus' structural changes is of a tendency
to simplify the plot, cast, and stage movement of his Greek source
where Terence seems, if anything, to like to complicate it further.

---

[119] The classic study here remains Wright 1974, amplified now by Karakasis 2005.

Plautus will move onstage scenes offstage, strip scenes down, and delete entire characters and subplots (most notoriously in *Casina*, whose prologue cheerfully announces the wholesale removal of the title character, her lover, and the resolution of their story in a final recognition and betrothal). Any space thus freed up will generally be absorbed by more extended comic business of a verbal or knockabout kind. Terence, on the other hand, likes to bring additional subplots into the action, whether from offstage scenes in the Greek original, from his own invention, or, in at least three astonishing cases, by pasting in additional characters and scenes from a *second Greek source play*: the practice his rival Luscius stigmatized as *contaminatio*, 'messing'. Despite Terence's own protestations in the prologue to *Andria* (see below), no convincing evidence of such a practice in his predecessors has yet come to light; and it seems to be specifically associated with a marked Terentian preference (in five of the six plays) for what have come to be called 'double plots', intertwining the contrasting affairs, problems, characters, and fates of two pairs of lovers in an intricate dramatic dialogism. Yet at the same time these busy plays are comparatively short on the kind of flamboyant stage action associated with Plautus; in the *Hecyra* prologue, Ambivius classes the comedy as a 'standing-still' play (*stataria*; opposed by later critics to *fabula motoria*, a 'running-around play'). For Terence, the key action takes place not in the field of the visible but inside the characters' heads.

Four of the six plays are adapted from originals by Menander, and the other two from comedies by Apollodorus of Carystus, Menander's closest disciple in New Comedy's second generation; Menander is also the source for two of the three plays raided for additional material in the process of *contaminatio*. Of Plautus' twenty-one plays, in contrast, three are known to be from Menander, three from Diphilus, two from Philemon, one each from Alexis (probably) and the obscure Demophilus; other Menandrean adaptations may be hiding among the eleven plays without an attested source, but Plautus clearly felt no special predilection for Menander's comedies and, in the case of *Stichus*, he seems virtually to have excised Menander's entire plot. In contrast, Terence's regard for Menander goes deeper than mere choice of source, and deeper even than the attempt to capture in Latin dialogue the unsurpassed richness and naturalism of Menander's distillation of Athenian conversational speech. The texture of the comedy is Menandrean, with the expansive Plautine repartee reined severely in, and consistency and complexity of characterization restored. The lowlife leads, the clever slaves and parasites, are still there but have been largely displaced from their Plautine position at the centre of the action; the focus is now back on the citizen characters, and the one play to rely on a *Curculio*-style parasite hero, *Phormio*, presents the least generic instance of the type in extant New Comedy. For Terence, as for Menander, comedy is ultimately about the affirmation of citizen values, not about their subversion by figures of the demi-monde; citizen love, leading to marriage and the propagation of the *oikos*, displaces the purchased love that seeks to undermine it. Most of the plays involve a stark opposition on stage between the house of citizen duty and the house of pleasure of the kind we saw in Plautus' *Menaechmi*; but, where in the end Menaechmus abandoned his citizen place entirely, Terence's characters in the end choose well and fulfil their citizen obligations to family and state in the process.

Terence's plays proclaim themselves as Greek from their very titles, which, in all cases but one, are straight transliterations of the original Greek title, in contrast to Plautus' overwhelming preference for retitling as well as giving his play names in Latin. (The exception is *Phormio*, where Terence has substituted his hero's name Plautus-style for the obscurely technical Greek legal title *Epidikazomenos* – sensing, no doubt, that 'The Man Who Brought a Suit of Compulsory Uxoriation of Residuary Issue' lacked a certain ring to Roman ears.) Something similar is observable in the naming of characters, where both Plautus and Terence freely reassign names to the Menandrean named mask-characters; however, where Plautus coins absurd Greek polysyllables and speaking names, Terence simply draws at random from the New Comic repertory of everyday character names.

Above all, Terence delights in plotting: in convolutions of mistaken identity, bluffs and counter-bluffs, backfiring intrigues, and the audience's competence to work out what has to happen from genre rules alone, without needing to have the whole solution tiresomely announced in advance. Here his most radical move was the complete elimination of the divine prologue, strongly suspected to have explained all to the audience in some or all of his Greek source plays (as is the norm in the extant Greek Menander), leaving the audience to deduce the true situation from their familiarity with genre situations and conventions. In its place, Terence's comedies have a prologue of a quite different kind, separating out the extra-dramatic elements in Plautus' prologues from the expository material with which they there mingle, and devoting the formal prologue to a direct address to the audience by Ambivius or an anonymous member of his company, dealing with background information about the play and sparring with critics for the audience's favour, but giving away nothing at all about the storyline.[120]

The prologues

These fascinating, problematic prologues have, perhaps unfortunately, occasioned if anything more discussion than the plays to which they are attached, and are best considered as a group. All seem to be the composition of Terence himself but, like the parabatic anapaests of Aristophanes with which they are sometimes compared, are delivered not in the poet's own voice but by his players on his behalf, speaking of the dramatist in the third person and the audience in the second. Each is tied to the occasion of the play's first production or, in the case of *Hecyra*, to its final production in 160, with some lines preserved from the earlier unsuccessful production that year; the 165 prologue does not survive, but may have been recycled in part in the extant version. The remaining five prologues centre on responses to criticism of Terence's literary and professional practice. In four of the five, the criticism is specifically credited to an unnamed 'old poet', identified by Donatus as Luscius of Lanuvium, a minor comedian of the older generation.[121] *Adelphoe* does not specify the source, for reasons discussed below, but, since the points repeated are ones earlier credited to Luscius, he is clearly the target of rebuttal here as well.

The tone of these prologues is extremely hard to read – harder, for example, than that of Aristophanes' *parabases*. We should probably be wary of taking them too solemnly: these prologues were part of a scripted entertainment, and build a relationship with the audience through a mixture of jokes, badinage, and extra-dramatic comment of a kind already present in Plautus' prologues – albeit without the close argumentative engagement with a single identified critic. The opening lines of the *Andria* prologue imply that it was still normal practice in Terence's day to set out the plot in such speeches, though here, as

---

[120] Plautus has divine prologues in *Rudens* (Arcturus), *Aulularia* (the Lar), *Trinummus* (Luxuria), *Cistellaria* (Auxilium, delayed), and the somewhat different case of Mercury in *Amphitruo*. An anonymous *prologus* introduces *Asinaria*, *Captivi*, *Casina*, *Menaechmi*, *Poenulus*, *Pseudolus*, *Truculentus*, and probably *Vidularia*; *Mercator* and *Miles Gloriosus* have prologues spoken by characters from the play, and five plays (*Curculio*, *Epidicus*, *Mostellaria*, *Persa*, *Stichus*) have no prologue (but may have had one at some stage in either or both of their Greek and Latin incarnations). *Bacchides* has lost its opening, but the fragments of the lost portion suggest either a postponed character prologue or none.

[121] What little we know of Luscius and his work is fleshed out, in perhaps optimistic detail, by Garton 1972.

throughout, it is dangerous to take Terence's words at face value: even the non-polemical prologue of *Hecyra*, which deals not with Luscius' complaints but with the play's own disaster-ridden production history, shows no interest at all in telling the audience what is going to happen, and Terence may be opportunistically repackaging a distaste for exposition as a response to pre-emptive bad-mouthing by Luscius.

Three kinds of charge are ascribed to Luscius, two of them surfacing repeatedly; and Terence's responses to the charges are masterpieces of obfuscation, disingenuousness, and evasion.

(i) **Contaminatio**. From his very first play, Terence is accused of the practice that Luscius calls by the verb *fabulas contaminare*, 'messing plays up'; Terence fastens on the term and quotes it back at *Andria* 16, *HT* 17. How Luscius was able to accuse Terence of this in his debut production is unclear, although the *Eunuchus* prologue reveals that there were preview performances for the aediles in charge of the festival, at one of which Luscius managed to wangle a place and promptly started to heckle. It is also not quite clear exactly what is being messed up; the *HT* prologue speaks of 'contaminating many Greek plays in making few Latin ones', which may mean simply that the integrity of the Greek plays is violated by recombination and excerption, or that the plays cherrypicked in this way become rapidly used up and unavailable for future translators in what was evidently a climate of professional hyperattentiveness to intellectual property rights. Terence cheerfully admits the charge on three occasions, and even names the second Greek play used as a source; but the three cases all seem different, and Terence's responses to the charge raise further questions that at least cast doubt on his frankness.

The first question is what Terence has actually done. *Adelphoe*'s single scene from Diphilus' *Commorientes* ('Death Pact') is easily identified, and indeed the prologue challenges the audience to spot the joins; but the other cases are more complex. The *Eunuchus* prologue admits, following exposure by Luscius, that the colourful soldier-parasite double-act of Thraso and Gnatho were not from Menander's *Eunuchos*, but from his *Kolax* or 'Toady'; evidently these characters, and dialogue scenes from the *Kolax* featuring them, have been grafted in to replace someone entirely different in the four scenes in which these characters appear, apparently with significant consequences for the ending. The earlier plays are more problematic still. In *Andria* 9–14, Terence states that 'Menander wrote *Andria* and *Perinthia*; who knows the one play knows the pair, for their plots are more or less the same, although dialogue and tone are different. The poet admits he has transferred material that fitted from the *Andria* to the *Perinthia*, and freely reused it'. This was a matter of some puzzlement to Donatus, who trawled through either a full text of *Perinthia* or the discussions of earlier scholars who had, and found only the idea of turning the opening monologue into a dialogue (but with a wife in Menander, a male freedman in Terence) and a couple of other brief passages; 'the rest is different', an impression now confirmed by a papyrus containing a scene of *Perinthia* where a slave takes refuge at an altar, something that does not happen in Terence at all. On 301 and 977, Donatus makes it clear that the figures of Charinus and Byrria were not in Menander's *Andria* – but the wording of both notes implies that they were not in *Perinthia* either, though many scholars remain nervous of the implication that they were therefore Terence's wholesale invention. As for *Heautontimorumenos*, the prologue's state-ment that the play has been 'made double from a single plot' has never been satisfactorily explained,[122] nor the reference to 'ruining many Greek plays to make a few Latin ones'; on the usual view, neither this play nor the earlier *Hecyra* are 'contaminated', but the remark is a strange one to find here of the lone offence, already three years past, of the three brief *Perinthia* borrowings in the *Andria*.

Terence's responses to the charge grow more sophisticated over time. The *Andria* prologue makes the mischievous claim that Terence is merely emulating the *neglegentia*, 'carelessness', of Naevius, Plautus, and Ennius, the classics of the previous generation – a remark which has sent modern scholars hunting for instances of *contaminatio*-style play-splicing in the extant plays of Plautus, though Terence carefully does not claim that Plautus' insouciance manifested in this exact form. The *HT* prologue repeats a version of this defence, this time boldly promising to repeat the offence with the precedent of classic authors before him. By the time of *Eunuchus* the charge has escalated from contamination to actual plagiarism (*furtum*, 'burglary'), on the interesting grounds that, in this case, the material taken from the second source, *Kolax*, had already been translated into Latin; Terence argues in response that he was unaware of the earlier Latin version (credited, intriguingly, to 'Naevius and Plautus' – in collaboration?)

---

[122] Interpretations include: a double plot from a single Greek source; a play spanning two days from a source spanning one; a plot into which a second deception has been grafted; a complicated, clever, or deceptive play from a single source; or a play in which additional speaking roles have been created by the promotion of Bacchis and Antiphila from offstage to onstage roles (so Brothers 1980: *q.v.* for a survey). This last founders on the impossible require-ment that the transfer of Bacchis from Chremes' house to Menedemus could have been 'covered' in the Greek by a choral break.

and so could not have plagiarized the earlier translation, and he goes on to argue with artful irrelevance that the whole genre is formulaic anyway, so that everything is a reuse of something. Needless to say, this dances elegantly around the nature of the charge here, which is the reuse *not* of stock characters and situations but of particular lines spoken by particular characters in a particular play that should be out of bounds. By the time of the masterly *Adelphoe* prologue, Terence has a dazzling defence prepared: Diphilus' play, from which the abduction scene has been taken, has indeed already been translated into Latin by Plautus – but *minus the scene* that Terence has now translated for the first time into Latin. In a particularly brilliant touch, he invites the audience to judge whether he has committed plagiarism or unearthed a lost classic, neither of which is the real issue here – but Terence has used the narrower charge of plagiarism to distract from the original accusation of cross-breeding mutant plays from multiple sources.

(ii) **Collaboration.** The second recurrent charge is more tantalizing still. By the time of *HT*, at least, Terence is having to defend himself against rumours (which he significantly never attributes to Luscius) that he is not the author of his own plays, but is instead a front for unnamed patrons in positions of power, identified by Donatus as Scipio Aemilianus and his brother, who three years later were the sponsors of the games at which *Adelphoe* was produced but whose association with Terence beyond and before that may be entirely inferred. Whoever Terence's patrons were, the charge would have been a difficult one to wriggle away from without deprecating the patronage on which he depended; in the event, he moves by an artful non sequitur to a counter-attack on Luscius' stagecraft without either confirming or denying the accusation. When the issue is recalled in the *Adelphoe* prologue, however, Terence is at his nimblest. That play was produced at the funeral games for Aemilius Paullus, sponsored by Paullus' two surviving sons; and whether or not those sons were the 'noble persons' (*homines nobiles*, *Ad.* 15) rumoured to have had a hand in the plays, Terence brilliantly points out that the whole festival is precisely a celebration of the achievements of the Roman nobility, so that the involvement of *nobiles* in his career is surely high praise and warmly to be welcomed.

(iii) **Style.** An issue mentioned in the prologue of *Phormio* only is Terence's conscious retreat from the full-blooded comic style of Plautine dialogue towards a radical naturalism of speech on the Menandrean model; here, where an actual defence could have been tedious, Terence spots that a stronger (and more amusing) tactic will be to launch a counter-attack on Luscius' own attempts to create Plautine imagery and emotion for an audience whose taste has presumably moved on.

Terence: individual plays

Andria.[123] Young Pamphilus has secretly fathered a child by the foundling Glycerium, and now has not only to trace her parents following the death of her fosterer, Chrysis of Andros, but to find a way out of the marriage arranged for him by his father, to the very bride his best friend Charinus seeks for his own. After a giddy series of bluffs and counter-bluffs over the on-again, off-again wedding, Glycerium is discovered to be the bride's long-lost sister, so that the two families can be united in marriage after all but with a different sister as the bride (Figure 9).

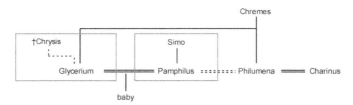

Figure 9

Terence's first production is an uncompromising showcase for the qualities that set him in opposition to the mainstream of Roman comedy: the intricate psychological plotting of motive and second-guessing; the obsession with symmetries and doublings (especially ironic and/or contrastive) in character, scene, and situation; the Menandrean return to the citizen characters and their emotional and ethical seriousness; the thematic opposition of *amor* and *pietas*, centred in the young lover and his conflicting sense of obligation.

Hecyra.[124] In a situation similar to that of Menander's *Epitrepontes*, Pamphilus has raped his bride-to-be with neither aware of the other's identity, and, during his absence abroad, she attempts to conceal the resulting pregnancy by moving back in with her mother; when

---

[123] McGarrity 1978; Goldberg 1981–2a; Richardson 1997; W. S. Anderson 2004.
[124] Sewart 1974; Gilula 1978, 1979–80, 1981; McGarrity 1980–81; Sandbach 1982; Konstan 1983: 130–41; Slater 1988a; Ireland 1990; Parker 1996; James 1998; Cabrillana 2000; Lada-Richards 2004; Penwill 2004.

Pamphilus returns to find she has borne another man's child, he tries to find pretexts of filial piety to explain his reluctance to take her back without exposing the fact of her rape. The couple's fathers wrongly blame, in turn, his mother for alienating her daughter-in-law; *her* mother for hostility to her son-in-law; and Pamphilus himself for continuing relations with his former mistress Bacchis, who turns out to hold the key to the recognition of rapist and victim and thus to the child's paternity (Figure 10).

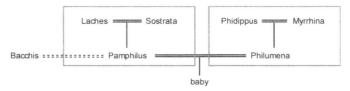

Figure 10

Terence's second play, but his last production, this complex psychological *stataria* was the play that took five years and three attempts simply to get to the end of a performance. Although it is his only play with a 'single' plot, in the sense that only one young couple is involved, the symmetries are if anything still more pronounced, as the ripples from Pamphilus' disintegrating marriage propagate to encompass relations between the two sets of in-laws in the two stage houses, and each mother-in-law in turn is mistakenly charged with attempting to sabotage the marriage out of stereotypical hostility to her child's spouse. Unlike in *Epitrepontes*, but in keeping with Terence's taste and practice, there is no omniscient prologue, at least in Terence's version; the audience is made to work hard to collate clues in the text with its general knowledge of genre situations to work out what is really going on. Even at Aemilius' funeral games, against a background of past and present success and the patronage of Aemilius' sons, the play seems to have been too much for its audience's patience.

Heautontimorumenos.[125] The self-tormentor of the title is Menedemus, who blames himself for his son Clinia's estrangement as a result of Menedemus' stern line on Clinia's relationship with the orphan Antiphila. His neighbour Chremes lectures him on tolerance, but is unaware that his own son Clitopho is embroiled in a far more extravagant affair with the courtesan Bacchis – allowing him to be

---

[125] Brothers 1980, 1988; Maltby 1984; Bond 1991; Konstan 1993b; Knorr 1995; J. C. B. Lowe 1998a; Dunsch 1999; Mauger-Plichon 2000; John Henderson 2004; Richardson 2006.

duped into installing Bacchis in his own house with Clitipho in the belief that she is Clinia's mistress, while his real mistress, Antiphila, poses as Bacchis' maid – but is ultimately recognized as Chremes' lost daughter, and allowed to marry Clinia (Figure 11).

Figure 11

Terence's remaining plays now fall into a consistent pattern: two young men collude in the pursuit of their two intertwined liaisons – one a pecuniary *meretrix* affair held back by parental or financial obstructions, the other a recognition or rape affair ending in citizen marriage. Here, however, the real dramatic centre is Chremes, whose famous motto *homo sum: humani nil a me alienum puto* ('I'm human, so any human business is my business') is a heavily ironic marker of Chremes' willingness to weigh in with judgments on others' affairs while blind to the lessons for his own. It is another play with a passion for paradox, multiple irony, and audacious inversions of reality, sustained by sometimes unintelligible lapses in exposition, motivation, and connection.

Eunuchus.[126] The courtesan Thais entertains the braggart soldier Thraso in preference to her lover Phaedria because she needs him to gift her the foundling slave Pamphila, who was sold to him by Thais' brother on their mother's death, and whom she is trying to reunite with her family. Phaedria's brother, Chaerea, infiltrates Thais' house in the guise of a eunuch and rapes Pamphila, but marries her when her living brother Chremes is tracked down, while Phaedria has to be content with sharing Thais with Thraso (Figure 12).

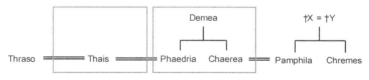

Figure 12

---

[126] Saylor 1975; Gilmartin 1975–6; J. C. B. Lowe 1983; Konstan 1986; Barsby 1993a, 1999; Frangoulidis 1993, 1994a, 1994b; L. P. Smith 1994; Dessen 1995; R. H. Martin 1995; Philippides 1995; Brothers 2000; M. Stein 2003.

This was the play that turned Terence's career around: Suetonius tells us that the play was awarded a record fee of 8,000 sesterces and a repeat performance (presumably at the same festival), and his output now shifts from three productions in six years to five productions in the space of eighteen months. The soldier-parasite double-act (specially imported from a play that had already worked for Plautus) and big visual set pieces suggest an attempt to accommodate the traditional tastes of Roman audiences while still retaining the Terentian focus on citizen relationships and ethics. The ending is a notorious problem: it is not clear whom Thraso has replaced in Menander's original or what kind of accommodation was reached at the end of Menander's play, but Phaedria's failure to win Thais for his exclusive own seems an odd reversion to the more cynical world of Plautus' *Truculentus*.

Phormio.[127] While their respective fathers Chremes and Demipho are away in Lemnos, cousins Phaedria and Antipho fall in love, Phaedria with the slave Pamphila and Antipho with the penniless orphan Phanium, whom he marries after engaging the professional freeloader Phormio to bring a bogus suit of *epidikasia*, the Athenian procedure under which an orphaned heiress is assigned in marriage to her nearest eligible male relative. When Demipho and Chremes return, they pay Phormio to dissolve the marriage; but he gives the cash to Phaedria to buy Pamphila, and, when it emerges that Phanium is Chremes' daughter by a bigamous marriage in Lemnos, Phormio enlists Chremes' Athenian wife, Nausistrata (whose dowry has financed Chremes' double life), to sanction his use of what is ultimately her money in the interests of her own children rather than her two-timing husband's (Figure 13).

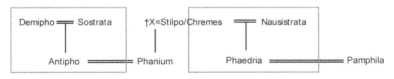

Figure 13

Like *Hecyra*, Terence's other adaptation from Apollodorus, *Phormio* engages its audience in a complex recognition puzzle without the

[127] R. H. Martin 1959; Arnott 1970; Büchner 1974: 484–97; Sewart 1974; Lefèvre et al. 1978; E. Segal and Moulton 1978; Konstan 1983: 115–29; Barsby 1993b; Frangoulidis 1996c, 1997: 77–132; J. A. Smith 2004.

assistance of an omniscient prologue. Phormio himself is a unique and impressive creation, Terence's only parasite hero in the mould of Curculio, and a fascinating recreation in citizen form of the mastery of improvisation and intrigue that characterizes the more usual slave incarnations of the comic hero, with access now to the full civic resources of law, dowries, betrothal, and marriage, while unencumbered by the rootedness in family and duty that ties down conventional citizen leads. Yet his unlikely alliance with Chremes' home wife, Nausistrata, against Chremes and his culpably complicit brother Demipho has the effect of actually reasserting and enforcing the familial responsibility that Chremes has spent the last fifteen years evading.

Adelphoe.[128] The brothers Micio and Demea conduct an intriguing social experiment on Demea's two sons: Demea raises Ctesipho in the country in austerity and strict discipline, while Aeschinus is given to the liberal bachelor Micio to raise his own way in the city. But Ctesipho, for all his father's efforts, falls for the slave prostitute Bacchis, while Aeschinus rapes and then promises to marry the fatherless Pamphila. To help Ctesipho keep his affair a secret from Demea, Aeschinus abducts Bacchis himself and pays off the pimp; and when Demea, always the last to the truth, finally catches up with what everyone else has been up to, he executes an extraordinary volte-face, bulldozes his brother into marriage with Pamphila's mother Sostrata, and showers alarming largesse on everyone in sight, before confiding in the final moments that his repentance has been less than total (we have certainly been fooled) and his aim to show by *reductio ad absurdum* that Micio's system alone is unworkable (Figure 14).

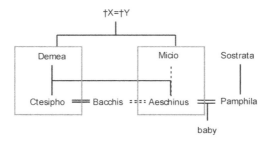

Figure 14

[128] Carruba 1968; Fantham 1968b, 1971; Johnson 1968; Grant 1971; Lloyd-Jones 1973; Goldberg 1975, 1980; R. H. Martin 1976; C. Lord 1977; Sandbach 1978; Greenberg 1979–80; Grant 1980; John Henderson 1988; Damen 1990; Gratwick 1992, 1999; J. C. B. Lowe 1998b; Leigh 2004: 158–91.

Some of this is not Menandrean (we know from Donatus that Micio did not raise objections to his own wedding as he does in Terence); how much, is the single most notorious crux in Terentian criticism.[129] Few would now endorse the old view of this play as showing the triumph of modern, Hellenizing, liberal attitudes to paternal authority and moral education over a more traditional and austere 'Catonian' stance, notwithstanding the parallels between Cato and Terence's Demea (and the fact that the name Micio seems to pun on Paullus). Nevertheless, Terence seems aware that Menander's play cannot be presented innocent of Hellenistic philosophical, ideological, and political baggage inconceivable to a fourth-century Greek. The antagonism of Epicurean and Stoic systems of practice, and the cultural gap between Greek and Roman consensus on paternal authority, both create an irresistible lobby for Demea against the dramatic grain of Menander's plot; and, as Terence goes out of his way to remind us in the prologue, the play was historically produced, and presumably selected for the purpose, by a pair of wealthy *adulescentes*, adopted into different families, in celebration of their blood father and the Roman aristocratic *familia*. Nobody in the audience could have failed to be struck by the invitation to draw connections, however bizarre or even tasteless the Aemiliani's choice of play may seem to us; but its celebration of Paullus is probably to be read in the dialectic between two sides of his complex public character, rather than in any simplistic identification with one or other figure.

After Terence

The most important writer of *palliatae* after Terence was the similarly Menandrophile **Turpilius** (d. 103), who ranks just below him in Volcacius' top ten and whose plays were still being performed in Cicero's day by his client, the great comic actor Roscius.[130] Plautus, too, was still in the repertoire at this late date; Cicero mentions the pimp Ballio from *Pseudolus* as another role in the Roscian canon. The age of Turpilius also saw the flowering of a new kind of literary comedy, the so-called *fabula togata* or plays in Roman dress, which took the conventions and situations of Greco-Roman New Comedy and adapted them to the composition of original Latin plays with

---

[129] Goldberg 1981–2b: 96–100 is a useful point of entry to the labyrinth.
[130] Cicero, *Pro Roscio comoedo* 7.20.

Italian characters and settings.[131] The master of this tradition was
L. Afranius, who claimed to draw on both Menander and Terence;
forty-four titles are attested, and the fragments amount to more
than four hundred lines. Two other poets of *togatae* are attested:
C. Quinctius Atta, who died in 77, and the more elusive **Titinius**,
who may have been the earliest, even the pioneer, in the form, and
whose titles include a majority referring to female characters, several
in or from provincial Italian settings. This repotting of New Comedy
in Italian soil had some interesting consequences: it was apparently
not done for Roman slaves to be cleverer than their masters,[132]
however willing the Roman audiences had been to laugh at such situations in a Greek setting; while Afranius, at least, allowed homosexual
as well as heterosexual love-plots.

By the time of Cicero's letters, new literary comedies for the stage
seem to have dried up, unless the **Quintipor Clodius** dismissed
by Varro as 'talentless' (*sine ulla musa*) was writing for performance.
Horace's friends **Fundanius** and **Aristius Fuscus** were still writing
palliatae in the Augustan era, but there is no sign that they were ever
intended for staging, let alone actually performed. Homegrown and
subliterary genres survived longer: the Atellana continued into the
empire; mime flourished in both Greek and Latin; and the shadowy
genres of mimetic dance, such as the mysterious *ludus talarius*, were
eventually to flower in the solo dance form known as pantomime,
which under the empire was to become the queen of the dramatic
genres.[133] But Greek and Latin comedies were now the property of
readers rather than spectators. It was the resilient and flexible mime
that provided actual continuity of ancient performance tradition into
the middle ages and beyond, while the job of literary comedy under
the empire was increasingly delegated to the non-theatrical genres of
prose and verse satire and the various experiments in humorous prose
that for us are visible primarily in the Roman novels and in the narrative and dialogue sketches of Lucian – themselves, of course, strongly
influenced by the Aristophanic revival of the early centuries AD.

[131] Beare 1964: 128–36; on the cultural implications, see Leigh 2004: 9–12.
[132] Donatus on Terence, *Eun.* 57.
[133] On pantomime, see now Lada-Richards 2007; Hall and Wyles 2008.

Bibliographic note

There are comprehensive bibliographies of Terence in Cupaiuolo 1984, 1992 and Lentano 1997, 1998. A new Budé edition is in preparation, but no immediate replacement is in prospect for the Oxford Text of Kauer and Lindsay 1926 (of which Reeve wrote a quarter-century ago, even before the major work of Grant 1986b, that 'a new edition, properly constituted and more critical than the OCT, is badly needed'[134]). Barsby's helpful Loeb edition (2001–2) replaces the badly dated earlier Loeb by Sargeaunt (1912). Radice's vintage Penguin translation (1965–7) now has a worthy competitor in Brown's version for World's Classics (2006), which is better annotated, though only Radice includes Suetonius' *Life*; note also Clayton's posthumously published verse translation (2006). There are outstanding Aris & Phillips editions of *Hecyra* (Ireland 1990), *HT, Eunuchus* (both by Brothers, 1988 and 2000), and *Adelphoe* (Gratwick 1999), with *Phormio* (Maltby) forthcoming, and the Cambridge green-and-yellow editions of *Adelphoe* (R. H. Martin 1976) and *Eunuchus* (Barsby 1999) are invaluable; the latter includes metrical markup, using Gratwick's system of underdots. For other plays, the student editions by R. H. Martin (*Phormio*, 1959) and Shipp (*Andria*, 1960) are still very useful. Barsby's *Companion* to the last three plays (1991) is one of the most helpful volumes of its kind on any classical author.

In comparison with Plautus, Terence remains a victim of quite serious critical neglect in English, where there is no counterpart to the classic study of Büchner 1974 or even to the excellent introduction by Kruschwitz 2004. But Goldberg 1986 is a useful general study, and Barsby 2002 a wonderfully crisp round-up of the state of the question on Terence's use of his Greek originals; Leigh's introduction to Clayton 2006 is also outstanding as a short overview. The most adventurous recent works have been collections of essays: particularly the special Terence issue of *Ramus* (2004, including articles by William Anderson, Boyle, John Henderson, Penwill, and Joseph Smith) and Kruschwitz et al. 2007. Terence's language has seen a series of substantial studies from Müller (1997), Bagordo (2001), and Karakasis (2005).

---

[134] Reeve 1983: 420.

BIBLIOGRAPHY

Adkins, A. H. W. 1970. 'Clouds, Mysteries, Socrates and Plato', *Antichthon* 4: 13–24.

Allison, Richard H. 1983. 'Amphibian Ambiguities: Aristophanes and his Frogs', *G&R* 30: 8–20.

Anderson, C. A. 1989. 'Themistocles and Cleon in Aristophanes' *Knights*', *AJP* 110: 10–16.

Anderson, Michael 1970. 'Knemon's *Hamartia*', *G&R* 17: 199–217.

Anderson, William S. 1972. 'The Ending of the *Samia* and Other Menandrian Comedies', in *Studi classici in onore di Quintino Cataudella*. 3 vols, Catania, Università di Catania: 155–79.

—— 1979. 'Plautus' *Trinummus*: The Absurdity of Officious Morality', *Traditio* 35: 333–45.

—— 1982. 'Euripides' *Auge* and Menander's *Epitrepontes*', *GRBS* 23: 165–77.

—— 1983. 'Chalinus *armiger* in Plautus' *Casina*', *ICS* 8: 11–21.

—— 1993. *Barbarian Play. Plautus' Roman Comedy.* Toronto, University of Toronto Press.

—— 2004. 'The Invention of Sosia for Terence's First Comedy, the *Andria*', *Ramus* 33: 10–19.

Andrews, N. E. 2004. 'Tragic Re-Presentation and the Semantics of Space in Plautus *Casina*', *Mnemosyne* 57: 445–64.

Arnott, W. G. 1964a. 'The Confrontation of Sostratos and Gorgias', *Phoenix* 18: 110–23.

—— 1964b. 'A Note on the Parallels between Menander's *Dyskolos* and Plautus' *Aulularia*', *Phoenix* 18: 232–7.

—— 1970. 'Phormio *parasitus*: A Study in Dramatic Methods of Characterization', *G&R* 17: 32–57.

—— 1972a. 'From Aristophanes to Menander', *G&R* 19: 65–90.

—— 1972b. 'Targets, Techniques, and Tradition in Plautus' *Stichus*', *BICS* 19: 54–79.

—— 1975. *Menander, Plautus, Terence. G&R* New Surveys 9. Cambridge, Cambridge University Press.

—— (ed. and tr.) 1979–2000. *Menander.* Loeb Classical Library. 3 vols, Cambridge, MA, Harvard University Press.

—— 1982. 'Calidorus' Surprise: A Scene of Plautus' *Pseudolus*, with an Appendix on Ballio's Birthday', *WS* 95: 131–48.

—— 1987. 'The Time-Scale of Menander's *Epitrepontes*,' *ZPE* 70: 19–31.

—— 1988. 'The Greek Original of Plautus' *Aulularia*', *WS* 101: 181–91.

—— 1989. 'A Study in Relationships: Alexis' *Lebes*, Menander's *Dyskolos*, Plautus' *Aulularia*', *QUCC* 62: 27–38.

—— (ed.) 1996. *Alexis. The Fragments*. Cambridge, Cambridge University Press.

—— 2004. 'Menander's *Epitrepontes* in the Light of the New Papyri', in D. L. Cairns and R. A. Knox (eds.), *Law, Rhetoric, and Comedy in Classical Athens. Essays in Honour of Douglas M. MacDowell*. Swansea, The Classical Press of Wales: 269–92.

Arrowsmith, William (tr.) 1961. *Aristophanes. The Birds*. Ann Arbor, MI, University of Michigan Press, 1961.

—— 1973. 'Aristophanes' *Birds*: The Fantasy Politics of Eros', *Arion* NS 1: 119–67.

Attardo, Salvatore 1994. *Linguistic Theories of Humor*. Berlin and New York, NY, Mouton de Gruyter.

Auhagen, Ulrike (ed.) 2001. *Studien zu Plautus' Epidicus*. Tübingen, Gunter Narr Verlag.

Austin, Colin and Olson, S. Douglas (eds.) 2004. *Aristophanes. Thesmophoriazusae*. Oxford, Oxford University Press, 2004.

Bagordo, Andreas 2001. *Beobachtungen zur Sprache des Terenz*. Hypomnemata 132. Göttingen, Vandenhoeck & Ruprecht.

Baier, Thomas (ed.) 1999. *Studien zu Plautus' Amphitruo*. Tübingen, Narr.

—— (ed.) 2004. *Studien zu Plautus' Poenulus*. Tübingen, Narr.

Bain, David M. 1979. '*Plautus vortit barbare*: Plautus, *Bacchides* 526–61 and Menander, *Dis Exapaton* 102–12', in David West and Tony Woodman (eds.), *Creative Imitation and Latin Literature*. Cambridge, Cambridge University Press: 17–34.

—— (ed. and tr.) 1983. *Menander. Samia*. Warminster, Aris & Phillips.

—— 1992. 'A Recent Suggestion about the Original of Plautus' *Aulularia*', *LCM* 17: 68–70.

Bakhtin, Mikhail M. 1984. *Rabelais and his World*. Bloomington, IN, Indiana University Press.

Bakola, Emmanuela 2006. *Cratinus and the Art of Comedy*. PhD dissertation, University College, London.

Balme, Maurice (tr.) 2001. *Menander. The Plays and Fragments*, with introduction and notes by Peter Brown. Oxford and New York, NY, Oxford University Press.

Banks, T. R. 1980. 'The Ephemeral, The Perennial, and the Structure of Aristophanes' *Wasps*', *CB* 56: 81–5.

Barkhuisen, J. H. 1981. 'The *Plutus* of Aristophanes', *AClass* 24: 17–22.

Barrett, David (tr.) 1964. *Aristophanes. The Frogs and Other Plays*. Harmondsworth, Penguin.

Barsby, John A. (ed.) 1986. *Plautus. Bacchides*. Warminster, Aris & Phillips.

—— 1991. *Terence. The Eunuch, Phormio, The Brothers. A Companion to the Penguin Translation*. Bristol, Bristol Classical Press.

—— 1993a. 'Problems of Adaptation in the *Eunuchus* of Terence', in Niall W. Slater and Bernhard Zimmermann (eds.), *Intertextualität in der griechisch-römischen Komödie*. Drama 2. Stuttgart, M&P: 160–79.

—— 1993b. 'The Stage Action of Terence, *Phormio* 979–89', *CQ* 43: 329–35.

—— 1995. 'Plautus' Pseudolus as Improvisatory Drama', in Benz et al. 1995: 55–70.

—— (ed.) 1999. *Terence. Eunuchus*. Cambridge, Cambridge University Press.

—— (ed. and tr.) 2001–2. *Terence*. Loeb Classical Library. 2 vols, Cambridge, MA, Harvard University Press.

—— 2002. 'Terence and his Greek Models', in C. Questa and R. Raffaelli (eds.), *Due seminari plautine*. Urbino, Edizione QuattroVenti: 251–77.

Beacham, Richard C. 1991. *The Roman Theatre and its Audience*. London, Routledge.

Beare, William 1964. *The Roman Stage. A Short History of Latin Drama in the Time of the Republic*. Third edition, London, Methuen.

Bennett, Larry J. and Tyrrell, Wm. Blake 1990. 'Making Sense of Aristophanes' *Knights*', *Arethusa* 23: 235–54.

Benz, Lore and Lefèvre, Eckard (eds.) 1998. *Maccus barbarus. Sechs Kapitel zur Originalität der Captivi des Plautus*. Tübingen, Narr.

——, Stärk, Ekkehard, and Vogt-Spira, Gregor (eds.) 1995. *Plautus und die Tradition des Stegreifspiels*. Tübingen, Narr.

Berg, Deena and Parker, Douglass (trs.) 1999. *Five Comedies. Plautus & Terence*. Indianapolis, IN, Hackett.

Bergson, Henri 1900. *Le Rire. Essai sur la signification du comique*. Paris. Translated as 'Laughter' in Sypher 1956: 61–190.

Beroutsos, Demetrios C. 2005. *A Commentary on the Aspis of Menander, Part One: Lines 1–298*. Hypomnemata 157. Göttingen, Vandenhoeck & Ruprecht.

Bertini, Ferrucio (ed.) 1968. *Plauti Asinaria*. Genoa, Università di Genova.

Bettini, Maurizio 1982. 'Verso un'antropologia dell'intreccio: le strutture semplici della trama nelle commedie di Plauto', *MD* 7: 39–101. Reprinted in Maurizio Bettini, *Verso un'antropologia dell'intreccio*, Urbino, QuattroVenti, 1991, 11–76.

Bieber, Margarete 1961. *The History of the Greek and Roman Theater*. Second edition, Princeton, NJ, Princeton University Press.

Bierl, Anton 2001. *Der Chor in der Alten Komödie. Ritual und Performativität*. Munich and Leipzig, Saur.

Biles, Zachary P. 2001. 'Aristophanes' Victory Dance: Old Poets in the Parabasis of *Knights*', *ZPE* 136: 195–200.

—— 2002. 'Intertextual Biography in the Rivalry of Cratinus and Aristophanes', *AJP* 123: 169–204.

Blanchard, Alain 2002. 'Moschion *ho kosmios* et l'interpretation de la *Samienne* de Ménandre', *REG* 115: 58–74.

—— 2007. *La Comédie de Ménandre. Politique, éthique, esthétique*. Paris, PUPS.

Blume, Horst-Dieter 1998. *Menander.* Erträge Der Forschung 293. Darmstadt, Wissenschaftliche Buchgesellschaft.

Bond, R. P. 1991. 'Approaches to a Production of Terence's *Heautontimorou-menos*', *Prudentia* 23: 4–18.

—— 1999. 'Plautus' *Amphitryo* as Tragi-comedy', *G&R* 46: 203–19.

Bonnamour, Jacqueline and Delavault, Huguette (eds.) 1979. *Aristophane, les femmes et la cité.* Fontenay aux Roses, École Normale Supérieure.

Borgogno, Alberto 2002. 'Per un'analisi dell'*Aspis* di Menandro', *Maia* 54: 243–58.

Borthwick, E. L. 1968. 'The Dances of Philocleon and the Sons of Carcinus in Aristophanes' *Wasps*', *CQ* 18: 47–51.

—— 1992. 'Observations on the Opening Scene of Aristophanes' *Wasps*', *CQ* 42: 274–8.

—— 1994. 'New Interpretations of Aristophanes *Frogs* 1249–1328', *Phoenix* 48: 21–41.

Bowie, A. M. 1982. 'The Parabasis in Aristophanes, Prolegomena: *Achar-nians*', *CQ* 32: 27–40

—— 1987. 'Ritual Stereotype and Comic Reversal: Aristophanes' *Wasps*', *BICS* 34: 112–25.

—— 1993. *Aristophanes. Myth, Ritual and Comedy.* Cambridge, Cambridge University Press.

Bowie, E. L. 1988. 'Who is Dicaeopolis?', *JHS* 108: 183–5.

Boyle, A. J. 2004. 'Introduction [to special issue on Terence]: Terence's Mirror Stage', *Ramus* 33: 1–10.

—— 2005. *Roman Tragedy.* London, Routledge.

Bremer, J. M. and Handley, E. W. (eds.) 1993. *Aristophane.* Entretiens Hardt 38.

Brock, R. W. 1986. 'The Double Plot in Aristophanes' *Knights*', *GRBS* 27: 15–27.

Brockmann, Christian 2003. *Aristophanes und die Freiheit der Komödie. Untersuchungen zu den frühen Stücken unter besonderer Berücksichtigung der Acharner.* Munich and Leipzig, Saur.

Brothers, A. J. 1980. 'The Construction of Terence's *Heautontimorumenos*', *CQ* 74: 94–118.

—— (ed. and tr.) 1988. *Terence. The Self-Tormentor.* Warminster, Aris & Phillips.

—— (ed. and tr.) 2000. *Terence. The Eunuch.* Warminster, Aris & Phillips.

Brown, P. G. McC. 1983. 'Menander's Dramatic Technique and the Law of Athens', *CQ* 33: 412–20.

—— 1990. 'Plots and Prostitutes in Greek New Comedy', *PLLS* 6: 241–66.

—— 1992. 'The Construction of Menander's *Dyskolos* Acts I–IV', *ZPE* 94: 8–20.

—— 1993. 'Love and Marriage in Greek New Comedy', *CQ* 43: 189–205.

—— (tr.) 2006. *Terence. The Comedies.* Oxford, Oxford University Press.

Büchner, Karl 1974. *Das Theater des Terenz*. Heidelberg, Winter.

Buck, Charles Henry, Jr 1940. *A Chronology of the Plays of Plautus*. Baltimore, MD, The Johns Hopkins University Press.

Butrica, James L. P. 2001. 'The Lost *Thesmophoriazusae* of Aristophanes', *Phoenix* 55: 44–76.

—— 2004. 'The Date of Aristophanes' Lost *Thesmophoriazusae*: A Response to Austin and Olson', *PLLS* 3.7: 1–5.

Cabrillana, C. 2000. 'Virtualités de l'espace extra-scénique dans l'*Hécyre* de Térence', *Pallas* 54: 269–87.

Calderan, Roberto (ed.) 2004. *Tito Maccio Plauto. Vidularia*. Ludus Philologiae 13. Urbino, QuattroVenti.

Canfora, Luciano 1987. *Biblioteca scomparsa*. Palermo, Sellerio. Translated by Martin Ryle as *The Vanished Library*, London, Hutchinson, 1989.

Cannata, Fabio 1995. 'La resa scenica del Paflagone nei *Cavalieri* di Aristofane', *MD* 35: 117–33.

Carey, Christopher 1993. 'The Purpose of Aristophanes' *Acharnians*', *RM* 136: 245–63.

—— 1994. 'Comic Ridicule and Democracy', in Robin Osborne and Simon Hornblower (eds.), *Ritual, Finance, Politics. Athenian Democratic Accounts Presented to David Lewis*. Oxford, Clarendon Press: 69–83.

Carruba, R. W. 1968. 'The Rationale of Demea in Terence's *Adelphoe*', *Dioniso* 42: 16–24.

Cartledge, Paul 1990. *Aristophanes and his Theatre of the Absurd*. Bristol, Bristol Classical Press.

Cassio, Albio Cesare (ed.) 1977. *Aristofane. Banchettanti*. Pisa, Giardini.

—— 1985. *Commedia e participazione. La Pace di Aristofane*. Naples, Liguori.

—— 2002. 'The Language of Doric Comedy', in Willi 2002: 51–83.

Chapman, G. A. H. 1978. 'Aristophanes and History', *AClass* 21: 59–70.

Chiarini, Gioachino 1979. *La recita. Plauto, la farsa, la festa*. Bologna, Patròn.

Christenson, David M. (ed.) 2000. *Plautus. Amphitruo*. Cambridge, Cambridge University Press.

—— 2001. 'Grotesque Realism in Plautus' *Amphitruo*', *CJ* 96: 243–60.

Clark, J. R. 1976. 'Structure and Symmetry in the *Bacchides* of Plautus', *TAPA* 106: 85–96.

Clayton, Frederick W. (tr.) 2006. *The Comedies of Terence*, introduced by Matthew Leigh. Exeter, University of Exeter Press.

Cody, Jane M. 1976. 'The Senex Amator in Plautus' *Casina*', *Hermes* 104: 453–73.

Compton-Engle, Gwendolyn 1999. 'From Country to City: The Persona of Dicaeopolis in Aristophanes' *Acharnians*', *CJ* 94: 359–73.

—— 2005. 'Stolen Cloaks in Aristophanes' *Ecclesiazusae*', *TAPA* 135: 163–76.

Connors, Catherine 1997. 'Scents and Sensibility in Plautus' *Casina*', *CQ* 47: 305–9.

Cornford, Francis M. 1914. *The Origin of Attic Comedy*. London, Arnold. Edited with foreword and additional notes by Theodor H. Gaster, Garden City, NY, Anchor, 1961. With new introduction by Jeffrey Henderson, Ann Arbor, MI, University of Michigan Press, 1993.

Courtney, Edward (ed.) 1993, with addenda 2003. *The Fragmentary Latin Poets*. Oxford, Clarendon Press.

Cox, Cheryl Anne 2002a. 'Crossing Boundaries through Marriage in Menander's *Dyskolos*', *CQ* 52: 391–4.

—— 2002b. 'Is Sostratus' Family Urban in Menander's *Dyskolos*?', *CJ* 97: 351–8

Craik, Elizabeth M. 1987. 'One for the Pot: Aristophanes' *Birds* and the Anthesteria', *Eranos* 85: 25–34.

Crichton, Angus 1991–3. '"The Old are in a Second Childhood": Age Reversal and Jury Service in Aristophanes' *Wasps*', *BICS* 38: 59–79.

Csapo, Eric 2000. 'From Aristophanes to Menander? Genre Transformation in Greek Comedy', in Mary Depew and Dirk Obbink (eds.), *Matrices of Genre. Authors, Canons, and Society*. Cambridge, MA, Harvard University Press: 115–33.

—— 2007. 'The Men who Built the Theatres: *Theatropolai, Theatronai*, and *Arkhitektones*', with an archaeological appendix by Hans-Rupprecht Goette, in Peter Wilson (ed.), *The Greek Theatre and Festivals. Documentary Studies*. Oxford Studies in Ancient Documents. Oxford, Oxford University Press: 97–121.

—— and Slater, William J. 1995. *The Context of Ancient Drama*. Ann Arbor, MI, University of Michigan Press.

Cupaiuolo, Giovanni 1984. *Bibliografia Terenziana (1480–1983)*. Naples, Società editrice napoletana.

—— 1992. 'Supplementum Terentianum', *BStudLat* 22: 32–57.

Cusset, Christophe 2000. 'La Fille d'à côté: symbolique de l'espace et sens du voisinage dans la *Samienne* de Ménandre', *Pallas* 54: 207–28.

—— 2003. *Ménandre ou la comédie tragique*. Paris, CNRS.

Damen, Mark 1988–9. 'Actors and Act-Divisions in the Greek Original of Plautus' *Menaechmi*', *CW* 82: 409–20.

—— 1990. 'Structure and Symmetry in Terence's *Adelphoe*', *ICS* 15: 85–106.

—— 1992. 'Translating Scenes: Plautus' Adaptation of Menander's *Dis Exapaton*', *Phoenix* 46: 205–31.

——1995. '"By the gods, boys, ... Stop bothering me! Can't you tell Menander from Plautus?" or How *Dis Exapaton* Does Not Help Us Understand *Bacchides*', *Antichthon* 29: 15–29.

Danese, Roberto M. (ed.) 2004. *Titus Maccius Plautus. Asinaria*. Editio Plautina Sarsinatis 2. Sarsina and Urbini, QuattroVenti.

David, Ephraim 1984. *Aristophanes and Athenian Society of the Early Fourth Century B.C. Mnemosyne* Supplementum 81. Leiden, Brill.

Davies, Malcolm 1990. '"Popular Justice" and the End of Aristophanes' *Clouds*', *Hermes* 118: 237–42.

De Lorenzi, Attilio 1952. *Cronologia ed evoluzione Plautina*. Naples, Ist. della stampa.

de Ste Croix, G. E. M. 1972. 'The Political Outlook of Aristophanes', Appendix 29 in *Origins of the Peloponnesian War*. London, Duckworth: 355–76.

Dearden, C. W. 1976. *The Stage of Aristophanes*. London, Athlone Press.

—— 1999. 'Plays for Export', *Phoenix* 53: 222–48.

Dedoussi, Christina 1988a. 'The Borrowing Play in *Dyskolos* 891–930', *BICS* 35: 79–83.

—— 1988b. 'The Future of Plangon's Child in Menander's *Samia*', *LCM* 13: 39–42.

del Corno, Dario (tr.) and del Corno et al. (eds.) 1985– . *Opere di Aristofane*. Fondazione Lorenzo Valla. Milan, Mondadori.

Dér, Katalin 1987. '*Vidularia*: Outlines of a Reconstruction', *CQ* 37: 432–43.

Dessen, Cynthia S. 1977. 'Plautus' Satiric Comedy: The *Truculentus*', *Philological Quarterly* 56: 145–68.

—— 1995. 'The Figure of the Eunuch in Terence's *Eunuchus*', *Helios* 22: 123–39.

Dettenhofer, Maria H. 1999. 'Praxagoras Programm: Eine politische Deutung von Aristophanes' *Ekklesiazusai* als Beitrag zur inneren Geschichte Athens im 4. Jahrhundert v. Chr', *Klio* 81: 95–111.

Deufert, Marcus 2002. *Textgeschichte und Rezeption der plautinischen Komödien im Altertum*. Berlin, de Gruyter.

Dickey, Eleanor 2007. *Ancient Greek Scholarship. A Guide to Finding, Reading, and Understanding Scholia, Commentaries, Lexica, and Grammatical Treatises, from Their Beginnings to the Byzantine Period*. Oxford, Oxford University Press.

Dillon, Matthew 1987a. 'The *Lysistrata* as a Post-Deceleian Peace Play', *TAPA* 117: 97–104.

—— 1987b. 'Topicality in Aristophanes' *Ploutos*', *Classical Antiquity* 6: 155–83.

Dobrov, Gregory W. 1990. 'Aristophanes' *Birds* and the Metaphor of Deferral', *Arethusa* 23: 209–33.

—— 1993. 'The Tragic and the Comic Tereus,' *AJP* 114: 189–234.

—— (ed.) 1997. *The City as Comedy. Society and Representation in Athenian Drama*. Chapel Hill, NC, and London, University of North Carolina Press.

—— 2001. *Figures of Play. Greek Drama and Metafictional Poetics*. Oxford, Oxford University Press.

Dover, K. J. (ed.) 1968. *Aristophanes. Clouds*. Oxford, Clarendon Press.

—— 1972. *Aristophanic Comedy*. Berkeley and Los Angeles, University of California Press.

—— 1993 (ed.). *Aristophanes. Frogs*. Oxford, Clarendon Press.

Dow, Sterling 1969. 'Some Athenians in Aristophanes', *AJA* 73: 234–5.

Duckworth, George E. (ed.) 1940. *Plautus. Epidicus*. Princeton, NJ, Princeton University Press.

—— 1994. *The Nature of Roman Comedy*. Second edition, with foreword and bibliographical appendix by Richard Hunter, Bristol, Bristol Classical Press. (First published 1952, Princeton, NJ, Princeton University Press.)

Dunbar, Nan (ed.) 1995. *Aristophanes. Birds*. Oxford, Clarendon Press.

—— 1996. '*Sophia* in Aristophanes' *Birds*', *SCI* 15: 61–71.

Dunsch, Boris 1999. 'Some Notes on the Understanding of Terence, *Heauton timorumenos* 6: *comoedia duplex, argumentum simplex*, and Hellenistic Scholarship', *C&M* 50: 97–131.

Dupont, Florence 1976. 'Significance comique du double dans *Amphitryon* de Plaute', *REL* 54: 129–41. Abridged version translated by Leofranc Holford-Strevens as 'The Theatrical Signifiance of Duplication in Plautus' *Amphitruo*' in Erich Segal 2001: 176–88.

Easterling, P. E. and Hall, Edith M. (eds.) 2002. *Greek and Roman Actors. Aspects of an Ancient Profession*. Cambridge, Cambridge University Press.

Edmonds, J. M. (ed. and tr.) 1957–61. *Fragments of Attic Comedy*. 4 vols, Leiden, Brill.

Edmonds, Radcliffe III 2004. *Myths of the Underworld Journey. Plato, Aristophanes, and the 'Orphic' Gold Tablets*. Cambridge, Cambridge University Press.

Edmunds, Lowell 1980. 'Aristophanes' *Acharnians*', *YCS* 26: 1–41.

—— 1987a. 'The Aristophanic Cleon's 'Disturbance' of Athens', *AJP* 108: 233–63.

—— 1987b. *Cleon, Knights, and Aristophanes' Politics*. Lanham, MD, University Press of America.

Ehrenberg, Victor 1951. *The People of Aristophanes. A Sociology of Old Attic Comedy*. Oxford, Blackwell.

Enk, P. J. 1964. 'Plautus' *Truculentus*', in Charles Henderson (ed.), *Classical, Mediaeval, and Renaissance Studies in Honor of Berthold Louis Ullmann*. 2 vols, Roma, Edizioni di storia e letteratura: i.49–65.

Epstein, P. D. 1981. 'The Marriage of Peisthetairos to Basileia in the *Birds* of Aristophanes', *Dionysius* 5: 6–28.

—— 1985. 'Dionysus' Journey of Self-Discovery in the *Frogs* of Aristophanes', *Dionysius* 9: 19–36.

Erbse, Hartmut 2002. 'Zur Interpretation der *Wolken* des Aristophanes', *Hermes* 130: 381–8.

Faller, Stefan (ed.) 2001. *Studien zu Plautus' Persa*. Tübingen, Narr.

Fantham, Elaine 1965. 'The *Curculio* of Plautus: An Illustration of Plautine Methods in Adaptation', *CQ* 59: 84–100.

—— 1968a. 'Act IV of the *Menaechmi*: Plautus and his Greek Original', *CP* 63: 175–83.

—— 1968b. 'Terence, Diphilus, and Menander: A Reexamination of Terence, *Adelphoe* Act II', *Philologus* 112: 196–216.

—— 1971. '*Hautontimoroumenos* and *Adelphoe*: A Study of Fatherhood in Terence and Menander', *Latomus* 30: 970–88.

—— 1973. 'Towards a Dramatic Reconstruction of the Fourth Act of Plautus' *Amphitruo*', *Philologus* 117: 197–214.

—— 1977. 'Philemon's *Thesaurus* as a Dramatisation of Peripatetic Ethics', *Hermes* 105: 402–21.

Faraone, Christopher A. 1997. 'Salvation and Female Heroics in the Parodos of Aristophanes' *Lysistrata*', *JHS* 117: 38–59.

—— 2006. 'Priestess and Courtesan: The Ambivalence of Female Leadership in Aristophanes' *Lysistrata*', in Christopher A. Faraone and Laura K. McClure (eds.), *Prostitutes and Courtesans in the Ancient World*. Madison, WI, University of Wisconsin Press: 207–23.

Fisher, N. R. E. 1993. 'Multiple Personalities and Dionysia Festivals: Dicaeopolis in Aristophanes' *Acharnians*', *G&R* 40: 31–47.

Fisher, Raymond K. 1984. *Aristophanes' Clouds. Purpose and Technique*. Amsterdam, Hakkert.

—— 1988. 'The Relevance of Aristophanes: A New Look at *Clouds*', *G&R* 35: 23–8.

Fitzgerald, William 2000. *Slavery and the Roman Literary Imagination*. Cambridge, Cambridge University Press.

Flashar, Hellmut 1967. 'Zur Eigenart der aristophanischen Spätwerks', *Poetica* 1: 154–75. Translated by Walter Moskalew as 'The Originality of Aristophanes' Last Plays', in Erich Segal 1996: 314–28.

Fletcher, Judith 1999. 'Sacrificial Bodies and the Body of the Text in Aristophanes' *Lysistrata*', *Ramus* 28: 108–125.

Foley, Hélène P. 1982. 'The "Female Intruder" Reconsidered: Women in Aristophanes' *Lysistrata* and *Ecclesiazusae*', *CP* 77: 1–21.

—— 1988. 'Tragedy and Politics in Aristophanes' *Acharnians*', *JHS* 108: 33–47.

Forehand, W. E. 1971. 'Irony in Plautus' *Amphitruo*', *AJP* 92: 633–51.

—— 1973a. 'Plautus' *Casina*: An Explication', *Arethusa* 6: 233–56.

—— 1973b. 'The Use of Imagery in Plautus' *Miles Gloriosus*', *RSC* 21: 5–16.

Forrest, W. G. 1963. 'Aristophanes' *Acharnians*', *Phoenix* 17: 1–12.

Fowler, Robert L. 1996. 'How the *Lysistrata* works', *EMC/CV* 15: 245–9.

Fraenkel, Eduard 1922. *Plautinisches im Plautus*. Berlin, Weidmann. Translated by Franco Munari with addenda as *Elementi Plautini in Plauto*, Florence, La Nuova Italia, 1960; and by Tomas Drevikovsky and Frances Muecke as *Plautine Elements in Plautus*, Oxford, Oxford University Press, 2007.

Frangoulidis, Stavros A. 1993. 'Modes of Metatheatre: Theatricalisation and Detheatricalisation in Terence, *Eunuchus*', *LCM* 18: 146–51.

—— 1994a. 'Performance and Improvisation in Terence's *Eunuchus*', *QUCC* 48: 121–30.

—— 1994b. 'The Soldier as Storyteller in Terence's *Eunuchus*', *Mnemosyne* 47: 586–95.

—— 1996a. 'Counter-Theatricalization in Plautus' *Captivi* III.4', *Mnemosyne* 49: 144–58.

—— 1996b. 'Food and Poetics In Plautus' *Captivi*', *AClass* 65: 225–30.

—— 1996c. '(Meta)theatre as Therapy in Terence's *Phormio*', *C&M* 47: 169–206.

—— 1996d. 'A Prologue-within-a-Prologue: Plautus, *Miles Gloriosus* 145–153', *Latomus* 55: 568–70.

—— 1997. *Handlung und Nebenhandlung. Theater, Metatheater und Gattungsbewußtsein in der romischen Komödie*. Drama Beiheft 6. Stuttgart, M & P. (The text of this book is in English.)

—— 1998. 'The Entrapment of Pyrgopolynices in Plautus' *Miles Gloriosus*', *PP* 53: 40–3.

Franko, George Fredric 1995. 'Fides, Aetolia, and Plautus' *Captivi*', *TAPA* 125: 155–76.

—— 1996. 'The Characterization of Hanno in Plautus' *Poenulus*', *AJP* 117: 425–50.

—— 1999. 'Imagery and Names in Plautus' *Casina*', *CJ* 95: 1–17.

Freud, Sigmund 1905. *Der Witz und seine Beziehung zum Unbewußten*. Leipzig, Deuticke. Translated by James Strachey as *Jokes and Their Relation to the Unconscious*. London, Routledge & Kegan Paul, 1960.

Frost, K. B. 1988. *Exits and Entrances in Menander*. Oxford, Clarendon Press.

Frye, Northrop 1957. *Anatomy of Criticism. Four Essays*. Princeton, NJ, Princeton University Press.

Gaertner, Jan Felix 1999. 'Der Wolken-Chor des Aristophanes', *RM* 142: 272–9.

Galinsky, G. K. 1966. 'Scipionic Themes in Plautus' *Amphitruo*', *TAPA* 97: 203–35.

Gamel, Mary-Kay (ed.) 2001. *Performing/Transforming Aristophanes' Thesmophoriazousai*, = *AJP* 123.2.

Garton, Charles 1972. *Personal Aspects of the Roman Theater*. Toronto, Hakkert.

Gelbart, Larry 1998. *Laughing Matters. On Writing M*A*S*H, Tootsie, Oh God!, and a Few Other Funny Things*. New York, NY, Random House.

Gelzer, Thomas 1960. *Der epirrhematische Agon bei Aristophanes*. Munich, C. H. Beck.

—— 1993. 'Feste Strukturen in der Komödie des Aristophanes', in Bremer and Handley 1993: 51–96.

Gentili, Bruno 1979. *Theatrical Performances in the Ancient World. Hellenistic and Early Roman Theatre*. Amsterdam, Gieben.

Giacomoni, Agnese 1998. 'Dike e adikia nel monologo di Trasonide (Menandro, *Misum*. P. Oxy. 3967)', *QUCC* 58: 91–109.

Gilmartin, Kristine 1975–6. 'The Thraso–Gnatho Subplot in Terence's *Eunuchus*', *CW* 69: 263–7.

Gilula, Dwora 1978. 'Where Did the Audience Go?', *SCI* 4: 45–9.

—— 1979–80. 'Terence's *Hecyra*: A Delicate Balance of Suspense and Dramatic Irony', *SCI* 5: 135–57.

—— 1981. 'Who's Afraid of Rope-Walkers and Gladiators? (Terence, *Hec.* 1–57)', *Athenaeum* 59: 29–37.

Gold, Barbara 1998. '"Vested Interests" in Plautus' *Casina*: Cross-Dressing in Roman Comedy', *Helios* 25: 17–29.

Goldberg, Sander M. 1975. 'The Ending of Terence's *Adelphoe* and the Menandrian Original', *AJP* 96: 42–60.

—— 1978. 'Plautus' *Epidicus* and the Case of the Missing Original', *TAPA* 108: 81–91.

—— 1980. *The Making of Menander's Comedy*. London, Athlone.

—— 1981–2a. 'The Dramatic Balance of Terence's *Andria*', *C&M* 33: 135–43.

—— 1981–2b. 'Scholarship on Terence and the Fragments of Roman Comedy: 1959–80', *CW,* 75: 77–115.

—— 1986. *Understanding Terence*. Princeton, NJ, Princeton University Press.

—— 1990. 'Act to Action in Plautus' *Bacchides*', *CP* 85: 191–201.

—— 1995. 'Improvisation, Plot, and Plautus' *Curculio*', in Benz, Stärk, and Vogt-Spira 1995: 33–41.

—— 1998. 'Plautus on the Palatine', *JRS* 88: 1–20.

—— 2004. 'Plautus and his Alternatives: Textual Doublets in *Cistellaria*', in Hartkamp and Hurka 2004: 385–98.

Goldhill, Simon D. 1991. 'Comic Inversion and Inverted Commas: Aristophanes and Parody', in *The Poet's Voice*. Cambridge, Cambridge University Press: 167–222.

Gomme, A. W. 1938. 'Aristophanes and Politics', *CR* 52: 97–109. Reprinted in *More Essays in Greek History and Literature*, Oxford, Blackwell, 1962, 70–91.

—— and Sandbach, F. H. 1973. *Menander. A Commentary*. Oxford, Clarendon Press.

Gosling, Ann 1983. 'A Rather Unusual Old Man: Hegio in Plautus' *Captivi*', *AClass* 26: 53–9.

Grant, John N. 1971. 'Notes on Donatus' Commentary on *Adelphoe*', *GRBS* 12: 197–209.

—— 1980. 'The Beginning of Menander, *Adelphoe* B', *CQ* 74: 341–55.

—— 1986a. 'The Father–Son Relationship and the Ending of Menander's *Samia*', *Phoenix* 40: 172–84.

—— 1986b. *Studies in the Textual Tradition of Terence*. Toronto, University of Toronto Press.

Gratwick, Adrian S. 1971. 'Hanno's Punic Speech in the *Poenulus* of Plautus', *Hermes* 99: 25–45.

—— 1973. 'TITVS MACCIVS PLAVTVS', *CQ* 23: 78–84.

—— 1982. 'Drama', in E. J. Kenney and W. V. Clausen (eds.), *The Cambridge History of Classical Literature. Volume 2: Latin Literature. Part 1: The Early Republic*. Cambridge, Cambridge University Press: 77–137.

—— 1992. 'Micion et Démea dans les *Adelphes* de Térence', *Pallas* 38: 371–8.

—— 1993 (ed.). *Plautus. Menaechmi*. Cambridge, Cambridge University Press.

—— 1999 (ed.). *Terence. The Brothers*. Second edition, Warminster, Aris and Phillips.

—— 2000. 'Brauchen wir einen neuen Plautus?', in Ekkehard Stärk and Gregor Vogt-Spira (eds.), *Dramatische Wäldchen. Festschrift für Eckard Lefèvre zum 65. Geburtstag*. Hildesheim, Olms: 321–44.

Green, Peter 1979. 'Strepsiades, Socrates and the Abuses of Intellectualism', *GRBS* 20: 15–25.

—— 1990. *Alexander to Actium. The Hellenistic Age*. London, Thames & Hudson.

Greenberg, N. A. 1979–80. 'Success and Failure in the *Adelphoe*', *CW* 73: 221–36.

Griffith, John G. 1988. 'Some Misgivings Concerning the Present State of Criticism of Plautus' *Pseudolus*', in *Festinat Senex*. Oxford, Oxbow: 50–63.

Groton, Anne H. 1987. 'Anger in Menander's *Samia*', *AJP* 108: 437–43.

—— 1990–1. 'Wreaths and Rags in Aristophanes' *Plutus*', *CJ* 86: 16–22.

Gruen, Erich S. 1990. 'Plautus and the Public Stage', in *Studies in Greek Culture and Roman Policy*. Leiden, Brill: 124–57.

—— 1993. 'The Theater and Aristocratic Culture', in *Culture and National Identity in Republican Rome*. London, Duckworth: 183–222.

Gurewitch, Morton 1975. *Comedy. The Irrational Vision*. Ithaca, NY, Cornell University Press.

Habash, Martha W. 1995. 'Two Complementary Festivals in Aristophanes' *Acharnians*', *AJP* 116: 559–77.

—— 1997. 'The Odd Thesmophoria of Aristophanes' *Thesmophoriazusae*', *GRBS* 38: 19–40.

—— 2002. 'Dionysos' Roles in Aristophanes' *Frogs*', *Mnemosyne* 55: 1–17.

Haberman, D. 1981. '*Menaechmi*: A Serious Comedy', *Ramus* 10: 129–39.

Haegemans, K. 2001. 'Character Drawing in Menander's *Dyskolos*: Misanthropy And Philanthropy', *Mnemosyne* 54: 675–96.

Hall, Edith M. 1989. 'The Archer Scene in Aristophanes' *Thesmophoriazusae*', *Philologus* 133: 38–54. Revised in Hall 2006: 225–54.

—— 2006. *The Theatrical Cast of Athens*. Oxford, Oxford University Press.

—— and Wrigley, Amanda (eds.) 2007. *Aristophanes in Performance 421 BC–AD 2007. Peace, Birds and Frogs*. London, Legenda.

—— and Wyles, Rosie (eds.) 2008. *New Directions in Ancient Pantomime*. Oxford, Oxford University Press.

Hall, F. W. and Geldart, W. M. (eds.) 1900–1. *Aristophanis Comoediae*. 2 vols, Oxford, Clarendon Press.

Hallett, Judith P. 1993. 'Plautine Ingredients in the Performance of the *Pseudolus*', *CW* 87: 21–26.

Halliwell, Stephen 1980. 'Aristophanes' Apprenticeship', *CQ* 30: 33–45.

—— 1991. 'Comic Satire and Freedom of Speech in Classical Athens', *JHS* 111: 48–70.

—— (tr.) 1998. *Aristophanes. Birds and Other Plays*. Oxford, Oxford University Press.

Halporn, James W. 1993. 'Roman Comedy and Greek Models', in Scodel 1993: 191–213.

Handley, E. W. (ed.) 1965. *The Dyskolos of Menander*. London, Methuen.

—— 1968. *Menander and Plautus. A Study in Comparison*. London, H. K. Lewis.

—— 1985. 'Comedy', in P. E. Easterling and B. W. M. Knox (eds.), *The Cambridge History of Classical Literature. Volume 1: Greek Literature. Part 2: Greek Drama*. Cambridge, Cambridge University Press: 355–425.

—— and Hurst, André (eds.) 1990. *Relire Ménandre*. Geneva, Droz.

Hansen, Hardy 1976. 'Aristophanes' *Thesmophoriazusae*: Theme, Structure, Production', *Philologus* 120: 165–85.

Hardy, Clara Shaw 2005. 'The Parasite's Daughter: Metatheatrical Costuming in Plautus' *Persa*', *CW* 99: 25–33.

Harriott, Rosemary M. 1982. 'The Function of the Euripides Scene in Aristophanes' *Acharnians*', *G&R* 29: 35–41.

—— 1985. '*Lysistrata*: Action and Theme', in James Redmond (ed.), *Themes in Drama 7. Drama, Sex and Politics*. Cambridge, Cambridge University Press: 11–22.

—— 1986. *Aristophanes. Poet and Dramatist*. London, Croom Helm.

Hartkamp, Rolf and Hurka. Florian (eds.) 2004. *Studien zu Plautus' Cistellaria*. Tübingen, Narr.

Harvey, David 2000. 'Phrynichos and his Muses', in Harvey and Wilkins 2000: 91–134.

—— and Wilkins, John (eds.) 2000. *The Rivals of Aristophanes. Studies in Athenian Old Comedy*. London, Duckworth & The Classical Press of Wales, 2000.

Harvey, F. D. 1994. 'Lacomica: Aristophanes and the Spartans', in Anton Powell and Stephen J. Hodkinson (eds.), *The Shadow of Sparta*. London and New York, NY, Routledge and The Classical Press of Wales: 35–58.

Havelock, Eric A. 1980. 'The Oral Composition of Greek Drama', *QUCC* 35: 61–113. Reprinted in *The Literate Revolution in Greece and its Cultural Consequences*, Princeton, NJ, Princeton University Press, 1982, 261–313.

Heath, Malcolm 1987. *Political Comedy in Aristophanes*. Hypomnemata 87. Göttingen, Vandenhoeck and Ruprecht.

—— 1990. 'Aristophanes and his Rivals', *G&R* 37: 143–58.

—— 1997. 'Aristophanes and the Discourse of Politics', in Dobrov 1997: 230–49.

Heiden, Bruce 1991. 'Tragedy and Comedy in the *Frogs* of Aristophanes', *Ramus* 20: 95–111.

Henderson, Jeffrey 1980a. *Aristophanes. Essays in Interpretation. YCS* 26.

—— 1980b. '*Lysistrate*: the Play and its Themes', in Henderson 1980a: 153–218.

—— 1987. *Aristophanes. Lysistrata*. Oxford, Clarendon Press.

—— 1989. 'The Demos and the Comic Competition', in John J. Winkler and Froma I. Zeitlin (eds.), *Nothing to Do with Dionysus?* Princeton, NJ, Princeton University Press: 271–313.

—— 1993a. 'Problems in Greek Literary History: The Case of Aristophanes' *Clouds*', in Ralph M. Rosen and Joseph Farrell (eds.), *Nomodeiktes. Studies Presented to Martin Ostwald*. Ann Arbor, MI, University of Michigan Press: 591–601.

—— 1993b: see Cornford 1914.

—— (ed. and tr.) 1998–2002. *Aristophanes*. Loeb Classical Library. 4 vols, Cambridge, MA, Harvard University Press.

—— 2007. 'Drama and Democracy', in Loren J. Samons II (ed.), *The Cambridge Companion to the Age of Pericles*. Cambridge, Cambridge University Press: 179–95.

Henderson, John 1988. 'Entertaining Arguments: Terence *Adelphoe*', in Andrew Benjamin (ed.), *Post-Structuralist Classics*. London and New York, NY, Routledge: 192–226. Revised version in John Henderson 1999: 38–66.

—— 1994. 'Hanno's Punic Heirs: Der Poenulusneid des Plautus', *Ramus* 23: 24–54. Revised in John Henderson 1999: 3–37.

—— 1999. *Writing Down Rome. Satire, Comedy, and other Offences in Latin Poetry*. Oxford, Clarendon Press.

—— 2004. 'Terence's *Selbstaussohnung*: Payback Time for the Self (*Hauton-timorumenus*)', *Ramus* 33: 53–81.

—— (ed. and tr.) 2006. *Plautus. Asinaria. The One about the Asses*. Madison, WI, The University of Wisconsin Press.

Henry, Madeleine M. 1985. *Menander's Courtesans and the Greek Comic Tradition*. Frankfurt-am-Main, Lang.

Hesk, Jon 2000. 'Intratext and Irony in Aristophanes', in Alison Sharrock and Helen Morales (eds.), *Intratextuality*. Oxford, Oxford University Press: 227–61.

Higgins, W. E. 1977. 'A Passage to Hades: The *Frogs* of Aristophanes', *Ramus* 6: 60–81.

Hofmann, Walter (ed.) 2001. *Plautus' Truculentus*. Darmstadt, Wissenschaftliche Buchgesellschaft.

Hokenson, Jan Marsh 2006. *The Idea of Comedy. History, Theory, Critique*. Madison, WI, and Teaneck, NJ, Fairleigh Dickinson University Press.

Holtermann, Martin 2004. *Der deutsche Aristophanes. Die Rezeption eines politischen Dichters im 19. Jahrhundert*. Hypomnemata 155. Göttingen, Vandenhoeck & Ruprecht.

Hooker, J. T. 1980. 'The Composition of the *Frogs*', *Hermes* 108: 169–82.

Horsley, G. H. R. 1982. 'Aristophanes' *Wasps*', in *Hellenika. Essays on Greek History and Politics*. North Ryde, New South Wales, Macquarie Ancient History Association: 69–96.

Hough, J. N. 1937. 'The Structure of the *Asinaria*', *AJP* 58: 19–37.

Hubbard, Thomas K. 1986 'Parabatic Self-Criticism and the Two Versions of Aristophanes' *Clouds*', *CA* 5: 182–97.

—— 1991. *The Mask of Comedy. Aristophanes and the Intertextual Parabasis*. Ithaca, NY, Cornell University Press.

Hubka, Karel 1984. 'The Dramatic Syllables and Hyper-Syllables of Menander's *Samia* and Plautus' *Mercator*', *Poetics* 13: 83–100.

Hughes, David 1984. 'The Character of Paegnium in Plautus' *Persa*', *RM* 127: 46–57.

Hulton, A. O. 1972. 'The Women on the Acropolis: A Note on the Structure of the *Lysistrata*', *G&R* 19: 32–6.

Hunter, Richard L. 1980. 'Philemon, Plautus, and the *Trinummus*', *MH* 37: 216–30.

—— 1981. 'The *Aulularia* of Plautus and its Greek Original', *PCPS* 27: 37–49.

—— (ed.) 1983. *Eubulus. The Fragments*. Cambridge, Cambridge University Press.

—— 1985. *The New Comedy of Greece and Rome*. Cambridge, Cambridge University Press.

Idle, Eric (ed.) 1971. *Monty Python's Big Red Book*. London, Methuen.

Ireland, Stanley (ed. and tr.) 1990. *Terence. The Mother-in-Law*. Warminster, Aris & Phillips.

—— 1993. *Menander. A Companion to the Penguin Translation*. Bristol, Bristol Classical Press.

—— (ed. and tr.) 1995. *Menander. The Bad Tempered Man*. Warminster, Aris & Phillips.

Iversen, Paul A. 2001. 'Coal for Diamonds: Syriskos' Character in Menander's *Epitrepontes*', *AJP* 122: 381–403.

Jacques, Jean-Marie (ed.) 1998. *Ménandre. Le Bouclier*. Paris, Les Belles Lettres.

—— 2004. 'Le *Dis exapaton* de Menandre, modèle des *Bacchides* de Plaute', *REA* 106: 23–47.

James, Sharon L. 1998. 'From Boys to Men: Rape and Developing Masculinity in Terence's *Hecyra* and *Eunuchus*', *Helios* 25: 31–48.

Janko, Richard 1984. *Aristotle on Comedy. Towards a Reconstruction of Poetics II.* London, Duckworth.

Jedrkiewicz, Stefano 2006. 'Bestie, gesti e logos: una lettura delle *Vespe* di Aristofane', *QUCC* 82: 61–91.

Jocelyn, H. D. 1984. 'Anti–Greek Sentiment in Plautus' *Menaechmi*?', *PLLS* 4: 1–25.

Johnson, W. R. 1968. 'Micio and the Perils of Perfection', *CSCA* 1: 171–86.

Karakasis, Evangelos 2005. *Terence and the Language of Roman Comedy.* Cambridge, Cambridge University Press.

Kassel, Rudolf and Austin, C. F. L. (eds.) 1983–2001. *Poetae Comici Graeci.* 8 vols, Berlin and New York, NY, de Gruyter.

Katsouris, Andreas G. 1975. *Tragic Patterns in Menander.* Athens, Hellenic Society for Humanistic Studies.

——— 1995. *Menander Bibliography.* Thessaloniki, University Studio Press.

Kauer, Robert and Lindsay, W. M. (eds) 1926. *P. Terenti Afri Comoediae.* Oxford, Clarendon Press.

Kerkhof, Rainer 2003. *Dorische Posse. Epicharm und attische Komödie.* Munich and Leipzig, Saur.

Keuls, Eva 1969. 'Mystery Elements in Menander's *Dyscolus*', *TAPA* 100: 209–20.

Kirkpatrick, John and Dunn, Francis M. 2002. 'Heracles, Cercopes, and Paracomedy', *TAPA* 132: 29–61.

Kleve, Knut 1996. 'How to Read an Illegible Papyrus: Towards an Edition of *PHerc.* 78, Caecilius Statius, *Obolostates sive Faenerator*', *CErc* 26: 5–15.

——— 2001. '*Caecilius Statius*, The Money-Lender (*PHerc.* 78)', in I. Andorlini, G. Bastianini, M. Manfredi, and G. Menci (eds.), *Atti del XXII Congresso Internazionale di Papirologia.* 2 vols, Florence, Istituto Papirologica G. Vitelli: ii.725.

Klose, Dietrich 1966. *Die Didaskalien und Prologe des Terenz.* Dissertation, University of Freiburg.

Knorr, Ortwin 1995. 'The Character of Bacchis in Terence's *Heautontimorumenos*', *AJP* 116: 221–35.

Koestler, Arthur 1964. *The Act of Creation.* London, Hutchinson.

Konstan, David 1983. *Roman Comedy.* Ithaca, NY, Cornell University Press.

——— 1985. 'The Politics of Aristophanes' *Wasps*', *TAPA* 115: 27–46. Revised in Konstan 1995: 15–28.

——— 1986. 'Love in Terence's *Eunuch*: The Origins of Erotic Subjectivity', *AJP* 107: 369–93. Revised version in Konstan 1995: 131–40.

——— 1987. 'Between Courtesan and Wife: Menander's *Perikeiromene*', *Phoenix* 41: 122–39. Revised in Konstan 1995: 107–19.

——— 1990. 'A City in the Air: Aristophanes' *Birds*', *Arethusa* 23: 183–207. Revised versions in Konstan 1995: 29–44 and Dobrov 1997: 3–22.

—— 1993a. 'Aristophanes' *Lysistrata*: Women and the Body Politic', in Sommerstein et al. 1993: 431–44. Revised in Konstan 1995: 45–60.

—— 1993b. 'The Young Concubine in Menandrian Comedy', in Scodel 1993: 139–60. Revised in Konstan 1995: 120–30.

—— 1995. *Greek Comedy and Ideology*. New York, NY and Oxford, Oxford University Press.

—— and Dillon, Matthew 1981. 'The Ideology of Aristophanes' *Wealth*', *AJP* 102: 371–94. Revised in Konstan 1995: 75–90.

Kopff, E. Christian 1990. 'The Date of Aristophanes, *Nubes* II', *AJP* 111: 318–29.

Koster, W. J. W. et al. 1960– . *Scholia in Aristophanem*. Groningen, Wolters/ Nordhoff/Forsten.

Kozak, Lynn and Rich, John (eds.) 2006. *Playing around Aristophanes*. Oxford, Aris & Phillips.

Kruschwitz, Peter 2002. 'Ist Geld die "Wurzel allen Ubels"? Zur Interpretation von Plautus' *Aulularia*', *Hermes* 130: 146–63.

—— 2004. *Terenz*. Olms Studienbücher Antike. Hildesheim, Olms-Weidmann.

——, Ehlers, Widu-Wolfgang, and Felgentreu, Fritz (eds.) 2007. *Terentius Poeta*. Zetemata 127. Munich, C. H. Beck.

Kyriakidi, Natalia 2007. *Aristophanes und Eupolis. Zur Geschichte einer dichterischen Rivalität*. Berlin and New York, NY, de Gruyter.

Lada-Richards, Ismene 1999. *Initiating Dionysus. Ritual and Theatre in Aristophanes' Frogs*. Oxford, Clarendon Press.

—— 2004. 'Authorial Voice and Theatrical Self-definition in Terence and Beyond: The *Hecyra* Prologues in Ancient and Modern Contexts', *G&R* 51: 55–82.

—— 2007. *Silent Eloquence. Lucian and Pantomime Dancing*. London, Duckworth.

Lamagna, Mario (ed.) 1998. *Menandro. La donna di Samo*. Naples, Bibliopolis.

Lange, D. K. 1975. 'The Identification of Plautus' *Cistellaria* with Menander's *Synaristosai*', *CJ* 70: 30–2.

Langer, Susanne 1953. *Feeling and Form. A Theory of Art Developed from 'Philosophy in a New Key'*. New York, NY, Scribner.

Lanza, Diego 2000. 'Entrelacement des espaces chez Aristophane: L'Exemple des *Acharniens*', *Pallas* 54: 133–9.

Lape, Susanne 2001. 'The Ethics of Democracy in Menander's *Dyskolos*', *Helios* 28: 141–72. Revised in Lape 2004: 110–36.

—— 2004. *Reproducing Athens. Menander's Comedy, Democratic Culture, and the Hellenistic City*. Princeton, NJ, Princeton University Press.

Leach, Eleanor Winsor 1969a. 'De exemplo meo ipse aedificato: An Organizing Idea in the Mostellaria', *Hermes* 96: 318–32.

—— 1969b. 'Ergasilus and the Ironies of the *Captivi*', *C&M* 30: 263–96.

—— 1969c. '*Meam quom formam noscito*: Language and Characterization in the *Menaechmi*', *Arethusa* 2: 30–45.

—— 1974. 'Plautus' *Rudens*: Venus Born from a Shell', *Texas Studies in Literature and Language* 15: 915–31.

—— 1980. 'The Soldier and Society: Plautus' *Miles Gloriosus* as Popular Drama', *RSC* 28: 185–209.

Leadbeater, L. W. 1986. 'Amphitryon, *Casina* and the Disappearance of Jupiter', in C. Deroux (ed.), *Studies in Latin Literature and Roman History IV.* Collection Latomus 196. Brussels: 135–50.

Lefèvre, Eckard 1982. *Maccus vortit barbare. Vom tragischen Amphitryon zum tragikomischen Amphitruo.* Wiesbaden, Steiner.

—— 1995. *Plautus und Philemon.* Tübingen, Narr.

—— 1997. *Plautus' Pseudolus.* Tübingen, Narr.

—— 1998. 'L'*Aulularia* de Plaute, l'*Avare* de Molière et la version originale grecque: Des formes différentes du comique', *Ktema* 22: 227–35.

—— 2001. *Plautus' Aulularia.* ScriptOralia 122. Tübingen, Narr.

——, Stärk, Ekkehard, and Vogt-Spira, Gregor 1978. *Der Phormio des Terenz und der Epidikazomenos des Apollodor von Karystos.* Zetemata 74. Munich, C. H. Beck.

—— —— —— (eds.) 1991. *Plautus barbarus. Sechs Kapitel zur Originalität des Plautus.* Tübingen, Narr.

Leigh, Matthew 2004. *Comedy and the Rise of Rome.* Oxford, Oxford University Press.

Lentano, Mario 1997. 'Quindici anni di studi terenziani, Parte I: Studi sulle commedie (1979–1993)', *BStudLat* 27: 497–564.

—— 1998. 'Quindici anni di studi terenziani, Parte II: Tradizione manoscritta ed esegesi antica (1979–1993)', *BStudLat* 28: 78–104.

Levine, Daniel 1987. '*Lysistrata* and *Bacchae*: Structure, Genre, and "Women on Top"', *Helios* 54: 29–38.

Lewis, D. M. 1955. 'Notes on Attic Inscriptions II: xxiii. Who was Lysistrata?' *ABSA* 50: 1–12. Reprinted in *Selected Papers on Greek and Near Eastern History*, Cambridge, Cambridge University Press, 187–202.

Lewis, Paul 1989. *Comic Effects. Interdisciplinary Approaches to Humor in Literature.* Albany, NY, State University of New York Press.

Lindsay, W. M. (ed.) 1903. *T. Macci Plauti Comoediae.* Oxford, Clarendon Press.

Littlefield, David J. 1968a. 'Metaphor and Myth: The Unity of Aristophanes' *Knights*', *Studies in Philology* 65: 1–22.

—— (ed.) 1968b. *Twentieth Century Interpretations of The Frogs.* Englewood Cliffs, NJ, Prentice-Hall.

Lloyd, R. B. 1963. 'Two Prologues: Menander and Plautus', *AJP* 84: 146–61.

Lloyd-Jones, Hugh 1966. 'Menander's *Sikyonios*', *GRBS* 7: 131–57. Reprinted in Lloyd-Jones 1990: 53–77.

—— 1971. 'Menander's *Aspis*', *GRBS* 12: 175–95. Reprinted in Lloyd-Jones 1990: 7–25.

—— 1972. 'Menander's *Samia* in the Light of the New Evidence', *YCS* 22: 119–44. Reprinted in Lloyd-Jones 1990: 31–52.

—— 1973. 'Terentian Technique in the *Adelphi* and the *Eunuchus*', *CQ* 67: 279–84. Reprinted in Lloyd-Jones 1990: 87–93.

—— 1990. *Academic Papers. Greek Comedy, Hellenistic Literature, Greek Religion, and Miscellanea*. Oxford, Clarendon Press.

Loraux, Nicole 1981. 'L'Acropole comique', *Ancient Society* 11/12: 119–50.

Lord, Carnes 1977. 'Aristotle, Menander, and the *Adelphoe* of Terence', *TAPA* 107: 183–202.

Lord, Louis E. 1925. *Aristophanes. His Plays and His Influence*. Boston, MA, Marshall Jones.

Louden, Bruce 1999. '*The Tempest*, Plautus, and the *Rudens*', *Comparative Drama* 33: 199–233.

Lowe, J. C. B. 1983. 'The *Eunuchus*: Terence and Menander', *CQ* 77: 428–44.

—— 1985a. 'The Cook Scene of Plautus' *Pseudolus*', *CQ* 35: 411–6.

—— 1985b. 'Plautine Innovations in *Mostellaria* 529–857', *Phoenix* 39: 6–26.

—— 1989. 'The *Virgo Callida* of Plautus, *Persa*', *CQ* 39: 390–9.

—— 1991. 'Prisoners, Guards, and Chains in Plautus, *Captivi*', *AJP* 112: 29–44.

—— 1992. 'Aspects of Plautus' Originality in the *Asinaria*', *CQ* 42: 152–75.

—— 1998a. 'The Intrigue of Terence's *Heauton Timorumenos*', *RM* 141: 163–71.

—— 1998b. 'Terence, *Adelphoe*: Problems of Dramatic Space and Time', *CQ* 48: 470–86.

—— 2001. 'Notes on Plautus' *Mercator*', *WS* 114: 143–56.

—— 2003. 'The Lot-Drawing Scene of Plautus' *Casina*', *CQ* 53: 175–83.

Lowe, N. J. 1987. 'Tragic Space and Comic Timing in Menander's *Dyskolos*', *BICS* 34: 126–38.

—— 1993. 'Aristophanes' Books', *Annals of Scholarship* 10: 63–83.

—— 2000a. *The Classical Plot and the Invention of Western Narrative*. Cambridge, Cambridge University Press.

—— 2000b. 'Comic Plots and the Invention of Fiction', in Harvey and Wilkins 2000: 259–72.

—— 2006. 'Aristophanic Spacecraft', in Kozak and Rich 2006: 48–64.

Luppe, Wolfgang 2000. 'The Rivalry between Aristophanes and Kratinos', in Harvey and Wilkins 2000: 15–21.

McCarthy, Kathleen 2000. *Slaves, Masters and the Art of Authority in Plautine Comedy*. Princeton, NJ, Princeton University Press.

MacCary, W. T. 1973. 'The Comic Tradition and Comic Structure in Diphilus' *Kleroumenoi*', *Hermes* 101: 194–208.

—— 1974. 'Patterns of Myth, Ritual, and Comedy in Plautus' *Casina*', *Texas Studies in Language and Literature* 15: 881–9.

—— 1979. 'Philocleon Ithyphallos: Dance, Costume and Character in the *Wasps*', *TAPA* 109: 137–47.

—— and Willcock, M. M. (eds.) 1976. *Plautus. Casina*. Cambridge, Cambridge University Press.

McDonald, Marianne and Walton, J. Michael (eds.) 2007. *The Cambridge Companion to Greek and Roman Theatre*. Cambridge, Cambridge University Press.

MacDowell, Douglas M. (ed.) 1971. *Aristophanes. Wasps*. Oxford, Clarendon Press.

—— 1982. 'Love versus the Law: An Essay on Menander's *Aspis*', *G&R* 29: 42–52.

—— 1983. 'The Nature of Aristophanes' *Akharnians*', *G&R* 30: 143–61.

—— 1995. *Aristophanes and Athens*. Oxford, Oxford University Press.

—— 1996. 'Aristophanes and Democracy', in F. R. Adrados and Michael B. Sakellariou (eds.), *Démocratie athénienne et culture*. Athens, Académie d'Athènes: 189–97.

McGarrity, T. 1978. 'Thematic Unity in Terence's *Andria*', *TAPA* 108: 103–14.

—— 1980–1. 'Reputation versus Reality in Terence's *Hecyra*', *CJ* 76: 149–56.

McGhee, Paul E. and Goldstein, Jeffrey H. (eds.) 1983. *Handbook of Humor Research*. 2 vols, New York, NY, Springer.

McGlew, James F. 1996. '"Everybody Wants to Make a Speech": Cleon and Aristophanes on Politics and Fantasy', *Arethusa* 29: 339–62.

—— 1997. 'After Irony: Aristophanes' *Wealth* and its Modern Interpreters', *AJP* 118: 35–53. Expanded in McGlew 2002: 171–211.

—— 2001. 'Identity and Ideology: The Farmer Chorus of Aristophanes' *Peace*', *SyllClass* 12: 74–97.

—— 2002. *Citizens on Stage. Comedy and Political Culture in the Athenian Democracy*. Ann Arbor, MI, University of Michigan Press.

—— 2004. '"Speak on my Behalf": Persuasion and Purification in Aristophanes' *Wasps*', *Arethusa* 37: 11–36.

McKeown, Niall 2007. *The Invention of Ancient Slavery?* London, Duckworth.

McLeish, Kenneth 1980. *The Theatre of Aristophanes*. London, Thames & Hudson.

Mahoney, Anne (ed.) 2004. *Plautus. Amphitryo*. Focus Classical Commentary. Newburyport, MA, Focus.

Major, Wilfred E. 1997. 'Menander in a Macedonian World', *GRBS* 38: 41–74.

—— 2006. 'Aristophanes and Alazoneia: Laughing at the Parabasis of the *Clouds*', *CW* 99: 131–44.

Malamud, Margaret 2001. 'A Funny Thing Happened on the Way from Brooklyn: Roman Comedy on Broadway and in Film', in Sandra Joshel, Margaret Malamud, and Donald T. McGuire, Jr. (eds.), *Imperial Projections. Ancient Rome in Modern Popular Culture*. Baltimore, MD, The Johns Hopkins University Press. Reprinted in *Arion* 8 2001: 33–51.

Maltby, Robert 1984. 'The Last Act of Terence's *Heautontimoroumenos*', *PLLS* 4: 27–41.

Marianetti, Marie C. 1992. *Religion and Politics in Aristophanes' Clouds*. Hildesheim, Olms.

—— 1993. 'Socratic Mystery-Parody and the Issue of *asebeia* in Aristophanes' *Clouds*', *SO* 68: 5–31.

Marshall, C. W. 2006. *The Stagecraft and Performance of Roman Comedy*. Cambridge, Cambridge University Press.

Martin, R. H. (ed.) 1950. *Terence. Phormio*. London, Methuen.

—— (ed.) 1976. *Terence. Adelphoe*. Cambridge, Cambridge University Press.

—— 1995. 'A Not-So-Minor Character in Terence's *Eunuchus*', *CP* 90: 139–51.

Martin, Richard P. 1987. 'Fire on the Mountain: *Lysistrata* and the Lemnian Women', *CA* 6: 77–105.

—— 1988–9. 'Rites of Passage in Aristophanes' *Frogs*', *CJ* 84: 308–24.

Martina, Antonio (ed.) 1997–2000. *Menandri Epitrepontes*. 3 vols, Rome, Kepos.

Mastromarco, Giuseppe 1979. 'L'esordio segreto di Aristofane', *QS* 10: 153–96.

Mattingly, Harold B. 1959. 'The Terentian Didascaliae', *Athenaeum* 37: 18–73.

—— 1963. 'The Chronology of Terence', *RCCM* 5: 12–61.

Mauger-Plichon, Brigitte 2000. 'Terence et le probléme de l'éducation: Réflexions sur les *Adelphes* et l'*Heautontimoroumenos*', *Latomus* 59: 802–18.

Maurach, Gregor 1988. *Der Poenulus des Plautus*. Heidelberg, Winter.

—— 2005. *Kleine Geschichte der antiken Komödie*. Berlin, Wissenschaftliche Buchgesellschaft.

Meineck, Peter (tr.) 2000. *Aristophanes. Clouds*. Indianapolis, IN, Hackett.

Meredith, George 1877. *On the Idea of Comedy, and of the Uses of the Comic Spirit*. London, Simmons and Botten. Reprinted as *An Essay on Comedy* in Sypher 1956: 3–57.

Miller, Norma (tr.) 1987. *Menander. Plays and Fragments*. Harmondsworth, Penguin.

Milnor, Kristina L. 2002. 'Playing House: Stage, Space, and Domesticity in Plautus' *Mostellaria*', *Helios* 29: 3–25.

Moellendorff, Peter von 1995. *Grundlagen einer Ästhetik der Alten Komödie. Untersuchungen zu Aristophanes und Michail Bachtin*. Tübingen, Narr.

—— 2002. *Aristophanes*. Olms Studienbücher 10. Hildesheim, Olms.

Monda, Salvator (ed.) 2004. *Titus Maccius Plautus. Vidularia et deperditarum fabularum fragmenta*. Editio Plautina Sarsinatis 21. Sarsina/Urbini, QuattroVenti.

Moore, Timothy J. 1991. '*Palliata togata*: Plautus, *Curculio* 462–86', *AJP* 112: 343–62.

—— 1998a. 'Music and Structure in Roman Comedy', *AJP* 119: 245–73.

—— 1998b. *The Theater of Plautus. Playing to the Audience*. Austin, TX, University of Texas Press.

Moorton, Richard F. 1999. 'Dionysus or Polemos? The Double Message of Aristophanes' *Acharnians*', in Frances B. Titchener and Richard F. Moorton (eds.), *The Eye Expanded. Life and the Arts in Greco-Roman Antiquity*. Berkeley, CA and London, University of California Press: 24–51.

Morreall, John 1983. *Taking Laughter Seriously*. Albany, NY, State University of New York.

—— (ed.) 1987. *The Philosophy of Laughter and Humor*. Albany, NY, State University of New York Press.

Muecke, Frances 1982. 'A Portrait of the Artist as a Young Woman', *CQ* 32: 41–55.

—— 1985. 'Names and Players: The Sycophant Scene of the *Trinummus*', *TAPA* 115: 167–86.

—— 1987. *Plautus, Menaechmi. A Companion to the Penguin Translation*. Bristol, Bristol Classical Press.

Mulkay, Michael 1988. *On Humour. Its Nature and Place in Modern Society*. Oxford, Blackwell.

Müller, Roman 1997. *Sprechen und Sprache. Dialoglinguistiche Studien zu Terenz*. Heidelberg, Winter.

Nelson, T. G. A. 1990. *Comedy*. Oxford, Oxford University Press.

Nesselrath, Heinz-Günther 1990. *Die attische mittlere Komödie*. Berlin and New York, NY, de Gruyter.

—— 1993. 'Parody and Later Greek Comedy', *HSCP* 95: 181–95.

—— 1995. 'The Polis of Athens in Middle Comedy', in Gregory W. Dobrov (ed.), *Beyond Aristophanes. Transition and Diversity in Greek Comedy*. Atlanta, Scholars Press: 271–88.

Nevola, Maria Lucia 1990–3. 'Meccanismi comici nelle *Nuvole* de Aristofane', *MCr* 25–28: 151–74.

Nilsen, Don L. F. 1993. *Humor Scholarship. A Research Bibliography*. Westport, CT, Greenwood.

Nixon Paul (ed. and tr.) 1916–38. *Plautus*. Loeb Classical Library. 5 vols, Cambridge, MA, Harvard University Press.

Norrick, Neal R. 1993. *Conversational Joking. Humor in Everyday Talk*. Bloomington, IN, Indiana University Press.

Norwood, Gilbert 1931. *Greek Comedy*. London, Methuen.

—— 1932. *Plautus and Terence*. New York, NY, Longmans, Green.

Nünlist, René 1999. 'Ein neu identifiziertes Buchfragment aus Menanders *Epitrepontes*', *ZPE* 128: 54–56.

—— 2003. '4641. Menander, *Epitrepontes*', *Oxyrhynchus Papyri* 68: 22–8.

Nussbaum, Martha 1980. 'Aristophanes and Socrates on Learning Practical Wisdom', in Henderson 1980a: 43–97.

Oakley, Stephen P. 1998. *A Commentary on Livy Books VI–X, Vol. 2: Books VII–VIII*. Oxford, Clarendon Press.

O'Bryhim, Shawn 1989. 'The Originality of Plautus' *Casina*', *AJP* 110: 81–103.

Olson, Elder 1968. *The Theory of Comedy*. Bloomington, IN, Indiana University Press.

Olson, R. 1984. 'Aristophanes and the Antiscientific Tradition', in Everett Mendelsohn (ed.), *Transformation and Tradition in the Sciences. Essays in Honour of I. Bernard Cohen*. Cambridge, Cambridge University Press: 441–54.

Olson, S. Douglas 1988. 'The 'Love-Duet' in Aristophanes' *Ecclesiazusae*', *CQ* 38: 328–30.

—— 1989a. *Aristophanes' Plutus*. 2 vols, Bryn Mawr, Bryn Mawr Commentaries.

—— 1989b. 'Cario and the New World of Aristophanes' *Plutus*', *TAPA* 119: 193–9.

—— 1989c. 'The Staging of Aristophanes, *Ec.* 504–727', *AJP* 110: 223–6.

—— 1990a. 'Dicaeopolis and Aristophanes in *Acharnians*', *LCM* 15: 31–2.

—— 1990b. 'Economics and Ideology in Aristophanes' *Wealth*', *HSCP* 93: 223–42.

—— 1990c. 'The New Demos of Aristophanes' *Knights*', *Eranos* 88: 60–3.

—— 1991a. 'Anonymous Male Parts in Aristophanes' *Ecclesiazusae* and the Identity of the *despotes*', *CQ* 41: 36–40.

—— 1991b. 'Dicaeopolis' Motivations in Aristophanes' *Acharnians*', *JHS* 111: 200–3.

—— 1994. '*Clouds* 537–44 and the Original Version of the Play', *Philologus* 138: 32–7.

—— 1996. 'Politics and Poetry in Aristophanes' *Wasps*', *TAPA* 126: 129–150.

—— (ed.) 1998. *Aristophanes. Peace*. Oxford, Clarendon Press.

—— (ed.) 2002. *Aristophanes. Acharnians*. Oxford, Clarendon Press.

—— (ed.) 2007. *Broken Laughter. Select Fragments of Greek Comedy*. Oxford, Oxford University Press.

O'Neill, Patrick 1993. *The Comedy of Entropy. Humour, Narrative, Reading*. Toronto, University of Toronto Press.

O'Neill, Peter 2003. 'Triumph Songs, Reversal and Plautus' *Amphitruo*', *Ramus* 32: 1–38.

O'Regan, Daphne Elizabeth 1992. *Rhetoric, Comedy, and the Violence of Language in Aristophanes' Clouds*. New York, NY, Oxford University Press.

Orin, Elliott 1992. *Jokes and their Relations*. Lexington, KY, University of Kentucky Press.

Owens, William M. 1994. 'The Third Deception in *Bacchides*: Fides and Plautus' Originality', *AJP* 115: 381–407.

—— 2000. 'Plautus' *Stichus* and the Political Crisis of 200 B.C.', *AJP* 121: 385–407.

Padilla, Mark 1992. 'The Heraclean Dionysus: Theatrical and Social Renewal in Aristophanes' *Frogs*', *Arethusa* 25: 359–84.

Papageorgiou, Nikolaos 2004. 'Prodicus and the Agon of the Logoi in Aristophanes' *Clouds*', *QUCC* 78: 61–9.

Parker, Holt N. 1996. 'Plautus vs. Terence: Audience and Popularity Re-examined', *AJP* 117: 585–617.

Parker, L. P. E. 1991. 'Eupolis or Dicaeopolis?', *JHS* 111: 203–8.

—— 1997. *The Songs of Aristophanes*. Oxford, Oxford University Press.

Pauw, F. R. 1996. 'Aristophanes' Nachleben and other post-Renaissance disasters', *Akroterion* 41: 161–86.

Pelling, C. B. R. 2000. *Literary Texts and the Greek Historian*. London, Routledge.

Penwill, J. L. 2004. 'The Unlovely Lover of Terence's Hecyra', *Ramus* 33: 130–49.

Perkell, Christine 1993. 'On the Two Voices of the Birds in *Birds*', *Ramus* 22: 1–18.

Petrone, Gianna 1977. *Morale e antimorale nelle commedie di Plauto*. Palermo, Palumbo.

Philippides, Katerina 1995. 'Terence's *Eunuchus*: Elements of the Marriage Ritual in the Rape Scene', *Mnemosyne* 48: 272–84.

Phillips, Jane E. 1985. 'Alcumena in the *Amphitruo* of Plautus: A Pregnant Lady Joke', *CJ* 80: 121–6.

Pickard-Cambridge, A. W. 1927. *Dithyramb, Tragedy and Comedy*. London, Oxford University Press. Second edition revised by T. B. L. Webster, Oxford, Clarendon Press, 1962.

Platnauer, Maurice (ed.) 1964. *Aristophanes. Peace*. Oxford, Clarendon Press.

Platter, Charles (ed.) 2003. *Aristophanes. Acharnians*. Bryn Mawr, Bryn Mawr Commentaries.

—— 2006. *Aristophanes and the Carnival of Genres*. Baltimore, MD, The Johns Hopkins University Press.

Porter, John R. 1999–2000. 'Euripides and Menander: *Epitrepontes*, Act IV', *ICS* 24–25: 157–73.

Post, L. A. 1969. 'Virtue Promoted in Menander's *Dyskolos*', *TAPA* 91: 152–61.

Pozzi, D. C. 1986. 'The Pastoral Ideal in the *Birds* of Aristophanes', *CJ* 81: 119–29.

Primmer, Adolf 1984. *Handlungsgliederung In Nea und Palliata. Dis Exapaton und Bacchides*. Vienna, Österreichische Akademie der Wissenschaften.

Purdie, Susan 1993. *Comedy. The Mastery of Discourse*. New York, NY and London, Harvester.

Questa, Cesare 1995. *Titi Macci Plauti Cantica*. Urbino, QuattroVenti.

—— (ed.) 2001. *Titus Maccius Plautus. Casina*. Urbino, QuattroVenti.

—— 2004. *Sei letture plautine*. Urbino, QuattroVenti.

—— 2007. *La metrica di Plauto e di Terenzio*. Urbino, QuattroVenti.

Radice, Betty (tr.) 1965–7, revised 1976. *Terence. The Comedies*. Harmondsworth, Penguin.

Raffaelli, Renato and Tontini, Alba (eds.) 1998– . *Lecturae Plautinae Sarsinates*. Urbino, QuattroVenti: *Amphitruo* (1998); *Asinaria* (1999); *Aulularia* (2000); *Bacchides* (2001); *Epidicus* (2006); *Captivi* (2002); *Casina* (2003); *Cistellaria* (2004); *Curculio* (2005); *Menaechmi* (2007).

Ramage, Edwin S. 1966. 'City and Country in Menander's *Dyskolos*', *Philologus* 110: 194–211.

Raskin, Victor 1985. *Semantic Mechanisms of Humor*. Dordrecht, Boston, and Lancaster, Reidel.

Rawson, Elizabeth 1985. *Intellectual Life in the Late Roman Republic*. London, Duckworth.

Reckford, Kenneth J. 1987. *Aristophanes' Old-and-New Comedy*. Chapel Hill, NC and London, University of North Carolina Press.

Reeve, M. D. 1983. 'Terence', in Reynolds 1983: 412–20.

Reinders, Peter 2001. *Demos Pyknites. Untersuchungen zur Darstellung des Demos in der Alten Komödie*. Stuttgart, Metzler.

Revermann, Martin 2006. *Comic Business. Theatricality, Dramatic Technique, and Performance Contexts of Aristophanic Comedy*. Oxford, Oxford University Press.

Reynolds, L. D. (ed.) 1983. *Texts and Transmission. A Survey of the Latin Classics*. Oxford, Clarendon Press.

Richardson, Lawrence Jr 1997. 'The Moral Problems of Terence's *Andria* and Reconstruction of Menander's *Andria* and *Perinthia*', *GRBS* 38: 173–85.

—— 2006. 'The Terentian Adaptation of the *Heauton Timorumenos* of Menander', *GRBS* 46: 13–36.

Richlin, Amy (tr.) 2005. *Rome and the Mysterious Orient. Three Plays by Plautus*. Berkeley, CA, University of California Press.

Roberts, Adam 2006. *The History of Science Fiction*. London, Palgrave Macmillan.

Robson, James 2006. *Humour, Obscenity and Aristophanes*. Drama: Studien zum antiken Drama und zu seiner Rezeption NS 1. Tübingen, Narr.

Rosellini, M. 1979. 'Lysistrata, une mise en scène de la feminise', in Bonnamour and Delevault 1979: 11–32.

Rosen, Ralph M. 1988. *Old Comedy and the Iambographic Tradition*. Atlanta, Scholars Press.

—— 1997. 'Performance and Textuality in Aristophanes' *Clouds*', *Yale Journal of Criticism* 10: 397–421.

—— 1999. 'Comedy and Confusion in Callias' *Letter Tragedy*', *CP* 94: 147–67.

—— 2004. 'Aristophanes' *Frogs* and the *Contest of Homer and Hesiod*', *TAPA* 134: 295–322.

Rosivach, Vincent J. 1998. *When a Young Man Falls in Love. The Sexual Exploitation of Women in New Comedy*. London and New York, NY, Routledge.

—— 2001. 'Class Matters in the *Dyskolos* of Menander', *CQ* 51: 127–34.

Rothwell, Kenneth S. Jr 1990. *Politics and Persuasion in Aristophanes' Ecclesiazusae. Mnemosyne* Supplementum 111. Leiden, Brill.

—— 2007. *Nature, Culture, and the Origins of Greek Comedy. A Study of Animal Choruses*. Cambridge, Cambridge University Press.

Ruch, Willibald 1998. *The Sense of Humor*. Berlin, Mouton de Gruyter.

Ruden, Sarah (tr.) 2003. *Aristophanes. Lysistrata*. Indianapolis, IN, Hackett.

Ruffell, Ian A. 2002. 'A Total Write-Off: Aristophanes, Cratinus and the Rhetoric of Comic Competition', *CQ* 52: 138–63.

—— 2006. 'A Little Ironic, Don't You Think? Utopian Criticism and the Problem of Aristophanes' Late Plays', in Kozak and Rich 2006: 64–104.

Russo, Carlo Ferdinando 1992. *Aristofane. Autore di teatro*. Third edition, Florence, Sansoni. Expanded and translated by Kevin Wren as *Aristophanes. An Author for the Stage*, London, Routledge, 1994.

Rusten, Jeffrey (ed.) in press. *The Birth of Comedy. Fragments of Greek Comic Theater, ca. 560–280 B.C.* Baltimore, MD, The Johns Hopkins University Press.

Saïd, Suzanne 1996. '*L'Assemblée des Femmes*: Les Femmes, l'économie et la politique', in Bonnamour and Delavault 1979: 33–69. Abridged and translated by Janice Orion as '*The Assemblywomen*: Women, Economy, and Politics', in Erich Segal 1996: 282–313.

Salamon, G. 2004. 'Le métathéâtre dans les *Bacchides* de Plaute', *VL* 170: 22–42.

Sandbach, F. H. 1973: see Gomme and Sandbach 1973.

—— 1977. *The Comic Theatre of Greece and Rome*. London, Chatto & Windus.

—— 1978. 'Donatus' Use of the Name Terentius and the End of Terence's *Adelphoe*', *BICS* 25: 123–45.

—— 1982. 'How Terence's *Hecyra* Failed', *CQ* 76: 134–5.

—— (ed.) 1990. *Menandri reliquiae selectae*. Oxford, Clarendon Press.

Sargeaunt, John (ed. and tr.) 1912. *Terence*. Loeb Classical Library, 2 vols, Cambridge, MA, Harvard University Press.

Saylor, C. F. 1975. 'The Theme of Planlessness in Terence's *Eunuchus*', *TAPA* 105: 297–311.

Scafuro, Adele C. 1997. *The Forensic Stage. Settling Disputes in Greco-Roman New Comedy*. Cambridge, Cambridge University Press.

Schmidt, Ernst A. 2003. 'Die Tragikomödie *Amphitruo* des Plautus als Komödie und Tragödie', *MH* 60: 80–104.

Schoeman, A. 1998. 'Mercury and Metatheatre I: The Antelogium in Plautus' *Amphitruo*', *Akroterion* 43: 32–42.

—— 1999. 'Mercury and Metatheatre II: The Argumentum in Plautus' *Amphitruo*', *Akroterion* 44: 38–55.

Scholtz, Andrew 2004. 'Friends, Lovers, Flatterers: Demophilic Courtship in Aristophanes' *Knights*', *TAPA* 134: 263–93.

Schutter, K. H. E. 1952. *Quibus annis comoediae Plautinae primae actae sint queritur*. Groningen, De Waal.

Scodel, Ruth (ed.) 1993. *Theater and Society in the Classical World*. Ann Arbor, MI, University of Michigan Press.

Sear, Frank 2006. *Roman Theatres. An Architectural Study*. Oxford, Oxford University Press.

Sedgwick, W. B. 1949. 'Plautine Chronology', *AJP* 70: 376–83.

Segal, Charles 1961. 'The Character and Cults of Dionysus and the Unity of the *Frogs*', *HSCP* 65: 217–23.

—— 1969. 'Aristophanes' Cloud-Chorus', *Arethusa* 2: 143–61.

Segal, Erich 1969. 'The *Menaechmi*: Roman Comedy of Errors', *YCS* 21: 75–93.

—— 1987a. 'Morality and Money: The Purpose of the *Trinummus*', in Erich Segal 1987b: 214–26.

—— 1987b. *Roman Laughter. The Comedy of Plautus*. Second edition, New York, NY, Oxford University Press. First edition Cambridge, MA, Harvard University Press, 1968.

—— 1991. 'Is the *Captivi* Plautine?', in *Studi di filologia classica in onore di Giusto Monaco*. Palermo, Università di Palermo: 553–68. Also published in Erich Segal 1987b: 191–214.

—— (ed.) 1996. *Oxford Readings in Aristophanes*. Oxford, Oxford University Press.

—— 2001. *The Death of Comedy*. Cambridge, MA, Harvard University Press.

—— (ed.) 2002. *Oxford Readings in Menander, Plautus, and Terence*. Oxford, Oxford University Press.

—— and Moulton, Carroll 1978. '*Contortor legum*: The Hero of the *Phormio*', *RM* 121: 276–88.

Sewart, D. 1974. 'Exposition in the *Hecyra* of Apollodorus', *Hermes* 102: 247–60.

Sfyroeras, Pavlos 1995. 'What *Wealth* Has to Do with Dionysus: From Economy to Poetics in Aristophanes' *Plutus*', *GRBS* 36: 231–62.

Sharrock, Alison 1996. 'The Art of Deceit: Pseudolus and the Nature of Reading', *CQ* 46: 152–74.

Sherk, Robert K. 1968. 'The Date of Menander's *Dyscolus*', *Arethusa* 1: 103–8.

Shipp, G. P. (ed.) 1960. *Terence. Andria*. Melbourne, Oxford University Press.

Sidwell, Keith 1990. 'Was Philocleon Cured? The *Nosos* Theme in Aristophanes' *Wasps*', *C&M* 41: 9–31.

—— 1993. 'Authorial Collaboration? Aristophanes' *Knights* and Eupolis', *GRBS* 34: 365–89.

—— 1994. 'Aristophanes' *Acharnians* and Eupolis', *C&M* 45: 71–115.

—— 1995. 'Poetic Rivalry and the Caricature of Comic Poets: Cratinus' *Pytine* and Aristophanes' *Wasps*', in A. Griffiths (ed.), *Stage Directions. Essays in Ancient Drama in Honour of E. W. Handley*. BICS Supplement 66. London, Institute of Classical Studies, University of London: 56–80.

—— 2000. 'From Old to Middle to New? Aristotle's *Poetics* and the History of Athenian Comedy', in Harvey and Wilkins 2000: 247–58.

Sifakis, G. M. 1971. *Parabasis and Animal Choruses*. London, Athlone.

—— 1992. 'The Structure of Aristophanic Comedy', *JHS* 112: 123–39.

Silk, M. S. 1988. 'The Autonomy of Comedy', *Comparative Criticism* 10: 3–30.

—— 1990. 'The People of Aristophanes', in C. B. R. Pelling (ed.), *Characterization and Individuality in Greek Literature*. Oxford, Oxford University Press: 150–73.

—— 2000. *Aristophanes and the Definition of Comedy*. Oxford, Oxford University Press.

Simon, Richard Keller 1985. *The Labyrinth of the Comic*. Tallahassee, FL, Florida State University Press.

Slater, Niall W. 1985. *Plautus in Performance. The Theatre of the Mind*. Princeton, NJ, Princeton University Press. Second edition, Amsterdam, Harwood.

—— 1988a. 'The Fictions of Patriarchy in Terence's *Hecyra*', *CW* 81: 249–60.

—— 1988b. 'Problems in the Hypotheses to Aristophanes' *Peace*', *ZPE* 74: 43–7.

—— 1992. 'Plautine Negotiations: The *Poenulus* Prologue Unpacked', *YCS* 29: 131–46.

—— 1993. 'Space, Character, and ἀπάτη: Transformation and Transvaluation in the *Acharnians*', in Sommerstein et al. 1993: 397–415.

—— 1996. 'Literacy and Old Comedy', in Ian Worthington (ed.), *Voice into Text*. Leiden, Brill: 99–112.

—— 1997. 'Waiting in the Wings: Aristophanes' *Ecclesiazusae*', *Arion* 5: 97–129.

—— 2002. *Spectator Politics. Metatheatre and Performance in Aristophanes*. Philadelphia, PA, University of Pennsylvania Press.

Slavitt, David R. and Bovie, Palmer (eds.) 1995. *Plautus. The Comedies*. 4 vols, Baltimore, MD, The John Hopkins University Press.

—— —— (eds.) 1998. *Menander*. Philadelphia, PA, University of Pennsylvania Press.

Smith, Joseph A. 2004. 'Buy Young, Sell Old: Playing the Market Economies of Phormio and Terence', *Ramus* 33: 82–99.

Smith, Louise Pearson 1994. 'Audience Response to Rape: Chaerea in Terence's *Eunuch*', *Helios* 21: 21–38.

Smith, Peter L. (tr.) 1991. *Plautus, Three Comedies. Miles Gloriosus, Pseudolus, Rudens*. Ithaca, NY, Cornell University Press.

Sommerstein, Alan H. 1977. 'Aristophanes and the Events of 411', *JHS* 97: 112–26.

—— 1980. 'The Naming of Women in Greek and Roman Comedy', *QS* 11: 393–418.

—— 1980–2002. *The Comedies of Aristophanes*. 12 vols, Warminster, Aris & Phillips. Second edition, Oxford, Oxbow/Aris & Phillips, 2005– .

—— 1984. 'Aristophanes and the Demon Poverty', *CQ* 34: 314–33.

—— 1986. 'The Decree of Syrakosios', *CQ* 36: 101–8.

—— 2002a. *Aristophanes. Lysistrata and Other Plays*. Second edition, London, Penguin.

—— 2002b. 'Comic Elements in Tragic Language', in Willi 2002: 151–68.

—— 2004. 'Harassing the Satirist: The Alleged Attempts to Prosecute Aristophanes', in Ineke Sluiter and Ralph M. Rosen (eds.), *Free Speech in Classical Antiquity*. Leiden, Brill: 145–74.

—— 2006. 'How Aristophanes Got his A&P', in Kozak and Rich 2006: 126–39.

——, Halliwell, Stephen, Henderson, Jeffrey, and Zimmermann, Bernhard (eds.) 1993. *Tragedy, Comedy and the Polis*. Bari, Levante.

Soubiran, J. 2003. 'Structure des *Bacchides* de Plaute', *VL* 169: 22–35.

Sparkes, B. A. 1975. 'Illustrating Aristophanes', *JHS* 95: 122–35.

Spielvogel, Jörg 2001. *Wirtschaft und Geld bei Aristophanes. Untersuchungen zu den ökonomischen Bedingungen in Athen im bergang vom 5. zum 4. Jh. v.Chr.* Frankfurter Althistorische Beiträge 8. Frankfurt-am-Main, Clauss.

Stanford, W. B. (ed.) 1963. *Aristophanes. Frogs*. Second edition, London, Macmillan.

Stärk, Ekkehard 1989. *Die Menaechmi des Plautus und kein griechisches Original*. Tübingen, Narr.

Starks, John H. Jr. 2000. '*Nullus me est hodie Poenus poenior*: Balanced Ethnic Humor in Plautus' *Poenulus*', *Helios* 27: 163–86.

Stehle, Eva 1984. '*Pseudolus* as Socrates, Poet and Trickster', in David F. Bright and Edwin S. Ramage (eds.), *Classical Texts and their Traditions. Studies in Honor of C.R. Trahman*. Chico, Scholars Press: 239–51.

Stein, J. P. 1970. 'Morality in Plautus' *Trinummus*', *CB* 47: 7–13.

Stein, Markus 2003. 'Der Dichter und sein Kritiker: Interpretationsprobleme im Prolog des Terenzischen *Eunuchus*', *RM* 146: 184–217.

Stewart, Zeph 1958. 'The *Amphitruo* of Plautus and Euripides' *Bacchae*', *TAPA* 89: 348–73.

Stockert, Walter 1997. 'Metatheatralisches in Menanders *Epitrepontes*', *WS* 110: 5–18.

Stone, Laura M. 1981. *Costume in Aristophanic Comedy*. New York, NY, Arno. Reprinted Salem, MA, Ayer, 1984.

Storey, Ian C. 1985. 'The Symposium at *Wasps* 1299ff.', *Phoenix* 39: 317–33.

—— 1987. 'Old Comedy 1975–1984', *Echos du Monde Classique/Classical Views* 6: 1–46.

—— 1992. '*Dekaton men etos tod*': Old Comedy 1982–1991', *Antichthon* 26: 1–29.

—— 1993. 'The Date of Aristophanes' *Clouds* II and Eupolis' *Baptai*: A Reply to E.C. Kopff', *AJP* 114: 71–84.

—— 2003. *Eupolis. Poet of Old Comedy*. Oxford, Oxford University Press.

—— and Allan, Arlene 2005. *A Guide to Ancient Greek Drama*. Oxford, Blackwell.

Strasburger, Hermann 1966. 'Der Scipionenkreis', *Hermes* 94: 60–72.

Stroup, Sarah Culpepper 2004. 'Designing Women: Aristophanes' *Lysistrata* and the 'Hetairization' of the Greek Wife', *Arethusa* 37: 37–73.

Sutton, Dana F. 1988. 'Dicaeopolis as Aristophanes, Aristophanes as Dicaeopolis', *LCM* 13: 105–8.

Sypher, Wylie (ed.) 1956. *Comedy*. Baltimore, MD and London, The Johns Hopkins University Press.

Taaffe, Lauren K. 1991. 'The Illusion of Gender Disguise in Aristophanes' *Ecclesiazusae*', *Helios* 18: 91–112.

—— 1993. *Aristophanes and Women*. London and New York, NY, Routledge.

Taplin, Oliver 1993. *Comic Angels and Other Approaches to Greek Drama through Vase-Paintings*. Oxford, Clarendon Press.

—— 2007. *Pots and Plays. Interactions between Tragedy and Greek Vase-Painting of the Fourth Century B.C.* Los Angeles, CA, Getty Publications.

Tarrant, Harold C. 1991. '*Clouds* I: Steps towards Reconstruction', *Arctos* 25: 157–81.

Tarrant, R. J. 1983. 'Plautus', in Reynolds 1983: 302–7.

Tatum, James (tr.) 1983. *Plautus. The Darker Comedies – Bacchides, Casina, Truculentus*. Baltimore, MD, and London, The Johns Hopkins University Press.

Telò, Mario (ed.) 2007. *Eupolidis Demi*. Florence, Le Monnier.

Thalmann, William G. 1996. 'Versions of Slavery in the *Captivi* of Plautus', *Ramus* 25: 112–45.

Thiercy, Pascal 1986. *Aristophane. Fiction et dramaturgie*. Paris, Les Belles Lettres.

—— and Menu, Michel (eds.) 1997. *Aristophane. La Langue, la scène, la cité*. Bari, Levante.

Tornau, Christian 2005. 'Pseudolus – der Blender. Bemerkungen zur Drama- turgie und Komik des Plautus', *A&A* 51: 43–68.

Torrance, Robert 1978. *The Comic Hero.* Cambridge, MA, Harvard Univer- sity Press.

Totaro, Piero 2000. *Le Seconde Parabasi di Aristofane.* Second edition, Stuttgart and Weimar, Metzler.

Traill, Ariana 2001. 'Knocking on Knemon's Door: Stagecraft and Symbol- ism in the *Dyskolos*', *TAPA* 131: 87–108.

Turner, E. G. (ed.) 1969. *Entretiens 16. Ménandre.* Vandoeuvres-Genève: Fondation Hardt.

—— 1977. 'The Lost Beginning of Menander, *Misoumenos*', *Proceedings of the British Academy* 73: 315–31.

Ussher, R. G. 1969. 'The Staging of the *Ecclesiazusae*', *Hermes* 97: 22–37.

—— (ed.) 1973. *Aristophanes. Ecclesiazusae.* Oxford, Clarendon Press.

—— 1979. *Aristophanes. G&R* New Surveys 13. Cambridge, Cambridge University Press.

Vaio, John 1971. 'Aristophanes' *Wasps*: The Relevance of the Final Scenes', *GRBS* 12: 335–51.

—— 1973. 'The Manipulation of Theme and Action in Aristophanes' *Lysistrata*', *GRBS* 14: 369–80.

—— 1985. 'On the Thematic Structure of Aristophanes' *Frogs*', in W. M. Calder III, U. K. Goldsmith and P. B. Kenevan (eds.), *Hypatia. Essays in Classics, Comparative Literature, and Philosophy Presented to Hazel E. Barnes on her Seventieth Birthday.* Boulder, CO, University of Colorado Press: 91–102.

Van Steen, Gonda A. H. 1994. 'Aspects of 'Public Performance' in Aristo- phanes' *Acharnians*', *AC* 63: 211–24.

—— 2000. *Venom in Verse. Aristophanes in Modern Greece.* Princeton, NJ, Princeton University Press.

Vander Waerdt, P. 1994. 'Socrates in the *Clouds*', in (ed.), *The Socratic Move- ment.* Ithaca, NY, Cornell University Press: 48–86.

Vickers, Michael 1995. 'Alcibiades at Sparta: Aristophanes *Birds*', *CQ* 45: 339–54.

—— 2001. 'Aristophanes' *Frogs*: Nothing to Do with Literature', *Athenaeum* 89: 187–201.

Viljoen, G. van N. 1963. 'The Plot of the *Captivi* of Plautus', *AClass* 6: 38–63.

Vogt-Spira, Gregor 1992. *Dramaturgie des Zufalls. Tyche und Handeln in der Komödie Menanders.* Zetemata 88. Munich, C. H. Beck.

Walton, J. Michael 2006. *Found in Translation. Greek Drama in English.* Cambridge, Cambridge University Press.

—— and Arnott, Peter D. 1996. *Menander and the Making of Comedy.* Westport, CT, Greenwood.

Watling, E. F. (tr.) 1964. *Plautus. The Rope and Other Plays*. Harmondsworth, Penguin Books.

—— (tr.) 1965. *Plautus. The Pot of Gold and Other Plays*. Harmondsworth, Penguin Books.

Way, Mahalia L. 2000. 'Violence and the Performance of Class in Plautus' *Casina*', *Helios* 27: 187–206.

Webster, T. B. L. 1960. *Studies in Menander*. Second edition, London, Methuen.

—— 1970. *Studies in Later Greek Comedy*. Ssecond edition, Manchester, Manchester University Press.

—— 1973. 'Woman Hates Soldier: A Structural Approach to Greek Comedy', *GRBS* 14: 287–99.

—— 1974. *An Introduction to Menander*. Manchester, Manchester University Press.

Welsh, David 1983a. 'The Chorus of Aristophanes' *Babylonians*', *GRBS* 24: 137–50.

—— 1983b. 'IG II.2 2343, Philonides and Aristophanes' *Banqueters*', *CQ* 33: 51–5.

—— 1990. 'The Ending of Aristophanes' *Knights*', *Hermes* 118: 421–9.

Whitehorne, John 2001. 'The Third Hypothesis of Aristophanes' *Peace* Again', *AC* 70: 143–6.

—— 2005. 'O City of Kranaos! Athenian Identity in Aristophanes' *Acharnians*', *G&R* 52: 34–44.

Wiles, David 1984. 'Menander's *Dyskolos* and Demetrios of Phaleron's Dilemma', *G&R* 31: 170–80.

—— (tr.) 1988a. *Brothers*, in Patric Dickinson and David Wiles (trs.), *Plautus. Two Plays*. Egham, Sutherland House: 63–76.

—— 1988b. 'Taking Farce Seriously: Recent Critical Approaches to Plautus', in James Redmond (ed.), *Themes in Drama 10: Farce*. Cambridge, Cambridge University Press: 261–71.

—— 1989. 'Marriage and Prostitution in Classical New Comedy', in James Redmond (ed.), *Themes in Drama 11. Women in Theatre*. Cambridge, Cambridge University Press: 31–48.

—— 1991. *The Masks of Menander. Sign and Meaning in Greek and Roman Performance*. Cambridge, Cambridge University Press.

—— 1997. *Greek Theatre Performance. An Introduction*. Cambridge, Cambridge University Press.

Wilkins, John 2001. *The Boastful Chef. The Discourse of Food in Ancient Greek Comedy*. Oxford, Oxford University Press.

Willcock, M. M. (ed.) 1987. *Plautus. Pseudolus*. Bristol, Bristol Classical Press.

—— 1995. 'Plautus and the *Epidicus*', *PLLS* 8: 19–29.

Willi, Andreas (ed.) 2002. *The Language of Greek Comedy*. Oxford, Oxford University Press.

—— 2003. *The Languages of Aristophanes. Aspects of Linguistic Variation in Classical Attic Greek*. Oxford, Oxford University Press.

Williams, Bronwyn 1993. 'Games People Play: Metatheatre as Performance Criticism in Plautus' *Casina*', *Ramus* 22: 33–59.

Williams, Gordon 1956a. 'Evidence for Plautus' Workmanship in the *Miles Gloriosus*', *Hermes* 84: 79–105.

—— 1956b. 'Some Problems in the Construction of Plautus' *Pseudolus*', *Hermes* 84: 424–55.

Williams, Robert I. 1993. *Comic Practice/Comic Response*. Newark, NJ, University of Delaware Press/London and Toronto, Associated University Presses.

Wilson, N. G. 1982. 'Two Observations on Aristophanes' *Lysistrata*', *GRBS* 23: 157–63.

—— 2007a. *Aristophanea. Studies on the Text of Aristophanes*. Oxford, Oxford University Press.

—— (ed.) 2007b. *Aristophanis fabulae*. 2 vols, Oxford, Clarendon Press.

Wilson, Peter 2000. *The Athenian Institution of the Khoregia*. Cambridge, Cambridge University Press.

Worthington, Ian 1987. 'Aristophanes' *Knights* and the Abortive Peace Proposals of 425 B.C.', *AC* 56: 56–67.

Woytek, Erich (ed.) 1982. *Plautus. Persa*. Vienna, Österreichische Akademie der Wissenschaften.

—— 2001. 'Sprach- und Kontextbeobachtung im Dienste der Prioritäts-bestimmung bei Plautus: Zur Datierung von *Rudens*, *Mercator* und *Persa*', *WS* 114: 119–42.

Wright, John 1974. *Dancing in Chains. The Stylistic Unity of the Comoedia Palliata*. Rome, American Academy.

—— 1975. 'The Transformations of Pseudolus', *TAPA* 105: 403–16.

—— (ed.) 1993. *Plautus' Curculio*. Norman, OK, University of Oklahoma Press.

Zagagi, Netta 1979. 'Sostratos as a Comic, Over-Active and Impatient Lover: On Menander's Dramatic Art in his Play *Dyskolos*', *ZPE* 36: 39–48.

—— 1988. '*Exilium amoris* in New Comedy', *Hermes* 116: 193–209.

—— 1994. *The Comedy of Menander*. London, Duckworth.

Zannini-Quirini, Bruno 1987. *Nephelokokkygia. La perspettiva mitica degli Uccelli di Aristofane*. Rome, Bretschneider.

Zeitlin, Froma I. 1982. 'Travesties of Gender and Genre in Aristophanes' *Thesmophoriazusae*', in Helene P. Foley (ed.), *Reflections of Women in Antiquity*. New York, NY: Gordon and Breach Science Publishers: 169–217. Reprinted in Zeitlin, *Playing the Other*, Chicago, University of Chicago Press, 1996, 375–416.

—— 1999. 'Aristophanes: The Performance of Utopia in the *Ecclesiazousae*', in Simon Goldhill and Robin Osborne (eds.), *Performance Culture and Athenian Democracy*. Cambridge, Cambridge University Press: 167–97.

Zetzel, James E. G. 1972. 'Cicero and the Scipionic Circle', *HSCP* 76: 173–9.

Zimmermann, Bernhard 1984–7. *Untersuchungen zur Form und dramatischen Technik der Aristophanischen Komödien*. 3 vols, Königstein, Hain.

—— 2006. *Die griechische Komödie*. Second edition, Frankfurt-am-Main, Verlag Antike.

Zwierlein, Otto 1990–2. *Zur Kritik und Exegese des Plautus*. 4 vols, Stuttgart, Steiner.

INDEX